Thought and Vision

A Critical Reading of H. D.'s Poetry

Angela DiPace Fritz

Printed in the United States of America

Library of Congress Cataloging-in-Publication Data

DiPace Fritz, Angela, 1944–
  Thought and vision.

  Bibliography: p.
  Includes index.
    1. H. D. (Hilda Doolittle), 1886–1961 — Criticism
and interpretation.   I. Title.
PS3507.0726Z617   1987   811'.52   87-13173
ISBN 0-8132-0642-1

To Tina Pappalardo DiPace
and Concetto DiPace
my parents

Contents

Preface

A survey of the growing field of H. D. studies (as indicated throughout this text) pinpoints significant phases and diversity of purpose in the scholarship of this major twentieth-century writer (poet, novelist, essayist). It also discloses the absence of a full-length study devoted to her daunting poetic achievement. This paucity of the scholarship suggests that the time is propitious for a critical reading of her entire poetic canon, especially now with the publication of Louis L. Martz's definitive edition *H. D. Collected Poems 1912–1944* and the fact that H. D.'s eminence as a modernist and feminist poet has been established by scholars like Susan Stanford Friedman, notably in *Psyche Reborn: The Emergence of H. D.* and by Rachael Blau Du Plessis in *H. D.: The Career of That Struggle.*

This study, moreover, intends to complement *H. D.: Woman and Poet,* published by the National Poetry Foundation, which reflects a wide spectrum of scholarship by contemporary scholars whose essays often go beyond the aims of this book and, in so doing, widen and deepen its significance. The biographical, historical, photographic (film and still photography), bibliographical, and critical works of Perdita Schaffner, Susan Stanford Friedman, Rachael Blau Du-Plessis, Alicia Ostriker, Barbara Guest, Albert Gelpi, L. S. Dembo, Adalaide Morris, Charlotte Mandell, Diana Collecott, Mary S. Mathis, and Michael King add further resonance to this text. Ultimately, this text is written as a tribute to Hilda Doolittle (1886–1961), whose centennial was appropriately celebrated in Bethlehem, Pennsylvania (the poet's birthplace), at Moravian College, commemorating the poet's religious origins and focusing on the connection between her life and work.

H. D. admittedly reveals a great deal about herself and her art in several unpublished and published autobiographical novels, such as *Palimpsest, Bid Me to Live (A Madrigal), HER*, and *The Gift*, which, in part, deal with growing up in Moravian Bethlehem; with her friendships and relationships with William Carlos Williams, Ezra Pound, Richard Aldington (whom she married and later divorced), Winifred (Bryher) Ellerman, D. H. Lawrence, and other literary figures; with her own personal problems; and with the outbreak of two world wars. The publication of two full-length biographies — Janice S. Robinson's *H. D. The Life and Work of an American Poet* (1982) and Barbara Guest's *Herself Defined: The Poet H. D. and Her World* (1984) — provides the necessary background for viewing the poetry.

H. D.'s elliptical prose pieces also offer points of entry into her poetry. Especially urgent to this study are *Notes on Thought and Vision* (1919); *Tribute to Freud*, consisting of "Writing on the Wall," written in 1944, and "Advent," a continuation of "Writing on the Wall," not written until 1948; *End to Torment* (1958), a memoir of Ezra Pound; and "Background Notes" to *Helen in Egypt*.

H. D., however, best defines her thought and vision throughout the development of her poetry. Progressively assimilating diverse mythical and religious contexts into the body of her poetry, she creates more than a private pursuit of spiritual reality and personal salvation. In her attempt to piece together the shards of her life, devastated by two world wars as well as personal adversity, H. D. creates a permanent vision of universal redemption amid the disruptions of the modern world, thus confronting and addressing central cultural issues of our era.

Acknowledgments

Thought and Vision would not have been possible without the personal and professional, emotional and intellectual support of many people. My debt originates with the poets Ezra Pound, Robert Duncan, and Denise Levertov, whose work introduced H. D.'s poetry to me. It extends to the many H. D. scholars whose work either complements or supplements mine. I am especially grateful to Louis L. Martz, since I am convinced that without his invaluable, intelligent, and tough criticism, this text would have suffered a great loss. And, I am very grateful to Perdita Schaffner, H. D.'s daughter, for allowing me to work with the H. D. papers in the Collection of American Literature, Beinecke Rare Book and Manuscript Library at Yale University. This book could not have existed without the enduring support of David J. McGonagle at The Catholic University Press. I am also thankful to Genevieve Bailey for her proficient typing of the various versions, and to Marjorie Sherwood for easing the labor of manuscript preparation. I am grateful to Sacred Heart University for a grant to help me complete the project. I am also thankful to my colleagues for all their support. During the research and the writing of *Thought and Vision,* many people provided a source of encouragement, and I am grateful to them. John Ehrstine, John Elwood, and Richard Haswell initially encouraged me with this project. Debbie Fausti, Roberta Wilkes, Marian Calabrese, Michelle Carbone Loris, and Millicent Metzger never seemed to have doubted my work-in-progress. My husband Barry Fritz and my son

Dylan Fitch have provided constant interest in my project; my mother Tina Pappalardo DiPace has taken great pride throughout the entire process; and Rita DiPace, Joey Di-Pace, Alfred de Palchi, and Mary Landers DiPace have been very supportive. Finally, my debt rests with H. D., whose poetry inspired me to write and persists in attaining my attention.

Abbreviations

Abbreviations and publication information for frequently cited editions are listed below. All citations from H. D.'s work are from these editions. The following abbreviations are used throughout this study.

CP: Collected Poems in *H. D. Collected Poems 1912–1944* (New York: New Directions, 1983)

RB: Red Roses for Bronze in *H. D. Collected Poems 1912–1944* (New York: New Directions, 1983)

Trilogy (New York: New Directions, 1973)
   WNDF: The Walls Do Not Fall
   TA: Tribute to the Angels
   FR: The Flowering of the Rod

HE: Helen in Egypt (New York: New Directions, 1961)
   P: Pallinode
   L: Leuké
   E: Eidolon

VA: Vale Ave in *New Directions Prose and Poetry* 44 (New York: New Directions, 1982). 18–68.

HD: Hermetic Definition (New York: New Directions, 1972)
   HD: "Hermetic Definition"   *SD:* "Star of Day"
   RRB: "Red Rose and a Beggar"   *S:* "Sagesse"
   GA: "Grove of Academe"   *WL:* "Winter Love"

TF: Tribute to Freud (Boston: David R. Godine, 1974)

1. Poetics: From *Sea Garden* to *Hermetic Definition* (1912–1961)

Beginning with the Imagist poems, written as early as 1912, and concluding with the epiphanic visions in *Hermetic Definition,* completed just before her death in 1961, this text aims to show that throughout the development of her poetry H. D. permanently carves a significant variant of the modern quest in terms of spiritual realism. By tracing the centrality of this movement toward such a reality in the poet's work, this text examines the poetry chronologically as documentation of this quest.

The first poetry, consisting of previously published and unpublished poems, appears in *The Collected Poems of H. D.* (1925) as follows: *Sea Garden* (1916); two sections entitled "The God" (1913–1917) and "Translations" (1915–1920); *Hymen* (1921); and *Heliodora* (1924). *Red Roses For Bronze* follows in 1931. Although H. D. continued to write poetry, no volume of poetry was published between 1931 and 1944. A few poems appeared in literary journals, and her own version of Euripides' *Ion* appeared in 1937. Approximately forty poems written during this period (mostly unpublished and uncollected) are now available in *H. D. Collected Poems 1912–1944*, bridging the chronological gap between 1925 and 1944. H. D.'s long poems include: *The Walls Do Not Fall* (1944), *Tribute to the Angels* (1945), and *The Flowering of the Rod* (1946), published posthumously as *Trilogy* in 1973; *Helen in Egypt,* written between 1951 and 1954 but published in 1961; *Vale Ave,* written in 1957 but published in 1982; and *Hermetic Definition* written between 1957 and 1961 and published in 1972.[1]

The early poems included in *Sea Garden* (1916) document H. D.'s spiritual drifting. The "sea garden" experience shows forth a drifting self surrounded by stagnant waters. Especially in it, she strives to attain continuity between the present and the ancient past, but this attempt is undercut by strong feelings of discontinuity and fragmentation, direct outcomes of a spiritually impoverished modern world.

A complex poetics of "spiritual realism," initiated in *Sea Garden,* underscores H. D.'s entire poetic career and lifelong attempt to arrive at a synthesis between objective reality and spirituality. In the early poem "The Shrine," subtitled ("She watches over the sea") (*CP* 7), she begins to establish a highly constructed system of signs. The goddess of the sea here manifests as the "spirit between the headlands / and the further rocks." In "Pursuit" (*CP* 11), "with short breath and gasp," she desperately implores the presences that inhabit and embody spiritual reality: "*wood-dæmons grant life — / give life — I am almost lost.*" Although inundated by sorrow, arising from personal and social misadventure, she resists being engulfed by this inner and "outer horror" ("The Gift" *CP* 15). It is also in "The Gift" that H. D. describes what she seeks in terms that begin to define her poetics of "spiritual realism." Living amid ruins "in this waste" of modern civilization, she searches for cities "*peopled / with spirits, not ghosts*" ("Cities" *CP* 39). While immersed, connected, and affected by this life, she seeks, finds, and creates "in rapt thought, / in vision" the embodiment "of that other life" ("The Gift"), the incarnation of spiritual reality.

1. The conventions noted on the Abbreviations page are used for the primary texts used in this study: Roman numerals within parentheses indicate sections of lyrics or cantos; arabic numbers refer, first, to lyrics within sequences or cantos; second, to lines; and, third, to page numbers.

In the polemic prose piece *Notes on Thought and Vision* (1919), from which the title of this text derives, H. D. locates the impetus of this quest as arising from an inordinate sense of discontinuity and fragmentation experienced as she lived through the desolation of World War I. A sense of lostness and drifting dominates the poems in *Sea Garden*. The failure of sexual love to overcome these feelings also prompts the poet to search for other kinds of love. Ironically, despair and paralysis initiate the poet's first voyage out, her first attempt to reconstruct her own "mysteries of vision," grounded in the pursuit of creativity, memory, thought, and love, albeit a regenerative kind of love.[2]

Although too often assigned a peripheral status in H. D. scholarship, *Notes* must be seen as the first of the poet's few statements on poetics. Albert Gelpi's "The Thistle and the Serpent" (1982), the introduction to the edition examined here, identifies the significance of these symbols (recurrent throughout H. D.'s *oeuvre*) as "a breakthrough into heightened consciousness" (9). *Notes*, Gelpi writes, "anticipates a lifetime spent in the divination of such epiphanical 'spots of time'" (9). Ascertaining the centrality of *Notes*, Rachael Blau DuPlessis in *H. D.: The Career of That Struggle* (1986) asserts that it is here that H. D. begins "to particularise what becomes a central motif in her *oeuvre*: the spiritual meaning of erotic passion."[3] In addition, *Notes* solidifies the thesis of this text that her poetics of quest has to be perceived as the integration of spirituality and mundane reality which, for her, is the key to personal and universal redemption. For H. D., "This thought is vision" (22).

In life, this thought is manifested in the "body, mind, and

2. The title of this study is borrowed from H. D.'s *Notes on Thought and Vision* (San Francisco: City Lights, 1982). All quotations are from this publication, p. 22.

3. Rachael Blau DuPlessis, *H. D. The Career of That Struggle* (Bloomington: Indiana University Press, 1986), p. 40.

over-mind" (17). It is the artist who, affected by these "three states or manifestations of life" (17), produced the "Charioteer at Delphi" (25) and the "Madonna of the Rocks" (18). No great art, for that matter, writes H. D., is created without "over-mind" (18), or "super-feelings" (19), which she envisions in the jelly-fish metaphor, and which enable the artist to begin with objective reality as a starting-point of his creative act and then to transcend it by including it, not excluding it, in the completed creative act.

The function of the artist, described in *Notes* and completely actualized in *Trilogy* and the great poems that follow it, is to bring "the whole force of this power back into the world" (27), a world given to the superiority of either sexual or intellectual motivation, while virtually excluding and ignoring the workings of the "over-mind." A close parallel to this kind of poetic infusion is that which occurs in Dylan Thomas' poetics, aptly expressed in "The Force That Through the Green Fuse Drives the Flower." Moreover, H. D. posits that the Hellenic "over-mind" conquered Egypt, as the Galilean conquered the Hellenic because Christ was "a great artist" (27) who, like those before and after him, effected a transformation of consciousness by bringing us, she imagines, "'into touch with the world of over-mind thought'" (28). The Eleusinian mysteries had previously served a similar transformational function: the initiates advanced through this life, overcoming obstacles of the "womb" and the "brain" (20–23), while envisioning "that other life" through "the world of over-mind thought."

This initiation (the artist's or initiate's) is repeatable and begins by getting "safely through the mere animal stage and the intellectual stage" (30). Another rite of passage into "over-mind consciousness" (31) is to realize that "vision is of two kinds — vision of the womb and vision of the brain" (20), since "the love-brain and over-brain are both capable of thought" (22). Using a "lens" as a metaphor for the "over-mind," H. D. at this point concludes that "when these lenses are properly adjusted, focused, they bring the world of vision into consciousness. The two work separately, perceive separately, yet make one picture" (23). Through the powers of love and the intellect we can begin to "understand the mysteries of vision" (22).

As noted in these statements, H. D.'s modernist poetics embraces cultural and personal points of view. Her signs are both universal and individualistic. Egypt, for instance, in *Notes* and elsewhere in the poetry is perceived "in terms of world consciousness [and] is the act of love," whereas "Hellas is a child born" (37). Yet she also writes: "We may enter the world of over-mind consciousness directly, through the use of our over-mind brain. We may enter it indirectly, in various ways. Every person must work out his own way" (23).

H. D.'s poetics of "spiritual realism," as decoded in *Notes* and observed throughout the development of the poetry, in both concrete and abstract expression, always oscillates between the two polarities of reality and spirituality, or, as she puts it, among

> Three worlds.
> 1. World of abstraction: Helios, Athene.
> 2. Intermediate or Nature world: Pan, the Naiads.
> 3. World of the uninitiate men and women. (37)

In her thought and vision of "spiritual realism," there are no walls among these worlds, and no one is prevented entrance or exit: "Spirits of a higher world have access into a lower world. Athene may appear to one in the next lower world" (38). In H. D.'s new mythology, divinities or human beings, demigods, heroes or heroines interpenetrate these three worlds of consciousness, whereas in contrast to previous mythologies, specifically Greek, "it was *de rigueur* for an Olympian not to appear to a mortal direct. Therefore Silene who requested this, was burned to ash" (38). Her revisionist mythmaking insists that we acknowledge the fact that "we have many records of Naiads, tree and river spirits, sea spirits and voices of the sea, and Centaurs holding friendly intercourse with mortals" (38). Immersed in revising Greek myth at this point of her poetic development, H. D. adds: "we also know that Pan appeared to those in pain or trouble, not only in dreams but 'visibly at mid-day.' Pan appeared at Marathon before all the Greeks. And I know of witnesses today who have had a vision of this god" (38). We may encounter Pan and other divinities in H. D.'s poetry "only insofar as we become identified with the highest in ourselves — 'our own familiar dæmon'" (37) and our own personal and cultural signs.

Whether it is a "bundle of myrrh" (*Trilogy*), a flower, a sea lily, a sea rose, its "fragrance," "form," or "colour" (32), a "thistle" (for H. D. a sign of "life, love, martyrdom" (40)), it "must lead in the logical course of events to death, paradise, peace. The world of death — that is, death to the stings of life, which is the highest life — may be symbolized by the serpent" (40). For H. D. the serpent also symbolizes the "over-conscious mind" (40) of the artist of "super-feelings" (19) whose function is "the realisation of this over-conscious world" (40), or spiritual reality, so that we may be "able to enter into a whole life" (42) as Lo-fu, Euripides, the Galilean, and Leonardo did, and as H. D. does, "as a means of completing" herself, "as a means of approach to ecstasy" (45) which she ultimately experiences and voices in one of the last poems "Winter Love" (1959): "I am delirious now and mean to be, / the whole earth shudders with my ecstasy."

What gives rise to this ecstasy? Certainly not the horror that exists in the modern world. What has nourished it? Given it birth? Again, it is in *Notes* that we begin to trace the process of this begetting, incipient in the flowering of "two forms of seed, one in the head and one in the body to make a new spiritual birth" (50) and to bring forth a new incarnation: "I am in my spiritual body" (50). The intensity of this experience is very acute for H. D. who describes it in *Notes* as this: "all the spiritual energy seemed concentrated in the middle of my forehead, inside my skull, and it was small and giving out a very soft light, but not scattered light, light concentrated in itself as the light of a pearl would be. So I understood exactly what the Galilean meant by the kingdom of heaven, being a pearl of great price" (51), because "the spirit, we realise, is a seed" (52) which fully blooms in *The Flowering of the Rod*: "Christ was the grapes that hung against the sunlit walls of that mountain garden, Nazareth. He was the white hyacinth of Sparta and the narcissus of the islands. . . . Christ and his Father, or as the Eleusinian mystic would have said, his mother, were one" (53).

Perceived, then, in the *Collected Poems* is H. D.'s attempt to overcome feelings of rejection and nothingness which turn her quest away from the world of men and women and toward nature, once inhabited by divinity. This seemingly extraordinary phenomenon, however, typifies the beginnings of women's spiritual quest. In *Diving Deep and Surfacing: Women Writers on Spiritual Quest*, Carol P. Christ notes that women writers, having been alienated by a patriarchal society that has denied them the right to search for their identity, turn to gods and goddesses because their "'sense of self and the world is created through them.'"[4]

H. D.'s search for divinity is not always successful during this phase of the quest, as noted between the poet's efforts to worship the gods and goddesses in her pantheon and her sense of futility in doing so. This tension appears in several ways but crystallizes in the attempt to write a communal poetry that is, in effect, to be "a meeting with others" through

4. Carol Christ, *Diving Deep and Surfacing: Women Writers on Spiritual Quest* (Boston: Beacon, 1980), p. 2. Christ here quotes Stephen Crites, "The Narrative Quality of Experience," *Journal of the American Academy of Religion* 39 (September 1971), p. 295.

prayer, and the realization that prayers, at this point of her poetic development (and spiritual pilgrimage), nearly always result as litanies of words laden with "the terrible weight of things," obstacles that obstruct transcendence and continuity.[5] Ultimately, however, the discovery of vestiges of divinity in nature, once inhabited by gods and goddesses, enables the poet to emerge from the stultifying "sea garden" experience.

Urgency and energy underscore the initial discovery that the numinous is the object of the search. This realization attains fruition as the poet increasingly identifies with the world of comparative myth. Perceiving correspondences between her life and the lives of goddesses and heroines, she begins to direct the course of her spiritual voyage. A progressively complex degree of mythical identification between the searching self and the world of myth, therefore, initiates the major thematic structures in H. D.'s poetry. By 1925, she begins to construct a view of the self and the world that serves as a preparation for the later major achievement. Through a progressive degree of mythical identification, she learns that the meaning of experience is best understood in relation to the ability to create one's myth, which, in turn, is valorized in terms of universal significance.

To understand the concept of H. D.'s lived myth a knowledge of the process of mythical identification, especially formulated by Mircea Eliade and Ernst Cassirer, is extremely helpful. Of particular importance to this study are Eliade's *The Sacred and the Profane; Myth, Dreams, and Mysteries; Myth and Poetry;* and Cassirer's *Language and Myth,* because they provide not descriptions but rather models for thinking about H. D.'s poetry and for critically reading it.

Her mythopoetic writing also shows that to the world of

5. Roland Barthes, "Is There Any Poetic Writing?" *Writing Degree Zero,* trans. Annette Lavers and Colin Smith (New York: Hill and Wang, 1983), p. 49.

paganism, she brings a sense of Christian morality and ethos rooted in Moravian theology. Although this synthesis is evident in many poems, it is particularly visible in poems like "The Mysteries Remain," where Demeter, Iacchus (Bacchus), and Christ all partake in recurring rituals of life, death, and resurrection. She superbly moves between pagan and Christian worlds, thereby achieving a most invigorating syncretism that deepens and enlarges in scope as she develops as a poet. Arthur Weigall's *The Paganism in Our Christianity* is very useful in ascertaining the agility with which H. D. fuses paganism and Christianity in the early poetry.

In *Red Roses For Bronze* (1931), the volume of poetry that follows the *Collected Poems,* the image of the self in search of transcendent reality supersedes that of a drifting self. The features of the numen, previously darkly and imperfectly perceived, now begin to pass over into the speaker who experiences them. The apperception of divinity in nature, the veneration of the gods and goddesses among the ruins, the function of the poet as initiate, all become appropriated as poetic signs, the hieroglyphics with which she begins to sculpt her self-myth.

A deepening sense of spiritual exploration and self-analysis (including her psychoanalysis with Freud in 1933–34, later recorded in her tour de force, *Tribute to Freud*) and the perceptible movement from private to communal prayer and worship characterize the poetry written between 1931 and 1944. Directly influenced and helped by Freud, H. D. gathers the fragments of her life and the world and reconstructs a new vision where words resonate the Word "which gratifies and fulfills like the sudden revelation of a truth . . . shines with an infinite freedom and prepares to radiate towards innumerable uncertain and possible connections."[6] As Bar-

6. Barthes, p. 47.

thes notes about modern poetry, the reader, too, discovers in
reading the poetry of the 1930s and 1940s that the poetic
Word "is reduced to a sort of zero degree, pregnant with
all past and future specifications. . . . The Word, here, is
encyclopaedic. . . ."[7]

In the Foreword to H. D.'s *Tribute to Freud*, Norman
Holmes Pearson writes that "Freud helped her to remember
and to understand what she remembered," and, as a record
of these memories, *Tribute* helps the reader to trace the poet's
transfiguration of words into the Word of encyclopaedic pro-
portions and universal significance.[8] As well as a tribute to
Freud's genius, this work is indispensable to the reader of
H. D.'s poetry because in tracing her "research into psychic
affinities" it documents the poet's transition from private to
communal redemption. *Tribute* substantiates the mapping,
synthesizing, and interpreting of private and communal real-
ities in the processes of perceiving and remembering them.
Dreams and reveries recorded in *Tribute* are not to be dis-
missed as mere aimless wanderings of the psyche, but to be
seen as the very experiences of a searching self, portents
which invite the reader to enter and share her thought and
vision. In his illuminating introduction to *Tribute*, Kenneth
Fields states that it "offers perhaps the best entry into poems
that for years people have found too difficult to read" (*TF* xlii).

Freud's use of classical and biblical myths to reconstruct
past rituals that directly pertained to significant cultural as-
pects of modern society solidified and codified H. D.'s para-
digm of the spiritual quest. For H. D., Freud verified that
memories (dreams, reveries, myths, visions — all interchange-
able terms for her) force themselves into consciousness as

7. Barthes, p. 48.
8. Norman Holmes Pearson, Foreword, *Tribute to Freud* (Boston: David
R. Godine, 1974) vii. All subsequent references to *Tribute to Freud* are from
this edition which has an Introduction by Kenneth Fields, xvii–xliv.

"priceless broken fragments" of the human psyche (*TF* 35). Freud's work, she writes, is a constant reminder that "the shape and substance of the rituals of vanished civilizations, were still inherent in the human mind — the human psyche" (*TF* 13).

During her sessions with Freud, H. D. learned to distinguish between significant and insignificant dreams and memories. They are significant when they pertain to our shared mythical past. These dreams "come from the same source as script or Scripture, the Holy Writ or Word" (*TF* 36). Such a dream fragment (or memory) functions as an "illumination," a "*hieroglyph of the unconscious*" (*TF* 93).

When she deems these fragments as significant signs (or epiphanies) she incorporates them into the content of her poetry. Her interpretation of dream-visions aligns itself, as Freud pointed out to her, to the ancient tradition of warnings and messages — "writing-on-the-wall" (*TF* 51). Thus, the poem is often perceived as "an extension of the artist's mind, a *picture* or an illustrated poem, taken out of the actual dream . . . content and projected from within (though apparently from outside)" (*TF* 51). The translatable value of dream-content, dreams not only of kings and pharoahs, but of the individual, empowered her with the possibility of limitless excavations of the human psyche, while simultaneously it enabled her to create a palimpsest view of self and humanity.

Such poems as "The Gift" and the longer sequence "A Dead Priestess Speaks" function as signs that simultaneously encapsulate the racial past and modernity. Importantly, too, they record H. D.'s break with Imagism, her revolt against its philosophical assumptions. In "A Dead Priestess Speaks," she sharply disengages herself from an exclusively isolationist and discontinuous view of the self and the world, a view supported by the Imagist tenets and credo that reflect a distrust of continuity and transcendence. Fields postulates that "Imagism was not simply a break with the exhausted poetic conventions of the end of the century. It was a thoroughly skeptical movement that grew out of a mistrust of the world and the mind, and a mistrust of the possibility of broadly sharable discourse" (xxi).

Adherence to Ezra Pound's restrictive Imagist credo would have prevented H. D. from pursuing her vision of spiritual realism as universal redemption dependent on recoverable loss. It would have prevented her from assuming the role of an ancient priestess, translator and interpreter of ancient wisdom in modern terms. In "Dodona" (*CP* 406), for instance, the poet-priestess' task is to create a poetry that ultimately aims to "defeat the tale of man fallen." In "The Dancer" and "The Poet," which approximate the world of *Trilogy*, H. D. fully relinquishes the Imagist world view. These and other poems, as Fields saw, "show a strength and determination to go her own way in pursuit of a life that was spiritually satisfying" (xli).

As the poetry becomes increasingly mythical and communal, it also becomes increasingly meditative. In the long poems of the late period (1944–1961) — *Trilogy, Helen in Egypt, Vale Ave,* and *Hermetic Definition,* H. D. achieves a heightened state of sustained meditation. The dynamics of meditation intrinsic in these poems align themselves with those expressed by Thomas Merton in *Contemplative Prayer* and his other works.

Indispensable to H. D.'s mythical-religious-meditative view is the knowledge that, for her, ordinary life is transcendent and enveloped in mystery, discerned partly through contemplation and prayer. The objectification of this seemingly non-rational factor and its relation to the rational underscores her greater poetic achievement. This paradoxical stance is explained by the religious thinker Rudolph Otto in his work *The Idea of the Holy.* For Otto, and by extension H. D., to participate within sacred, or holy, space and time is to experience *"das ganz andere"* ("the wholly other"), thus imparting to everyday existence a *mysterium tremendum et fascinans.*[9]

In *Trilogy,* the self's encounter with a manifested "wholly other" reality accounts for the poem's complexity and depth. The spiritual quest begun in the early poetry here proceeds by various degrees and varieties of spiritual experience, at once contemplative, magical, and sacramental, effecting a major turn in the poet's thought and vision. The quest for the "Father" and the "Lady" through the desert world of *Trilogy* (1944–46) establishes it as one of this century's most important war poems and as the epitome of the modern quest poem. The search for identity and for the meaning of poetry in the modern world renders *Trilogy* both a war poem that deals with the dire consequences of war and a quest poem within a war-minded society that devaluates the role of the poet and the relevance of poetry.

It is in *Trilogy,* then, that H. D. fully expands and elaborates her poetics of "spiritual realism," originated in *Sea Garden* and first put forth as a statement of poetics in *Notes on Thought and Vision.* But her approach to a "wholly other" reality is also evident in many poems written after *Sea Garden* and before *Trilogy.* For example in "Charioteer" (*CP* 190) the poet hopes ("I myself on earth pray") that her "mere mortal prayer" for deliverance "from disenchanted days" in "Prayer" (*CP* 141) is heard by the gods. By 1944, however, she is sickened by the prevalent disenchantment of the modern world that prevents the hidden seed to flower and flourish.

Determined to leave "The place-of-a-skull / to those who have fashioned it" (2), she now creates her own garden in *The Flowering of the Rod.* Regeneration leads to resurrection and creativity: "this is the flowering of the rood, / this is the flowering of the reed" (7) in *Tribute to the Angels.* The gods

9. Otto, Rudolf, *The Idea of the Holy,* trans. John W. Harvey, 2nd ed. (London: Oxford University Press, 1928), pp. 1–40 and *passim.*

and goddesses, angels, magi, and the lady help her enter the world of "spiritual realities" (38) in *The Walls Do Not Fall*. In turn, H. D. shows us where to *"pause to give / thanks that we may rise again from death and live"* (*TA* 43). In her book, which "is our book" (*TA* 39), H. D. provides her "peculiar intricate map" (*WDNF* 38) to spiritual realism:

> Let us substitute
> enchantment for sentiment,
>
> re-dedicate our gifts
> to spiritual realism,
>
> scrape a palette,
> point pen or brush,
>
> prepare papyrus or parchment,
> offer incense to Thoth,
>
> the original Ancient-of-days,
> Hermes-thrice-great,
>
> let us entreat
> that he, by his tau-cross,
>
> invoke the true-magic,
> lead us back to the one-truth,
>
> let him (Wisdom),
> in the light of what went before,
>
> illuminate what came after,
> re-vivify the eternal verity,
>
> *be ye wise*
> as asps, scorpions, *as serpents.*
> (*WDNF* 35)

The search for identity; the role of the woman poet; the significance of dream visions; the adventures and misadventures of the questing self: these are the concerns in *Helen in Egypt*. Adaptation, recreation, and transformation of the Helen-Achilles-Paris myth in relation to a vision of Helen symbolizing universal recoverable loss bring forth the possibility of rebirth and resurrection. *Helen in Egypt*, a work of sustained meditation and mythmaking, culminates in perceiving the object of the multiple quests as the different kinds of love associated with the goddess of ancient myth.

In *Helen in Egypt*, H. D.'s densest and most difficult poem, the search for spiritual reality simultaneously reveals invariance of self, while furthering transformation that allows the self to attain new levels of consciousness. Denis de Rougemont's theory of love in *Love in the Western World*, a book much read by H. D., closely approximates the many kinds of love experienced and symbolized by Helen, who incorporates both humanity and divinity. The multiple love-masks bring Helen close to *The White Goddess* by Robert Graves. Helen's identification with Isis illustrates yet another kind of love, central in D. H. Lawrence's *The Man Who Died*, a book H. D. believed Lawrence had written for her. In assimilating the Helen myth to her own lived myth, H. D. clearly retains certain invariances of identity, while she undergoes several transformations. In creating her own self-myth as a woman-poet in the lineage of the goddess of many forms and shapes, her *Helen* is a modern testament of what takes place in the modern psyche between a tale and its user, a concept discussed by Walter Burkert in *The Structure and History of Greek Myth and Ritual*.

The attempt to attain secret knowledge that would lead the poet to an understanding of the goddess' wisdom is at the core of *Vale Ave*, dominated by portent and mystery. A woman's search for knowledge kept secret by a patriarchal tradition results in meetings and partings between lovers

whose attempt to obtain this knowledge leads them to Lu-
cifer and Lilith. Through Lilith's prophetic script, the poet
learns to read occult and hermetic signs. Their significance
unlocks the doors previously closed to women questers of
spiritual realism.

The resolution of her spiritual pilgrimage finds final ex-
pression in the epiphanic visions in *Hermetic Definition* (1957–
1961). In *Hermetic Definition,* H. D. creates her own signs to
reach the goddess. Religious intensity, authentic prayer, and
invocation of angels, who pay tribute to the poet, give rise to
creativity and knowledge. The Cabala, Christianity, and
Greek myth, all interiorized, substantiate H. D.'s view of the
goddess-poet-woman as creatrix. During moments of height-
ened meditation, poetry gives way to epiphany.

H. D.'s hermeticism relies heavily on Robert Ambelain's
esoteric text *La Kabbale pratique,* made accessible by Susan
Stanford Friedman in *Psyche Reborn.* Gustav Davidson's *Dic-
tionary of Angels,* moreover, elucidates the poet's complex an-
gelology which directly bears upon the works of cabalists.

More significantly, *Hermetic Definition* documents H. D.'s
poetic development and crystallizes the meaning of her be-
ginnings, the early poems, which are somewhat hard to grasp.
The red roses sculpted in bronze, hard and seemingly un-
approachable in 1931, fully blossom and unfold in *Hermetic
Definition:* "So my *Red Roses for Bronze* (1930) / bring me to-
day, a prophecy, / so these lyrics . . . / perhaps reach further
into the future." It seems as if it took more than "30 years"
for the poetry to find its "exact image," and more than thirty
years for that image to find its place among modern readers
("Hermetic Definition" 14).

Such a sequential analysis of H. D.'s poetic achievement
reinforces the contention that a definite intercourse exists
among her poetic texts, thereby providing several interstices
between these periods (1912–1925; 1931–1944) and the late

period (1944–1961), when the major long poems are written. *Trilogy, Helen in Egypt, Vale Ave,* and *Hermetic Definition* cannot be fully explicated or received without approaching them as growing from the earlier. To note this origin, continuity, and transformation adds a dimension not previously observed in her poetry.

Throughout the poetry H. D. creates a personal and communal vision of the self in search of spirituality and creativity. This text, then, explores the progression toward transcendence within mundane reality as it finds dominant expression in the poet's paradigm of the search for "spiritual realities" (perceived in "historical parallels" and "psychic affinities," *WDNF*). In the process, H. D. reveals her thought and vision, a veritable record of lived myth embedded in a poetics of actual experience.

A close reading of her poetry reveals that as she moves away from strict Imagist boundaries, the poetry becomes increasingly mythical, meditative, and communal, revealing a concern for universal redemption. The later poetry retains the evocative tone of the earlier verse, but, on the whole, it is a more inclusive poetry. If the early poetry seems devoid of conclusions about art and human experience, to the later poetry are added human judgments, criticisms, and evaluations. In the long poems, H. D. becomes perceivably attuned to the very concerns that characterize the major poetry of the twentieth century.

To disclose the nature of her thought and vision, therefore, a close reading of her poetry is both necessary and rewarding. The poetry of the 1910s, 1920s, and 1930s serves as an essential preparation for the poetry of the major period. The quest begun in the early poetry continues in *Trilogy* and the subsequent poems. Throughout her "personal approach / to the eternal realities" (*WDNF* 38), H. D. invites us to journey with her:

we are voyagers, discoverers
of the not-known,

the unrecorded;
we have no map;

possibly we will reach haven,
heaven.

(*WDNF* 43)

A full-length, chronological study of the poetry reveals not only a private quest for "spiritual realism" and universal redemption, but a communal and cultural quest as well. Discovering the nature of this poetic quest is essential to an understanding of H. D.'s overall thought and vision. We now embark, therefore, on the first phase of the voyage, the origin of her first meditation and projection of a self-myth.

2. Matrix: *Collected Poems* (1925)

The poems in the *Collected Poems*, written between 1912 and 1924, constitute the core from which the later poetry evolves. In "Notes" to *H. D. Collected Poems 1912–1944*, Louis L. Martz remarks that in this volume she brings "together all the poems of her early books, but she has rearranged some of them to form the two sections ("The God" [1913–1917] and "Translations" [1915–1920]) that lie between *Sea Garden* (1916) and *Hymen* (1921)."[1] *Heliodora* (1924) concludes the 1925 volume. This poetry centers on two primary concerns: to carve an Imagist style, and to formulate a mythical meditative context.

H. D.'s impeccable Imagist style is indubitably responsible for the success of this poetry. Ezra Pound and others saw in her first poetry the makings of modern poetry. The publication of "Priapus / Keeper-of-Orchards" in *Poetry* in 1913, one of the poems sent by Ezra Pound to Harriet Monroe, initiated years of success and critical acclaim.

Critical appraisal of H. D.'s first poetry extols her contribution to the Imagist movement. F. S. Flint, a fellow Imagist, coins for her the epithet of the "perfect imagist," and Ezra Pound and Amy Lowell point to her distinctively modern

---

1. Louis L. Martz, *H. D. Collected Poems 1912–1944* (New York: New Directions, 1983), p. 615. All references to the poems in this chapter are made to this new edition, abbreviated *CP*.

style.[2] Pound's letters, written before 1917 and addressed to Harriet Monroe, praise H. D.'s early verse above all for its modernity: it is "modern" in the sense that it is "objective — no slither, direct — no excessive use of adjectives, no metaphors that won't permit examination. It's straight talk, straight as the Greek!"[3] In *Tendencies in Modern American Poetry* (1919), Amy Lowell defines other aspects of modernism: perfect cadences that approximate the rhythm of speech; subtle changing rhythms; and carefully crafted free verse.[4] Heavy reliance on active verbs, on the sentence as the sole unit of meaning, and on reiteration of syntactical structures result in a poetry that approximates a Greek lyrical strain while expressing a distinctively modern sensibility and style.

In 1914, Pound also sent H. D.'s "Oread" to Harriet Monroe for publication in *Poetry,* and from this time onward this one-sentence poem has been much admired and anthologized. "Oread" clearly fulfills Pound's dictum of the image, expressed in his 1913 manifesto, where he defines the image as "that which presents an intellectual and emotional complex in an instant of time." In "Oread" (as in "The Pool," and "Sea Rose," and other poems) the image, a paradoxically restrained outburst of emotional and intellectual energy, is the sole unit of meaning, producing a precise moment of fusion among diverse perceptions:

> Whirl up, sea —
> whirl your pointed pines,
> splash your great pines

2. The phrase was coined originally by F. S. Flint, *Egoist* (1 May 1915), p. 72.

3. D. D. Paige, ed. *The Letters of Ezra Pound, 1907–1941* (New York: Harcourt and Brace, 1950), p. 50. Letter to Harriet Monroe, dated 12 October 1912.

4. Amy Lowell, *Tendencies in Modern American Poetry* (New York: Macmillan, 1969), p. 256 and *passim.*

on our rocks,
hurl your green over us,
cover us with your pools of fir.
(*CP* 55)

The energy in the poetry, however, arises from perceiving and interpreting experience from a mythical viewpoint by simultaneously merging and focusing all feeling and thought on a single object in a moment of time. In *Language and Myth* (1946) Ernst Cassirer states that "This focusing of all forces on a single point is the prerequisite for all mythical thinking and mythical formulation."[5]

H. D.'s use of the image in the early poetry functions at this level of mythmaking. By fusing imagism and myth, she creates a poetry of marked immediacy and intensity. These characteristics are also evident in the first stage of mythical formulation. Cassirer points out that during this phase, "Instead of a widening of intuitive experience, we find here its extreme limitation; instead of expansion that would lead to greater and greater spheres of being, we have here an impulse toward concentration."[6] What results is an accumulation of carved and differentiated images, which demonstrate H. D.'s superb ability to objectify her perceptions of self in relation to the world of myth.

In many of the lyrics where a synthesis between Imagist style and mythical thinking occurs, she plants the seed from which the later poetry springs. In these lyrics, myth does not serve to explain nor echo personal experience; rather, it is the experience of the poem. Similarly, Cassirer explains that "The mythical form of conception is not something superadded to certain definite elements of empirical existence; in-

5. Ernst Cassirer, *Language and Myth*, tr. Susanne Langer (New York: Dover, 1946), p. 33.
6. Cassirer, p. 33.

stead, the primary 'experience' itself is steeped in the imagery of myth and saturated in its atmosphere."[7]

The world of Greek myth provides spiritual and aesthetic direction. H. D.'s first poetry reveals not only a knowledge of Greek myth and the mastery of allusion but also a personal interpolation of myth. In *Imagism and Imagists: A Study in Modern Poetry* (1931), Glenn Hughes notes this modern use of myth in her early work. Her knowledge of Greek poetry also finds approval among classical scholars. In "The Classics and Our Twentieth-Century Poets" (1927), the eminent American classicist Henry Rushton Fairclough places H. D.'s chiseled verses among the best of modern poetry. Of particular significance he finds her assimilation of epic theme to lyric form in the manner of Bacchylides, Pindar, and Stesichorus. Nearly fifty years later, H. D. was to incorporate the epic theme of the Trojan war into her full-length book *Helen in Egypt* which would assimilate the vision of Helen presented by Euripides and Stesichorus, thereby creating a modern poem, "epic in substance but lyric in form."[8] In *The Classical World of H. D.*, Thomas Swann focuses on H. D.'s use of Greek myth. Greek myth, Swann notes, offered her not only "moral" and "intellectual" illuminations, but also a "healing alternative" to the modern malaise that surrounded her.[9]

Sea Garden and the other early poems depict a world of stark pristine beauty threatened by spiritual degeneration, epitomized first in the image of absconding gods and second in the image of a drifting self surrounded by whirlpools, stagnation, heat, and ruin. H. D.'s overwhelming sense of drifting reflects personal adversity as well as universal dislocation and discontinuity.

7. Cassirer, p. 10.
8. Henry Rushton Fairclough, *The Classics and Our Twentieth-Century Poets* (Stanford: University of California Press, 1927), p. 299.
9. Thomas Swann, *The Classical World of H. D.* (Lincoln: University of Nebraska Press, 1962), pp. 185–186.

It is this sense of drifting which occasions the despondency expressed in "Mid-day" (*CP* 10) where the speaker feels "vanquished" and "defeated." Her dejection is caused by experiencing infrequent spells of inspiration and concentration. Her thoughts are spent and scattered "as the black seeds." Like the seeds, she sees her self dispersed and fragmented: "I am scattered like / the hot shrivelled seeds." Instead of being flung "among the crevices of the rocks," she wishes to be "deep-rooted." The speaker's despair is explicit.

Her dejection, on the other hand, abates whenever she is able to recreate the beauty manifested by the gods. The beauty which, for instance, incandescently emanates from the flowering "Pear Tree" (*CP* 39) is proof that a god has taken refuge within it. The tree in bloom, a symbol of divine beauty, uplifts the speaker's soul because it reaffirms a spiritual fruition to come. It generates hope for the future and facilitates the emergence from a state of spiritual aridity to one of spiritual growth.

This fluctuation of mood is evident throughout *Sea Garden,* where the sense of drifting motivates her emergence from a state of aimless spiritual wandering and initiates her search for the gods who have hidden themselves from the hearts of men. Only engagement in active ritual and deeply felt worship will insure their reappearance. Worship of the gods is expressed in images of flowers and in rituals which reflect the progressive regenerative process of the self. In *Sea Garden* the flower poems take the quester from "sea-grass" to "shore-grass" ("Hermes of the Ways," *CP* 37).

"Sea Rose" (*CP* 5) symbolizes a harsh existence: the rose is "marred with stint of petals, / meagre flower, thin / sparse of leaf." It is "caught in the drift;" it is "flung on the sand," "lifted" and caught in a whirlpool. The "Sea-Lily" (*CP* 14) is also caught in the whirlpool and is "slashed and torn" by it. The "Sea-Violet" (*CP* 25), however, is strong enough to front the wind; its exposure to the elements augments its beauty as it catches "the light — / frost, a star edges with its fire." The "Sea-Iris" (*CP* 36) a "brittle flower," "tangled in sand," resists the onslaught of the wind by its "rigid myrrh-bud," while its "camphor-flower" assures healing. Ignored by those who seek gold, the "Band of iris-flowers" bloom undaunted by the heavy winds. "Sea-Poppies" (*CP* 21) possesses the colors and texture which strongly appeal to H. D. The poppies are "Amber husk / fluted with gold" and are "fruit on the sand / marked with a rich grain." The poppies are a "treasure" which banks the shores and spills "near the shrub-pines." They have survived the onslaught by rooting on shore: "your stalk has caught root." To stop drifting and to reach shore become the quester's goals.

She combs through every stream bank and wood path to search for signs of the gods. In "Pursuit" (*CP* 11) she discovers that the "sand on the stream-bank / still holds the print of your foot." The smashed stalk of a hyacinth is proof that a god has passed by: "the purple buds — half ripe — / show deep purple / where your heel pressed." Although the poem ends in defeat ("I can find no trace of you / in the larch-cones and underbrush"), the speaker actively searches for other signs of the gods hidden in their sacred altars.

This despairingly intoned pursuit gives way to an ecstatic idiom in "The Gift" (*CP* 15), which introduces the role of the speaker as initiate. The initiate "in rapt thought / in vision" speaks with "another race, / more beautiful, more intense than this." She is certain that "another life holds what this lacks" and resolves to experience this other state of existence by engaging in contemplative prayer, thus becoming fully immersed in the ritual of prayer. From this point onward, she becomes increasingly aware that prayer is a significant ritual:

> I have lived as they
> in their inmost rites —

they endure the tense nerves
through the moment of ritual.
(61–64)

Spiritual intensity underlies her best lyrics and under-
scores the major movement toward authentic (genuine)
prayer. In this first poetry, H. D. engages both in private
prayer ("the holy particularity of the soul in need") and in
communal prayer (or "corporate focus").[10]

H. D.'s involvement with prayer arises from inward crisis
and the need for spiritual direction. Her movement toward
prayer is best understood in terms of Thomas Merton's *Con-
templative Prayer*, where he states that "the climate in which
prayer flowers is that of the desert," and that its 'movement'
is "a kind of descent into our own nothingness, a recognition of
helplessness, frustration, infidelity, confusion, ignorance."[11]
Particularly in *Sea Garden*, prayer arises from the need to stop
drifting and from the desire to experience spiritual growth.
Yet, the anguish in many of these prayer-poems objectifies a
lack of authenticity, an emptiness and lostness which not
only reflect the speaker's state of mind but also typify the
spiritual disorientation experienced by the modern age. Simi-
larly, it is Merton's belief, and a thematic structure in H. D.'s
poetry, that the "option of absolute despair is turned into
perfect hope by the pure and humble supplication of . . .
prayer."[12] Through prayer, the speaker finds herself "in a
position of working out [her] own salvation and that of the
world."[13] Prayer brings forth a transformation of conscious-

10. Douglas V. Steere, "Foreword," *Contemplative Prayer* by Thomas
Merton (New York: Herder and Herder, 1969), p. 9.

11. Thomas Merton, *Contemplative Prayer* (New York: Herder and
Herder, 1969), p. 29 and p. 40.

12. Merton, p. 28.

13. John J. Higgins, S.J., *Thomas Merton on Prayer* (New York:
Doubleday, 1973), p. 22. Higgins here quotes Merton's *Seeds of Destruction*
(New York: Farrar, Straus and Giroux, 1964), p. 322.

ness — the transition from a death-in-life existence to a trans-figuration of self.

The quester begins to experience this transformation in "Adonis," (the second poem in the section entitled "The God," *CP 47*) where the self, like the god, partakes in the cycle of birth-death-rebirth. Resurrection is moving beyond a death-in-life existence, as it is attaining a higher state of existence exemplified in "The Gift." Resurrection in these poems may be perceived in terms analogous to Merton's definition of "conversion," a definition that suggests that it is a "deep change of heart in which we die on a certain level of our being in order to find ourselves alive and free on another more spiritual level."[14]

The prayer poems dispersed throughout the *Collected Poems* also parallel the direct and personal prayers of the monks who follow the most rudimentary liturgy. Prayer, for the early monks, consisted of memorizing and repeating Biblical words and phrases "with deep and simple concentration, 'from the heart.'"[15] Reiteration of words which connote divinity expresses this kind of worship. This constant invocation of divinity forces a "concentration of one's entire being upon a prayer stripped of all non-essentials and reduced to nothing but the invocation . . . a simple petition for help."[16] For the poet, the constant search of one's deepest center entails consciously making the divine entity invoked the supreme goal of the search. Prayer, as such, is not so much a method as it is a point of view and an orientation.

Although in many of these lyrics H. D. is engaged in private prayer, she also progressively shows a strong need for communal prayer. The importance of communal worship is evident in "The Wind Sleepers" (*CP 15*), a collective cry for spiritual direction:

14. Merton, p. 89.   15. Merton, p. 22.
16. Merton, p. 22.

> Tear —
> tear us an altar,
> tug at the cliff-boulders,
> pile them with the rough stones —
> we no longer
> sleep in the wind,
> propitiate us.
>
> (10–16)

Despite their suffering and hardships, suggested by the rough coastal terrain, the worshipers are adamant in their commitment to perpetual ritual and prayer: they "Chant in a wail / that never halts / pace a circle and pay tribute / with a song." "The Helmsman" (*CP* 5) continues the theme of communal worship. The invocation "O be swift" is reiterated nineteen times, thus stressing the urgency of the quest and emphasizing the importance of communal experience: "we fled," "we pastured," "we wandered," and "we worshipped." Joy in the pursuit, however, is not sustained, and the poem ends with a shift in tone from ecstasy and enchantment to defeat and hesitancy:

> But now, our boat climbs — hesitates — drops —
> climbs — hesitates — crawls back —
> climbs — hesitates —
>
> (39–42)

Nonetheless, in the "Huntress" (*CP* 23) the poet invites other worshipers to join her search for spiritual reality:

> Come, blunt your spear with us,
> . . .
> *Can you come,*
> *Can you come. . . .*
>
> (1:6–7)

The invitation extends to the search for beauty amid untamed nature. The beauty of "Pear Tree," its color, mass, promise; of the resilient sea flowers; and of the terrain, in general, stands diametrically opposed to the artificial beauty eschewed in "Sheltered Garden" (*CP* 19), where the "border-pinks" and the "wax-lilies" are stifling and suffocating. Nothing is less desirable than this manicured beauty. Instead, the speaker craves for "some sharp swish of a branch" or "coarse weeds." She wishes to eradicate artificial beauty and to supplant it with natural beauty:

> O to blot out this garden
> to forget, to find new beauty
> in some terrible
> wind-tortured place.
>
> (55–58)

The urge is to rediscover a garden suitable to our authentic nature, not to manufacture a false one. H. D.'s epitome of spiritual beauty embodied in nature is found in "Orchard" (*CP* 28), previously entitled "Priapus / Keeper-of-Orchards." Here autumnal beauty is too much to bear for the speaker, who, confronted by its splendor, feels inferior and inadequate. She is overwhelmed by natural beauty:

> I saw the first pear
> as it fell —
> the honey-seeking, golden-banded,
> the yellow swarm
> was not more fleet than I,
> (spare us from loveliness)
> and I fell prostrate
> crying:
> you have flayed us
> with your blossoms,
> spare us the beauty
> of fruit-trees.
>
> (1–12)

The fall of the pear underscores H. D.'s belief in the paradox of the fortunate fall, since fruition symbolizes resurrection. Again, a divine entity — the "rough-hewn / god of the orchard" — facilitates the manifestation of beauty, which occasions the speaker's supine position of devotion and offering, a catalog which symbolizes the abundance of autumnal (spiritual) fruition:

> these fallen hazel-nuts,
> stripped late of their green sheaths,
> grapes, red-purple,
> their berries
> dripping with wine,
> pomegranates already broken,
> and shrunken figs
> and quinces untouched,
> I bring you as offering.
>
> (18–26)

The existence of spiritual beauty sustains the speaker's search for the goddess. In "The Shrine" (*CP 7*) subtitled ("She watches over the sea") the goddess evoked is a composite of Thetis and Aphrodite. The goddess' power over the sea outlasts human worship. The ruined shrine demonstrates mankind's irreverence and ignominy. Instead of freshly strewn flowers, there are seaweed and broken shells. In contrast to others' forgetfulness, the speaker and the questers affirm their worship of the goddess: "You are not forgot." They have come to make their offering, and during their journey they have "dared deeper than the fisher-folk" in their attempt to gather sea-flowers. The goddess is not indifferent to their effort and responds by rekindling a spiritual awakening in them:

> Flame passes under us
> and sparks that unknot the flesh,
> sorrow, splitting bone from bone,
> splendour athwart our eyes. . . .
>
> (57–60)

Their song, "we hail this shore / we sing to you, / spirit between the headlands / and the further rocks" brings forth the goddess' forgiveness — her eyes "have pardoned our faults."

Although the shrine is usually a perilous obstacle to un-believers, it is a sanctuary for those who come to affirm the existence and the power of her divinity.

"The Cliff Temple" (*CP* 26) offers another sanctuary for the questing worshiper. Its beauty, "shelf of rock," "silver granite," "clean cut, white against white," is purifying and sacramental. The altar stands as "the world-edge," serving as "pillar for the sky-arch."

Affirmation of spiritual reality is also the theme in "Sea Gods" (*CP* 29), a powerful credo which extols the gods, while undermining all of those who "say there is no hope" (reiterated throughout the poem) in the efficacy of gods and goddesses. These are the alienated and the estranged whose faith in divinity is shaken because they perceive the gods as vulnerable and unable to heal their suffering. They no longer worship because divinity symbolizes futility and vulnerabil-ity. The speaker cries out:

> They say you are twisted by the sea,
> you are cut apart
> by wave-break upon wave-break,
> that you are misshapen by the sharp rocks,
> broken by the rasp and after-rasp.
>
> That you are cut, torn, mangled,
> torn by the stress and beat,
> no stronger than the strips of sand
> along your ragged beach.
>
> (I, 11–19)

In the first part of the poem, accusations are leveled against the gods by those who no longer find their actions efficacious. The poet, however, pleads for the gods' appearance which would negate the accusations made against them. In the sec-ond part, the speaker pays tribute by offering a catalog of vio-lets: "we bring violets, / great masses — single, sweet, / wood-violets, stream-violets, / violets from a wet marsh." And the third sequence is a refusal to mourn the gods' inefficacy:

> For you will come,
> you will come,
> you will answer our taut hearts,
> you will break the lie of men's thoughts,
> and cherish and shelter us.
>
> (III, 21–25)

Her worship of divinity is likened to the emergence from a prison peopled by all those who either reject the gods or are rejected by them, as seen in "Prisoners" (*CP* 33). In contrast to the poet, these individuals remain in bondage and do not experience the freedom she attains during her spiritual advancement. She sees herself and other worshipers as the chosen people: "Fate — God sends this as a mark, / a last token that we are not forgot, / lost in this turmoil," and she describes her new-found life as "a strange life, / patterned in fire and letters / . . . written on the walls."

The culmination of her sea-garden experience is celebrated in the pivotal "Hermes on the Ways" (*CP* 37). Hermes stands between shore and land, fronting an orchard. He is the god of "the triple path-ways" who awaits the questers:

> Dubious,
> facing three ways,
> welcoming wayfarers,
> he whom the sea-orchard
> shelters from the west,
> from the east
> weathers sea-wind;
> fronts the great dunes.
>
> (I, 17–23)

Hermes holds a special place in H. D.'s pantheon and, in this lyric, he is the god of spiritual direction. Associated with the arts in both Egyptian and Greek myth, Hermes is the poet's patron, the guiding luminary who awaits the quester "where sea-grass tangles with / shore-grass."

In naming the gods and goddesses, locating their places of worship and manifestation, H. D. clearly furthers her mythmaking. Hermes, Adonis, Thetis, and other divinities reveal a particular aspect of her mythmaking consciousness. Cassirer explains this process in these terms:

The notion that the name and essence [of the deity] bear a necessary and internal relation to each other, that the name does not merely denote but actually is the essence of its object, that the potency of the real thing is contained in the name — that is one of the fundamental assumptions of the mythmaking consciousness itself.[17]

By naming, placing, and describing their attributes, she creates a group of personal deities who provide a link between the past and her present state of mind, making the past reappear in the present.[18] Cassirer calls this a "dynamic concept of deity," one which gives full reign to the laws of the divine origins and becoming.[19]

The origin of a particular divinity and its attributes serves as a focus in many poems. Typically, the particular legends associated with a given deity are epitomized before any addition or change is made by the poet. The consolidation of legends that span centuries into a few lines establishes her ability to condense myth, which often occurs, as Cassirer states, when "phases of reality that are temporally widely separated become connected and linked for historical conception and understanding."[20]

H. D.'s special (or personal) gods and goddesses live in a particular milieu. In order to bring forth their response, the individual must enter their milieu and insure their divine protection. A way of imaginatively entering their world is through prayer, which explains the formulaic nature of many poems. The formulae (petition and invocation) are reiterated every time a divinity is addressed, since as Cassirer points out, "every act of devotion to the god, every appeal directed to him, commands his attention only if he is invoked by his

17. Cassirer, p. 3.   18. Cassirer, p. 21.
19. Cassirer, p. 23.   20. Cassirer, p. 27–28.

appropriate name."[21] Hermes, for example, is one of H. D.'s special gods.

H. D.'s mythical mythmaking noticeably assimilates diverse spiritual contexts. For instance, she fuses Graeco-Christian myths with the Cabala, and she shares with the cabalist the supreme urge to attain a constant state of meditation through prayer. In this aspect she approximates the initiates of Greek mysteries and Christian contemplatives who place a strong emphasis on the efficacy of prayer. She also discovers that prayer is of extreme importance in the Cabala, where it furthers the ascent toward spiritual reality. It is Gershom Scholem's contention in *Kabbalah* that "Above all, in the Kaballah it is prayer that serves as the principal realm for this ascent" and that "The greatest kabbalists were all great masters of prayer."[22]

In the Cabala prayer directs the ascent to higher levels of existence, imaged as an inward journey, "a spiritual peregrination among the supernal realms. . . . Its field of activity in kabbalistic thought is entirely in the inward worlds and in the connections between them."[23] For the cabalist, and by extension H. D., the words of prayer repeat the mysterious processes of the universe. Scholem states that:

the ontological hierarchy of the spiritual worlds reveals itself to the kabbalist in the time of prayer as one of the many Names of God. This unveiling of a divine 'Name' through the power of the 'word' is what constitutes the mystical activity of the individual in prayer. . . . Divine names are . . . aroused through meditative activity directed toward them. The individual in prayer pauses over each word and fully gauges the *kavvanah* [specific content] that belongs to it. The actual text of the prayer, therefore, serves as a kind of bannister onto which the kabbalist holds as he makes his not unhazardous ascent, groping his way by the words.[24]

21. Cassirer, p. 55.
22. Gershom Scholem, *Kabbalah* (New York: New American Library, 1974), p. 176.
23. Scholem, p. 177.   24. Scholem, p. 177.

The poems in "The God" point to this ascent, thereby implicitly defining the sea garden experience as a descent, characterized by withdrawal and emptiness. "I had drawn away into the salt, / myself, a shell / emptied of life," she writes in the title poem "The God" (*CP* 45). But how can individuals construe their own salvation (ascent), and how can divinity dwell in their hearts, if they are "given over to evil" (descent)? H. D.'s answer is that those who are engulfed by evil possess stone hearts and cannot but perceive stone in a statue of a god; consequently, they are incapable of perceiving a statue as a symbolic manifestation of divinity. On the contrary, the speaker's transformation of consciousness allows her to envision the carved stone as an expression of spiritual reality. The carved grapes which adorn the god suggest "wine spilled."

In "Adonis" (*CP* 47), the god's sacrifice is epitomized in the cycles of nature. His sacrifice and resurrection are both particularized and universalized:

> Each of us like you
> has died once,
> each of us like you
> has passed through drift of wood-leaves,
> cracked and bent
> and tortured and unbent
> in the winter frost,
> then burnt into gold points,
> lighted afresh,
> crisp amber, scales of gold-leaf,
> gold turned and re-welded
> in the sun heat. . . .
>
> (I, 1–12)

The resurrection of god and humanity, symbolized in the renewal in nature, signifies a golden rebirth: "each of us has crossed an old wood-path / and found the winter leaves / so golden in the sun-fire." Because of our potential for experiencing resurrection, we are like the gods and goddesses, "fit to be worshipped" and capable of attaining transcendence.

The pagan gods, although heroic, are not always perfect. The reality of imperfection, juxtaposed to the urge to attain perfection, is illustrated in "Pygmalion" (*CP* 48), a poem about creativity. In Pygmalion, the divine potential, creation, is on the verge of corruption. He is caught in a web and finds it impossible to extricate himself from the intricate threads spun by his own vainglorious ego. The danger lies in being trapped by his ego: "Shall I let myself be caught / in my own light?" His creativity serves as his nemesis, and his unchecked narcissism causes overwhelming anguish. Who or what is more powerful — inspiration, the creator, or the product:

> does this fire thwart me
> and my craft,
> or does my work cloud this light?
> which is the god,
> which is the stone
> the god takes for his use?
>
> (I, 8–13)

For Pygmalion, the creative process is one of agony and ambiguity. The inability to ascertain control poses a perpetual dilemma: "am I the god? / or does this fire carve me / for its use?" Is the artist a victim of her own creation? Which is real, the power of the muse who inspires her or the finished product? Where is the artist's place in the process of creation? These questions plague the poet.

Further anguish is reflected in many of the monologues in this volume. In "Romantic Thralldom in H. D." Rachael Blau DuPlessis provides an accurate accounting for the suffering experienced by betrayed women and goddesses. DuPlessis' insights fully apply to much of the early poetry where women are victims of "romantic thralldom," defined as "an all-encompassing, totally defining love between unequals.

The lover has the power of conferring self-worth and pur-
pose upon the loved one. Such love is possessive, and while
those enthralled feel it completes and even transforms them,
they are also enslaved."[25]

"Helen" (*CP* 154), "Circe" (*CP* 118), "Evadne" (*CP* 132),
"Leda" (*CP* 120), "Phaedra" (*CP* 135) and other rejected
women suffer the consequences of "romantic thralldom"
which, as DuPlessis states, "insists upon the differences be-
tween the sexes, encouraging a sense of mystery surrounding
the motives and powers of the lover: thus it begins with and
ends in sexual polarization. Viewed from a critical, feminist
perspective, the sense of completion or transformation that
often accompanies thralldom in love has a price of oblitera-
tion and paralysis, for the entranced self is entirely defined
by another."[26] In two of H. D.'s most successful monologues,
"Eurydice" (*CP* 51) and "Demeter" (*CP* 111), the script of
"romantic thralldom" is fully acted out and experienced, but
also rejected.

The numerous allusions to Thetis, Achilles, and Helen
clearly suggest the importance of this relationship to H. D.
In "Helen" *CP* 154) she depicts the degeneration of Greece.
Helen is a product of Greece's beauty and corruption. After
the war, she is Greece's enigma:

> All Greece hates
> the still eyes in the white face,
> the lustre as of olives
> where she stands,
> and the white hands.
>
>   (1–5)

Her beauty goads the survivors: "All Greece reviles / . . . re-
membering past enchantments / and past ills." Greece wants

25. Rachael Blau DuPlessis, "Romantic Thralldom in H. D." *Contem-
porary Literature*, 20 (2), 1979, pp. 178–179.
26. Blau DuPlessis, p. 179.

to sacrifice Helen in order to atone for the war. Once, Greece was moved by love for Helen; now Greece remains "unmoved" by Zeus' daughter "born of love." Only a sacrificial pyre would move Greece, "only if she were laid, / white ash amid funereal cypresses." By wishing for Helen's death, Greece prepares its own entombment.

Propitious, too, is "Egypt" (*CP* 140), which foreshadows *Helen in Egypt*. Here, Egypt is the seductive force which has caused Greece's fall: "Egypt had maimed us, / offered dream for life, / an opiate for a kiss, / and death for both." The fault, however, may not rest with Egypt but with Greece in the sense that "Egypt had given us knowledge, / and we took, blindly, / through want of heart. . . ." In creating a spiritual context, the poet assimilates pertinent aspects of Egyptian religion to Greek myth. "Egypt," in this sense, foreshadows the very concerns at the center of *Helen in Egypt,* where Helen, the victim and personification of Greece's "days of trance, / shadow, fore-doom of death," achieves the transformation H. D. believes to be the very heart of spirituality — *"passionate grave thought, / belief enhanced, / ritual returned and magic"* (emphasis mine). In "Egypt," amid corruption and desecration, the poet foresees a renaissance for Greece, and a kind of rebirth envisioned in the flowering of the red rose in the desert:

> the grey eyes following
> in the mid-most desert —
> great shaft of rose,
> fire shed across our path,
> upon the face grown grey, a light,
> Hellas re-born from death.
>
> (28–30)

The corruptive force of seductive love is obvious in "Circe" (*CP* 118). The goddess-lover's enchantments are frustrated by Odysseus. In this monologue, the goddess seeks to re-

trieve the lost lover. Her magic, however, is useless in regard
to Odysseus, even though it is powerful enough to summon
most men from the edges of the earth. Aroused, they are
quick to answer her call:

> they prayed for a touch,
> they cried for the sight of my face,
> they entreated me
> till in pity
> I turned each to his own self.
>
> (17–21)

Their bellows and snarls (panthers, leopards, hounds) echo
in her chambers of perfect beauty, surrounded by "sea stars."
Yet, she would gladly relinquish her magical arts and her
sanctuary for another tryst with Odysseus:

> But I would give up
> rock-fringes of coral
> and the inmost chamber
> of my island palace
> and my own gifts
> and the whole region
> of my power and magic
> for your glance.
>
> (52–59)

"Evadne" (*CP* 132) is a companion poem to "Circe."
Evadne, a sea-nymph, is loved by Apollo. Their consum-
mation is rendered in a perfect image of flowers and hair.
Nothing can destroy the vitality of this poignantly desolate
memory:

> Still between my arm and shoulder,
> I feel the brush of his hair,
> and my hands keep the gold they took
> as they wandered over and over
> that great arm-full of yellow flowers.
>
> (17–21)

"Leda" (*CP* 120) deals with the rape of Leda (lily) by Zeus (swan). Here, their consummation is attuned to the rhythm of the river:

> Where the slow river
> meets the tide,
> a red swan lifts red wings
> and darker beak,
> and underneath the purple down
> of his soft breast
> uncurls his coral feet.
>
> (1–7)

The Phaedra monologues that follow depict her tragic nature. The first monologue, "Phaedra" (*CP* 135) reveals the heroine's passionate self pitted against her concern for spiritual growth. This realization occasions an anxious return to her past in Crete:

> Think, O my soul,
> of the red sand of Crete;
> think of the earth; the heat
> burnt fissures like the great
> backs of the temple serpents[.]
>
> (1–5)

The only deliverance she foresees from the depth of frustrated and enmeshed passions is to retrieve a sense of lost spiritual reality:

> Think, O my soul —
> what power has struck you blind —
> is there no desert-root, no forest-berry
> pine-pitch or knot of fir
> known that can help the soul
> caught in a force, a power,
> passionless, not its own?
>
> (10–16)

Although passion and lust have blinded her, prayer restores vision. She now implores the gods, enlists their help: *"grant answer to my prayer."*

In the second monologue, "She Contrasts Herself with Hippolyta" (*CP* 136), Phaedra wonders if she can attain this transformation. Hoping to subdue her passion, she asks, "Can flame beget white steel —" Hippolyta, although temporarily submissive to Theseus, was able to retain her true nature; in fact, Hippolytus, from Phaedra's point of view, was "born of hate."

Her attempt to lessen her passion by reducing it to the Amazon's steel-like character is the subject of the third monologue, "She Rebukes Hippolyta" (*CP* 138). Phaedra does not believe that Hippolyta remains unaffected by the encounter; is she after all so chaste? Hippolyta is seen to be as wanton as herself, except that Hippolyta's eroticism is directed toward nature rather than men. Phaedra interprets her natural exploits as sexual encounters. Her "galloping up the slope / between great boulder and rock" is perceived as a consummation between herself and the sun god:

> Who can say —
> the broken ridge of the hills
> was the line of a lover's shoulder,
> his arm-turn, the path to the hills,
> the sudden leap and swift thunder
> of mountain boulders, his laugh.
> (35–40)

Phaedra's belief is that Hippolyta, like herself, suffers from self-deception and, therefore, that neither can achieve transformation of self.

Eurydice's complaint, in H. D.'s successful monologue "Eurydice" (*CP* 51), is that Orpheus' arrogance is the cause of her grief. Had it not been for his inordinate pride, she would not be found in Hades; instead, she "could have walked with the live souls / above the earth." His arrogance damned her:

> so for your arrogance
> and your ruthlessness
> I am swept back
> where dead lichens drip
> dead cinders upon moss of ash[.]
>
> (I, 6–10)

In place of this subterranean existence, Eurydice yearns for human love and earthly beauty. Flowers, for her, symbolize the epitome of earthly existence.

> What had my face to offer
> but reflex of the earth,
> hyacinth colour
> caught from the raw fissure in the rock
> where the light struck,
> and the colour of azure crocuses
> and the bright surface of gold crocuses
> and of the wind-flower,
> swift in its veins as lightning
> and as white.
>
> (II, 21–30)

In contrast to the colors of the flowers which give meaning to life, she inhabits a colorless nothingness: "everything is crossed with black, / black upon black / and worse than black, / this colourless light." By looking back, Orpheus condemns her to an agonizing existence. Had he forgotten her, she thinks that she would have been able to succumb to an eternal nothingness which she would have transformed, in time, to eternal peace, but he has aroused within her the thirst for life, and, consequently, her plight is unbearable. She wishes to smell the flowers that will give her a new breath of life: "if I could have taken once by breath of them, / enough of them," she thinks that she could have taken life beneath within her. A catalog of what could have been follows:

> if I could have caught up from the earth,
> the whole of the flowers of the earth,
> if once I could have breathed into myself
> the very golden crocuses
> and the red,
> and the very golden hearts of the first saffron,
> the whole of the golden mass,
> the whole of one great fragrance,
> I could have dared the loss.
>
>   (IV, 14–22)

Through suffering she realizes that her hell is no worse than Orpheus' hell on earth. By internalizing her love for life, she recreates the flowers she longs for; moreover, these flowers bloom more resplendently within her than those without. She regains more than she has lost:

> At least I have the flowers of myself,
> and my thoughts, no god
> can take that;
> I have the fervour of myself for a presence
> and my own spirit for light;
>
> and my spirit with its loss
> knows this;
> though small against the black,
> small against the formless rocks,
> hell must break before I am lost;
>
> before I am lost,
> hell must open like a red rose
> for the dead to pass.
>
>   (VII, 1–13)

In "Eurydice," H. D. reaches the point where the self transforms reality. Eurydice attains a sense of spirituality that enhances knowledge of self ("and my spirit with its loss / knows this") and that allows for transformation of reality: "before I am lost, / hell must open like a red rose / for the dead to pass." In "Eurydice," H. D. breaks from the entrapment of "romantic thralldom," by shifting, as DuPlessis observes, "the perspective of this familiar myth."[27] Betrayed but refusing to succumb to Orpheus' arrogance and egoism, Eurydice asserts her own identity in hell. This defiance may be read, DuPlessis suggests, as an affirmation of "the splendor of her essential life."[28]

The self must be either the agent of transformation as is Eurydice, or must emulate the transformational powers exhibited by gods and goddesses, such as Demeter. Love and death are the subjects of many poems but are especially dominant in "Demeter" (*CP* 111). The mother goddess views Persephone's union with Pluto as a rape (a death and a wintry experience). In this monologue, H. D. succeeds in presenting several aspects of Demeter. At first Demeter is viewed as a dolorous mother, establishing, from the goddess' point of view, the futility of men's worship: their prayers do not abate her grief nor compensate for her loss. Nothing can assuage her inconsolable sorrow: "power and wealth, purpose and prayer alike, / (men, fires, feasts, temple steps)" are "useless." Nothing enables her to regain possession of Persephone.

In her grief, Demeter voices a diatribe against fraudulent ritual and prayer, practiced by those worshipers who seek to fulfill their own needs and ask for proof of fulfillment in terms of "scroll, / parchment, oracle, prophecy, precedent;"

> do you ask for tablets marked with thought
> or words cut deep on marble surface,
> do you seek measured utterance or the mystic trance?
>
> (II, 1–5)

The above lines convey the poet's self-warning against the dangers she may succumb to in her search for spiritual reality. There is danger for the poet-worshiper who needs the trappings of ritual in order to deepen her belief in divinity.

Demeter, at this point, issues the commandments that facilitate worship and admonishes the worshipers (II). Wor-

27. Blau DuPlessis, p. 184.   28. Blau DuPlessis, p. 185.

ship entails suffering; it requires concentration and distance; and it subsumes absolute supremacy of the goddess. The object of the quester is always the divinity invoked. The efficacy of worship is to meditate on the tributes of the divine presence. In this lyric it is Demeter who is the greatest nature goddess; she is least only in her loss of Persephone and her inability to retrieve her from Pluto's underworld. Her profound love for Persephone gives her the strength "to keep back the winter / when winter tracks too soon" so that spring may come. Her only recompense is Zeus' promise to have Persephone leave the underworld for six months. Because of her happiness, Demeter makes flowers bloom when Persephone is with her.

She cannot, however, accept the fact that her Primavera, in her union with Pluto, is also the "mistress of Death" (IV). Demeter offsets this harsh reality by remembering the time before the rape when she indulged in motherly love and was herself a young goddess: *"What of her — / mistress of Death?*

> From a golden wreath
> were my hands that girt her head,
> fingers that strove to meet,
> and met where the whisps escaped
> from the fillet, of tenderest gold,
> small circlet and slim
> were my fingers then.
>
> (IV, 1–7)

Sorrow brings about a drastic change in the goddess whose fingers now

> . . . are wrought of iron
> to wrest from earth
> secrets; strong to protect,
> strong to keep back the winter
>
> (IV, 10–13)

so that "hope of spring / rise in the hearts of men."

Hymen concludes with "Prayer" (*CP* 141) and "Helios"

(*CP* 142), which serve to emphasize H. D.'s continued search for spirituality and creativity, also dominant in *Heliodora*. "Prayer" is a petition for spiritual and artistic reawakening:

> Give back the glamour to our will,
> the thought; give back the tool,
> the chisel; once we wrought
> things not unworthy,
> sandal and steel-clasp;
> silver and steel, the coat
> with the white leaf-pattern
> at the arm and throat:
> silver and metal, hammered for the ridge
> of shield and helmet-rim;
> white silver with darker hammered in,
> belt, staff and magic spear-shaft
> with the gilt spark at the point and hilt.
>
> (17–19)

"Helios" (also known as Hyperion) is hailed as the god of light, artistic inspiration, and regeneration. This poetic urge to chisel and hammer poems that embody spiritual fervor and creative energy extends to *Heliodora* (1924). In "Wash of cold river" (*CP* 147), H. D. reiterates a familiar yearning:

> *that I would take*
> *to mold a clear*
> *and frigid statue;*
>
> *rare, of pure texture,*
> *beautiful space and line,*
> *marble to grace*
> *your inaccessible shrine.*
>
> (21–27)

She would mold into permanence "*Ionian water, / chill, snow-ribbed sand, / drift of rare flowers.*" This landscape mirrors the "*intimate thoughts*" or "*the treasure of* [her] *mind.*"

Of the poems in this brief volume, "Heliodora" (*CP* 151) is perhaps the most important one in the sense that it is H. D.'s most intimate poem in the early work. Ostensibly, the poem deals with a competition between two poets who seek the most suitable name for a little girl. "Heliodora," however, is important because it sets the context for later poems which deal with the difficulties encountered by a woman poet.

"Lais" (*CP* 149) deals with the transition from youth and beauty into maturity and old age. At one time (as described in the *Greek Anthology*), Lais was a beautiful and powerful courtesan. Now old, through a mirror she contrasts the pageant of her past life with her present condition. The "now and then" structure divides the poem into two sections: lines 1–36 reflect the tyrannical attraction of Lais' youth and beauty, and lines 37–58 mirror her old age and maturity. At first Lais' tone is triumphant: "Let her who walks in Paphos / take the glass, / let Paphos take the mirror." The city basks in her beauty. She is exultant in her tyranny of Greece: "Lais who kept her lovers in the porch, / lover on lover waiting." Now, her mirror reflects a ruined city and the decline of a great beauty.

"Nossis" (*CP* 155), also culled from the *Greek Anthology*, is about poetry, creativity, the Muse, and love for Greek poetry. Its imagery is one of haunting beauty, often associated with the visitation of the Muse. The setting is a moonlit garden. The speaker, a woman, overhears a man as he nervously paces the garden; his voice is powerful, enchanting, and arresting. As he calls out the name of Nossis, the speaker feels as if "the girl might rise / and make the garden silver, / as the white moon breaks." Here, the speaker provides a provokingly ironic commentary of the poet in the garden and his invocation of the muse — Nossis:

> 'a girl that's dead
> some hundred years;
> a poet — what of that?
> for in the islands,
> in the haunts of Greek Ionia,

Rhodes and Cyprus,
girls are cheap.'
                    (7-13)

Why should a contemporary poet choose a minor Greek
love-poet as his muse, except for the fact that he, too, is
affected by Greek poetry, especially love poetry. With the
flame of love and poetry burning within him, she overhears
his piercing cry: "'I want a garden'" where the spirit of Nos-
sis dwells. The speaker comments:

His was no garden
bright with Tyrian violets,
his was a shelter
wrought with flame and spirit,
and as he flung her name
against the dark,
I thought the iris-flowers
that lined that path
must be the ghost of Nossis.
                    (31-39)

It is this kind of garden, symbolic of the ghost of Greece,
which H. D. avoids. Instead of specters from the past,
she evokes the lingering presentness of a meaningful spiri-
tual past.

The muse also appears in the form of a special goddess in
"Thetis" (*CP* 159), favored by the poet. In the first poem
about Thetis (*CP* 116), in *Hymen,* the sea, the goddess, and
the sun's courtship of the goddess govern the lyric. Here,
however, H. D. focuses on the love between Thetis and Pel-
eus (Achilles' father) and their palace under the sea. Her
metamorphoses are infinite and perfect, as she easily changes
from a "crescent," or "a curve of a wave," to "a glistening
fish." The goddess "flung from the crest / of the wave," strings
a necklace "to mark the beat and the stress / of the lilt" of the
songs that she sings—she "*Who dreams of a son.*" She con-
stantly searches for Achilles, awaiting his "rare foot-fall."

Other poems in *Heliodora* cluster around the aftermath of Troy and the poet's attempt to achieve creative rebirth. "After Troy" (*CP* 168) underscores the tragedy of the fallen heroes. Another victim of the war is heard in the poem "At Ithaca" (*CP* 163). Penelope's monologue is keyed to the rhythm of the ocean and the loom. "Over and back, / the long waves crawl / and track the sand with foam," as her fingers weave "Over and back, / the tangled thread falls slack." She wishes for someone to intervene, for some force to manifest itself so that she can relinquish this death-in-life existence of endless waiting: "I wish some fiery friend / would sweep impetu-ously / these fingers from the loom."

In the monologues (love-petitions) that follow, love is seen as both redemptive and destructive. "Telesila" (*CP* 184) is a love-poet and warrior whose epitaph in Argos reads: "*at her feet the scroll of her love-poetry, in her hand a helmet.*" H. D., as a love poet, identifies with this carved warlike image of Tele-sila, which reveals love's leveling power. As a votary of love, the poet approximates the priestess of Greek mysteries, since love is at the center of the mysteries. Telesila projects a per-fect embodiment of H. D.'s ideal as a poet.

In the early poetry H. D. clearly assumes the role of vo-tary of love poetry, engaging in all its mysteries and espous-ing its devotional and sacramental nature. In "At Eleusis" (*CP* 179), she reaches the "altar step" in a trance and dreams of approximating divine existence: "(I a mortal, set in the god-dess' place?)" In "Charioteer" (*CP* 190), she associates love with the mysteries. In this poem, an extended prayer to the gods and goddesses, she celebrates the creative powers of Apollo and vows: "I will fashion a statue / . . . out of thought, / and the strength of my wrist / and the fire of my brain." Her poetic credo is expressed in this lyric, her "mortal prayer":

> I will strive night and day
> till I mould from the clay,
> till I strike from the bronze,

till I conjure the rock,
the chisel, the tool,
to embody this image[.]
(54–59)

In the *Collected Poems,* H. D. creates images that startle, capture, and transform the self on its first voyage out. In "The Look-out" (*CP* 197), a complex and pivotal poem, she reiterates her poetic dictum by proclaiming "I'd gladly die / if I did not love the quest / . . . the god-like quest." The lyrics dispersed throughout the *Collected Poems* demonstrate the poet's deep involvement with myth, love, and poetry. The petition heard in "Holy Satyr" (*CP* 148) poignantly expresses H. D.'s achievement in the *Collected Poems:*

hear this our song,
accept our leaves,
love-offering,
return our hymn,
like echo fling
a sweet song,
answering note for note.
(24–30)

It is apparent that creativity and spirituality sustain her through the inward struggles encountered on the initial phase of the quest. Immense inner reserve commands her dedication as a poet, and deeply felt worship guides her progress toward achieving regeneration and reconstruction of self. With relentless precision, she creates a personal and contemplative vision of the self in search of spirituality and creativity.

3. Transcendence:
Red Roses For Bronze (1931)

The function of the poet and poetry, rejection and isolation incurred by unrequited love, and the need for spirituality direct H. D.'s focus in *Red Roses for Bronze* (1931). The *Greek Anthology* inspires many of the essentially nondramatic monologues which closely approximate the tone and fervor of Greek poetry. However, her monologues — complaints, addresses, prayers — also reflect the subjectivity and introspection prevalent in modern poetry. These poems not only function as a perfect vehicle for self-expression and subjective utterance, but they also further H. D.'s mythopoeic mode and contemplative stance. Many of the prayers, addressed to her special gods, are a concrete realization of the synthesizing activity of a self involved in ritualistic acts aimed toward transcendence. Her twofold aim in *Red Roses for Bronze*, then, is to sculpt a durable poetry and to dwell among the "host of the immortals" ("Calliope," *RB* 286).[1]

The progression toward transcendence, or the pursuit of a transcendent self, is, in essence, a movement toward understanding the mystery that envelops all life, as evinced in the concluding lyric of *Red Roses For Bronze* entitled "The Mys-

1. All subsequent line and page references from *Red Roses For Bronze* are from Louis L. Martz's *H. D. Collected Poems 1912–1944* (New York: New Directions, 1983), p. 286. The abbreviation *RB* is used for *Red Roses For Bronze*.

teries" (*RB* 300), where there is no distinction between
Greek and Christian myth. As a result, a new spiritual height
is reached. Through a constantly reiterated "I am," the name
of the deity addressed becomes synonymous with the self
["The mysteries remain" (Part VI of "The Mysteries")]. The
speaker proclaims: "'I am red wine and bread'" and "'*I am
the vine, / the branches, you / and you.*'" Cassirer in *Language
and Myth* points out that in this progressive development of
mythical identification a sense of unity between objective and
subjective experience is achieved, so that "the meaning of di-
vinity is approached not through the existence of things, but
through the being of the Person, the Self."[2] H. D.'s insistence
on concreteness of presentation and sharpness of image also
substantiates her process of mythmaking. Cassirer's com-
ments shed light on this aspect of H. D.'s poetics:

Here, again, the mythmaking mind exhibits a sort of consciousness
of the relationship between its product and the phenomenon of lan-
guage, though characteristically it can express this relationship not
in abstract logical terms, but only in images. . . . This emergence
from the vague fullness of existence into a world of clear, verbally
determinable forms, xs represented in the mythic mode, in the
imagist fashion peculiar to it.[3] . . .

The mythopoetic stance acts as a liberating force. "This
liberation," Cassirer explains, "is achieved not because the
mind throws aside the sensuous forms of word and image,
but in that it uses them both as organs of its own, and
thereby recognizes them for what they really are: forms of its
own self-revelation."[4] In *Contemplative Prayer*, Merton sug-
gests that, at this level, image and ritual enable "the inner
self of the contemplative to incorporate the senses and the
body in the totality of the self-orientation . . . that is neces-

---

2. Ernst Cassirer, *Language and Myth*, tr. Susanne Langer (New York:
Dover, 1946), p. 76.

3. Cassirer, p. 81.   4. Cassirer, p. 99.

sary for worship and for meditation."[5] In this sense, Merton sees that objectivity and concreteness bring forth an extraordinary flowering of inner reality, "a flowering of the 'spiritual senses' and the aesthetic awareness," which is at once a sensuous and spiritual heightening of experience.[6] In *Red Roses For Bronze*, H. D. uses myth, prayer, image, and ritual to attain an aesthetically and spiritually liberated life rooted in permanence.

The title poem "Red Roses For Bronze" (*RB* 211) expresses the poet's urge to create a durable poetry —

> If I might take a weight of bronze
> and sate
> my wretched fingers
> in ecstatic work[.]
>
>   (I, 1–4)

Her intent is to "hammer" perfectly clear lines:

> if I might ease my fingers and my brain
> with stroke,
> stroke,
> stroke,
> stroke,
> stroke at — something (stone, marble intent,
> stable, materialized)[.]
>
>   (I, 13–18)

After a brilliant beginning, the poem begins to falter. The conversational idiom seems contrived and diffused, and the aim of making her poet-lover equal the gods results in a rather tiresome Part II. The unresolved tension that exists throughout this five-part poem arises from the futile search for a perfect earthly lover. Although she confronts a rival

5. Thomas Merton, *Contemplative Prayer* (New York: Herder and Herder, 1969), p. 106.
6. Merton, p. 106.

poet-lover who rejects her love and her verse, she does not abandon the search for the quintessential lover.

H. D.'s view of love closely resembles Denis de Rougemont's view in *Love in the Western World,* a book she later says that she had read many times. Love is so glorified that it becomes "infinite transcendence, man's rise into his god. And this rise is without return."[7] Love is a "divinizing of desire," in the sense that "Eros has pursued infinite becoming."[8] Because sexual desire is utterly frustrated, it is sublimated into the desire for divinity and eternity. Since she finds no recompense in sexual love, she turns to the love of the gods, thus writing a love poetry that will endure — "my roses would endure, / while others / . . . must fall and sift and pale."

"In the Rain" (*RB* 215) exposes the speaker's disenchantment with an irritable, jealous, and often absent lover (I–III). Here she concludes that sexual "(love is a trap, / a snare)" (III). As a result, she finds solace in poetry: "no pain of love" (IV) silences the rhythm in her brain, and it does not obscure "the way to the temple" (IV). She knows that her poetic quest will prove to be more successful than her love experiences (IV). The "way to the temple" is yet another apt metaphor for H. D.'s quest. Her fortitude resides in the progressive reawakening of the spiritual self: "then, / the air / will be full of multiple wings" (IV). Then, too, a more encompassing kind of love will be experienced and the god of love will stand at the square. Presently, however, she will "walk by the shrine / and the sacred rows" (IV) and recreate the god of love and poetry in her own verse:

> I will bow
> to one God;
> (O intimate song,

---

7. Denis de Rougemont, *Love and Death in the Western World,* tr. Montgomery Belgion (New York: Pantheon, 1956), p. 62.
8. de Rougemont, p. 68.

>   my Lord,
>   O fire
>   and the Word).
>   (V, 20–25)

The wound of love has maimed her (VII), but she seeks res-
toration, "sustenance" and "shelter" (V) in poetry and in her
special god, Hermes. As "a god above / and a god below"
(VI), Hermes will guide her through the passage from death-
in-life to one of spiritual flowering. "Hermes, / Lord-of-the-
dead" (VI) will aid her. "Defamed," "maimed," and "lost,"
the speaker seeks Hermes' healing powers.[9]

"If You Will Let Me Sing" (*RB* 222) is a lucid, nine-line
sentence image in which she prays for inspiration so that her
songs will be worthy of the gods.

>   If you will let me sing,
>   That God will be
>   gracious to each of us,
>   who found his own wild Daphne
>   in a tree,
>   who set
>   on desolate plinth,
>   image
>   of Hyacinth.

The suffering of the gods and their mysteries completely dom-
inates H. D.'s imagination. The mysteries associated with Di-
onysus and his suffering, for instance, are the themes of her
"Choros Translations" from *The Bacchae* (*RB* 223). Assuming
the role of bacchant, she states: "I cry with every note / of
concentrated speech / my song to Dionysos." Blessed is the

----

9. Robert Graves, *The White Goddess* (London: Faber and Faber, 1948),
p. 173. In *The White Goddess*, Robert Graves refers to one of the doctrines
of mystical paganism which stresses the belief that when men died their
souls were carried to eternity by Hermes, "the conductor of souls." The
Greek also identified Hermes with the Egyptian Thoth, so that among his
multiple attributes he is also the god of healing.

individual who reenacts the rituals associated with the wor-
ship of gods and goddesses:

> O happy, happy each
> man whom predestined fate
> leads to the holy rite
> of hill and mountain worship;
> O blessed, blessed spirit
> who seeks the mountain goddess,
> Cybele mother-spirit. . . .
> (I, 16–19)

Those who reject the gods, a theme originating in *Sea Garden*,
in actuality, reject wisdom, beauty, and holiness. Even if "the
way to the temple" is extremely difficult and lonely, the gods'
existence cannot be denied:

> mysterious,
> mystical happiness,
> this one
> who finds
> day by day,
> hour by hour,
> mysterious,
> mystical,
> not to be spoken
> bliss.
> (IV, Epode, 20–30)

The search for creative silence, solitude, and permanence,
is the subject of "Chance Meeting" (*RB* 231). The poet-
lover's aim is to focus on the evanescent, and "translatable /
things," whereas her aim is to grasp the eternal mysteries of
things that

> are nameless,
> old and true;
> they may not be named;
> few may live and know.
> (I, 18–22)

Mystery mesmerizes her completely and her spirit is caught in it. Had she and the other poet reached this level of communication, they might have constructed another world together: "Our hands might have crushed / red petal / of an island rose" (II). They would have imaginatively traveled to the islands (H. D.'s version of the Holy Land), where "heaven" might be "a near / translatable thing" (II). Although they both deal with Greek myth, he seems to take "'whatever fire there was'" (IV), out of it: his gods are left "'without love / and without power'" (IV). Instead of perceiving a permanent reality, he focuses on "'things that otherwise must perish / in the wind / and fire'" (IV).

Unlike her, he is blind to spiritual reality:

> You didn't know
> those Gods that pass,
> those feet that come and go,
> the parting of the curtain
> where waves swell,
> the holy sands,
> the sunken holy well,
> the wave that burns
> and breaks a sharper blue
> because for just one moment
> some deft thought
> severed the curtain
> of that 'then' and 'now.'
>   (V, 1–13)

In her conception of spiritual reality, there is no break between the past, present, and future. The gods have not vanished; instead they have retreated into the human psyche. Under their spell, she perceives a "sense of the wings beyond the gate" (V) that promises universal transcendence and redemption.

H. D.'s pursuit of transcendence in *Red Roses For Bronze* is imaged as a journey through the islands ["Sea-Choros" translation from *Hecuba*, RB 237)]. She identifies her search with

Hecuba's. Like Hecuba, exiled and unfortunate, she wonders where her quest will take her — "where, / where in the land of the Greek, / do you take me?"

The first sojourn on the islands, marked by a shifting state of consciousness, is ushered in by wine and sleep. In the sacramental poem "Wine Bowl" (*RB* 241), she sculpts a bowl engraved with images of nymph, satyr, and naiad. Inspired, she will sing songs, accompanied by reed and lyre, that will affect men's hearts so as to direct them toward a similar quest. In a trance-like state ("Trance," *RB* 244), she imagines herself to be in a ". . . bare, bare open court, / (geometric, / with circumspect wing)" and confronts a "naked plinth, / the statue's rare, / intolerant grace."

In the movement from trance to the sleep, she invokes Morpheus [in "Chorus Sequence," from *Morpheus* (*RB* 253)] because she is tired of "protestation," "argument," and the "brain's intricacies." She seeks the wisdom that transpires in Morpheus' dreams because it "has driven deeper / than the lordliest tome / of Attic thought / or Cyrenian logic." She craves for the poppies that would:

> still my ambition
> that would rear and chafe
> like chariot horses
> waiting for the race;
> let me forget
> the spears of Marathon.
> (I, 37–42)

She seeks respite from Morpheus, whom she perceives as offering an entrance into a transcendent reality.

She hopes that this abandonment will enable her to cast aside the curtain separating self from self. The poppies bring her closer to her inner self: "we near heaven's hills with this, / God's asphodels." She is willing to forego all of her previous experiences "for just one grain / of [his] enchantment" and prays to Morpheus to "lift / the veil, / dividing me

from me." This shift of consciousness would stimulate her
creativity:

> *I would revive the whole*
> *of Ilium*
> *and in sacred trance,*
> *show Helen*
> *who made Troy*
> *a barren town.*
>   (III, 35–40)

She hopes that this magic would lift the veil which shrouds
the Eleusinian mysteries, associated with Dionysus, Deme-
ter, and Persephone:

> *the lost and lovely Daughter*
> *must arise*
> *and God must quicken hell*
> *and Paradise*
> *must be revealed to all*[.] (Emphasis mine)
>   (VI, 14–18)

Such a transformation of consciousness brings an end to one
world and ushers in another: "So having died, / raise me
again, / again" (VIII).

This new shift in consciousness furthers H. D.'s mythical
identification. Within Morpheus' "fringe of consciousness,"
she assumes the role of Thetis (Achilles' "lover-mother"). She
is also aware that unless she translates these thoughts into
controlled verse or song wrought in enchantment (XII) she
will inhabit a state of madness (XI). Using her poetic pow-
ers, she transforms her dreams into verses that are "sac-
rosanct / and blest" (XII). Her obsession with Achilles and
Helen has to be transmuted into poetry (XIII). Presently
awake, she resumes the task before her to re-envisage those
who accomplished the "Delphic quest" (XII).

This aim is visible in "Myrtle Bough" (*RB* 245). The motto
("*'I'll wreathe my sword in a myrtle-bough'*") derived from the
Greek Anthology expresses her admiration for the valor of

these heroes (in particular that of Harmodius and Aristogiton) who bravely waged battles alongside Perseus. The heroes' valor affects the gods, who ultimately bring forth the ascendancy of worship over war: her "manifold power / of song / and verse / and prayer" (IV). The supremacy of love, worship, and art brings about apotheosis:

> O Tyrian shoot,
> I would impregnate you
> with sacredness
> so that you never, never could be free
> but loom
> and waver
> and waft terribly
> white wings and wings of gold
> across bright skies
> be Eros to all eyes.
>
> (VI, 42–51)

She evokes the return of halcyon days and attempts to retrieve the loss of peace incurred by unrequited love. In "Halcyon" (*RB* 270) she laments the loss of love and begs for the power to overcome her discontentment.[10] Without love the landscape of her mind is desolate and arid,

> . . . like a desert apart
> without hope of oasis
>
> or a grot lacking water
> or a bird with a broken wing
> or some sort of withered Adon-garden[.]
>
> (VI, 19–23)

The power of love is celebrated in "Songs From Cyprus" (*RB* 277), which originate in H. D.'s translation-recreation

---

10. Thomas Bulfinch, *The Age of Fable* (Philadelphia: David McKay, 1898), p. 94; see: pp. 88–94. Her wailing cry was heard by the gods who changed her and her husband into birds who yearly mate, and "for seven placid days, in winter time, Halcyone broods over her nest, which floats upon the sea."

Hippolytus Temporizes (1927) dedicated to Aphrodite. "Songs From Cyprus" include "Gather for festival"; "White rose, O white"; "Where is the nightingale"; "Bring myrrh and myrtle bud"; and "In Cyprus."

The first song, "Gather for festival," is a preparation for the celebration of the goddess' feast. Appropriately, the offerings are associated with the sea. The worshipers are to gather "bright weed and purple shell" and are to dance rhythmically on "holy sand," making a

> pattern as one might make
> who tread, with rose-red heel,
> a measure
> pleasureful[.]
>
> (I, 4–7)

They are also to gather rose and myrtle, sacred to Aphrodite.[11]

In the citron glade, the erotic bower of the goddess, red and white roses are spread before her feet (I). The change from white to red roses, symbolized by the stain of cyclamen, is accounted for by the birth of Eros (II). The celebrant is to "Bring fluted asphodel" and "silver" (III) and "fling them before Love's Shrine" (III), where the white flowers turn to red. The association of love with night brings forth the song of the nightingale (IV): "Where is the nightingale, / in what myrrh-wood and dim?" (IV). Part V furthers the preparation for Aphrodite's festival: the celebrants are to "Bring myrrh and myrtle bud," "white violet," "white citron" and "whitest rose, / (myrrh leaves, myrrh leaves enclose)."

The contrast between the offerings made in Cyprus and Greece poignantly points to two different kinds of love. In Cyprus (the topos in "The Shrine," "Cliff Temple," and "Sea Gods" in *Sea Garden*), love is associated with the Adongarden: "In Cyprus, / we sought lilies for her shrine, / (white and dark-petalled where Adonis bled)" (VI). In Greece,

11. Graves, pp. 168–213, *passim.*

however, love tyrannizes men's hearts and is "scarred with fire" (VI). This antinomy is obvious:

> . . . here in Greece,
> love is a torment
> and they drive him out, far out,
> and sue for peace.
>
> (VI, 11–14)

The poet concludes that no one should reject Aphrodite's kind of love since it governs the universe: "there is no escape / from her who nurtures, / who imperils all" (VI).

Her dedication to this kind of love is evident in "Let Zeus Record" (*RB* 281), where she does not apologize for her poetry, which "outlines simply / Love's authority" (II), made concrete in an ideal lover unaffected by inconstancy. The poet's role is similar to that of "one who sets a statue on a height / to show where Hyacinth or Pan have been" (III). In this particular poem, the idealized lover is Theseus (IV–V) whose celebrated battles are the subject of the bas-reliefs of the Parthenon (I).

None, however, equal the ideal lover in "Stars wheel in purple" (VI), who is the epitome of beauty, youth, and spring. (It is interesting to note that in *Palimpsest* [1926] this poem was dedicated to Bryher). "Stars wheel in purple" is a springboard to her invocation of "Calliope" (*RB* 286), the muse of epic poetry. She invokes Calliope so as "To climb the intricate heights / of unimpeded rapture" and to transform carnal to sacred love. Then, she will overcome "blackest despair" and retreat from "the intolerable host / and throng of mortals spoil." Her desire is to dwell among "the white throng, / the host of the immortals," who like the "stars, swing free / and need no lamp of silver work or bronze." Her verse removes the temporal curtain (the "fleshly portal)."

"All Mountains" (*RB* 288), a version of Artemis' hymn to Zeus, provides the landscape that she seeks. Like Artemis, she seeks a rarefied existence — "give me the islands of the upper air." She wishes to dwell apart and worship in "secret altars," surrounded by snow and "threatened with wave of pine, / with wash of alder." H. D.'s use of these particular trees suggests a knowledge of mystic lore associated with the worship of deities. In *The White Goddess*, Graves traces the worship of goddesses associated with specific trees. In Greece, for instance, the alder is associated with goddesses of death and resurrection, whereas the pine, associated with Artemis, is sacred to her.[12]

The concluding poems in *Red Roses For Bronze* are, in essence, petitions to sustain the poet's "mystic lore." They reveal H. D.'s obsession with and dedication to the goddess-muse, addressed as "O spirit, white, / and versed in mystic lore" ("Calliope"). She hopes to produce a poetry ("a few rare songs and some philosophising," "Let Zeus Record" IV) that will further her knowledge of the goddess.

In "Triplex," subtitled "A Prayer" (*RB* 291), H. D. discloses the triple nature of the goddess, a composite of Athena-Artemis-Aphrodite. She asks for a peaceful coexistence of the goddess' triple nature within herself: "Let them not war in me, / these three." Pallas-Athena is the "Saviour-of-cities, / Flower-of-destiny"; Artemis-Diana, the "Twinborn-with-Phoebus," is the "Maid / of the luminous grey-eyes"; and the rose of the Cyprian coast refers to Aphrodite-Venus.

"Birds in Snow" (*RB* 292) suggests that the durability of her poetry stems from its being devoted to the gods. Her images, *"in carven hieroglyph,"* (emphasis mine) adorn temples with "ancient writ" (12). Her "hieratic" symbols trace the myths of the past, and her poetry "proclaims what's left unsaid."

H. D.'s "mystic's lore" is also rooted in white magic associated with nature and divinity.[13] The seven "seals" begun in

12. Graves, p. 197, *passim*.   13. Cassirer, pp. 44–62.

"Sigil" (*RB* 294) are later added to in the sequence *A Dead Priestess Speaks,* where she adds lyrics VIII–XIX (*CP* 411). She is inspired by "grass-blade" (V), "fern / and moss" and "every wind-flower." In "Epitaph" (*RB* 299), she hopes to be immersed into this world:

> "Greek flower; Greek ecstasy
> reclaims for ever
>
> one who died
> following
> intricate songs' lost measure."
> (8–12)

Her affinity and identification with flowers and trees stress her keen devotion to the mysteries which hold sacred the trees and flowers associated with the veneration of particular deities.

In "The Mysteries" (*RB* 300), subtitled "Renaissance Choros," H. D. espouses the celebration of Greek and Christian mysteries. The apocalyptic nature of the poem, symbolic of external cataclysms and catastrophes, is subdued only by the inner strength of a self involved in the celebration of the mysteries. External chaos and turmoil give way to a spiritual flowering of the self:

> then voice within the turmoil,
> that slight breath
> that tells as one flower may
> of winter past
> (that kills
> with Pythian bow,
> the Delphic pest;)
> one flower,
> slight voice,
> reveals
> all holiness
> with
> "peace
> be still."
> (I, 26–29)

The poet ("enchanter / and magician," II) sanctifies the past and reenacts the death and resurrection witnessed in the Adonis experience (III). The sanctity of love is celebrated (IV), and the poet's function is to keep the mysteries alive ("'Not to destroy, / nay, but to sanctify / the fervour / of all ancient mysteries'" (V) by making the spiritual evident in the actual. Spiritual reality is concrete and accessible ("'the grain is gold, / blade, / stalk / and seed within; / the mysteries / are in the grass / and rain'" (V).

Because she possesses new insight, she does not draw a disingenuous distinction between pagan and sacred myth:

> "The mysteries remain,
> I keep the same
> cycle of seed-time
> and of sun and rain;
> Demeter in the grass
> I multiply,
> renew and bless
> Iaccus in the vine;
> I hold the law,
> I keep the mysteries true,
> the first of these
> to name the living, dead;
> I am red wine and bread."
>
> (V, 1–13)

The worship of Demeter, the earth-mother associated with grain, harvest, and the renewal of nature, is associated with that of her daughter, Persephone. Because of her anguish over Persephone's rape, Demeter is also the Mother of Sorrows.

In the Eleusinian mysteries, the worship of Demeter is also associated with that of Dionysus (Bacchus, Iaccus, or Bromios), the god of wine, upholder of the law, and the lover of peace. In addition to the orgiastic rituals celebrated by the Bacchants, a wine festival, variously called "cask-opening day" or "pouring day," was celebrated annually and a miracle was believed to take place at one of Dionysus' places of worship.[14] The association between Dionysus and Christ was made by the early Christians, who saw the pagan god as a prototype of Christ who changed water into wine.[15] The biblical Christ is also known as the vine. Demeter, Dionysus, and Christ are assimilated and, therefore, she proclaims:

> "*I keep the law,*
> *I hold the mysteries true,*
> *I am the vine,*
> *The branches, you*
> *and you.*"
>
> (VI, 14–18)

By keeping and celebrating the mysteries, the poet-celebrant discovers the path toward transcendence. The second phase of the quest, then, effects a transformation from objective to subjective experience. In *Red Roses For Bronze*, H. D. accomplishes the task of making the personal pronoun, "I keep the law, / I hold the mysteries true, / I am the vine," analogous with "I am he; I am the first, I also am the last" (Isaiah 48:12; 43:10) of the Prophetic Books, thus attaining transcendence.

14. Bulfinch, p. 473.
15. Arthur Weigall, *The Paganism in Our Christianity* (London: Hutchinson, 1928), p. 63; *passim*.

4. Hieroglyphs: "Uncollected and Unpublished Poems" (1912–1944)

Bridging the chronological gap in H. D.'s poetic canon are forty pivotal poems, some previously published and others withheld from publication by H. D., but all are now collected together for the first time in Louis L. Martz's *H. D. Collected Poems 1912–1944*.[1] These poems not only strengthen the thematic structures begun in *Sea Garden*, but also provide thematic continuity and progression between *The Collected Poems* (1925) and *Red Roses For Bronze* (1931). Moreover, some of these poems eradicate the notion of H. D.'s silent years, 1925–1931 and 1931–1944, periods of no major poetic publication, but during which she wrote a great deal and discovered her own voice. These poems cumulatively create a self-reflexive discourse definitive of mythical-meditative poetry. The outcome of contemplation in these poems is the discovery of a distinctive poetic voice heard as it pierces through several masks which she begins to shatter for the first time.

In relation to H. D.'s entire poetic canon, these poems offer a repository of metonymy, providing several metaphors of filiation to the early and later poetries. They are essential

1. Martz's edition (New York: New Directions, 1983) also includes a noteworthy Introduction, pp. xi–xxxvi, and invaluable Notes, pp. 613–624. All quotations and page references to the poems in this chapter refer to this new edition, abbreviated *CP*.

in reconstructing her concept of spiritual realism. "Late Spring," for instance, affirms the existence of divinity in nature theme, whereas "I Said" clearly points to the poet-as-seer, fully developed in the later poetry. Because of their metonymy, their ability to stand for whole complexes of thought, these poems become permanent hieroglyphs of H. D.'s poetics, moving the reader backward and forward within her poetic discourses while simultaneously providing the necessary interstices.

"Late Spring," "Helios and Athene," "The Shepherd," "At Croton," "Projector," "Projector II (Chang)," and "Other Sea-Cities" reiterate the central themes found in the first poetry: the visibility of gods and goddesses to the select and elect quester-worshipers; the manifestations of deities — their presence — in their special places of worship; the gods and goddesses' gifts to the quester-worshipers; and the tributes paid to the divinities by the worshipers.

The themes of lostness, the search for the perfect god-like lover, the lament of the deserted and betrayed lover, the poet-as-seer, and the supremacy of the goddess crystallize in the triadic poems, "Amaranth," "Eros," and "Envy," as well as in "I Said," "Gift," and "Psyche."

A formidable group of nine poems prepared for eventual publication by H. D. is found in the sequence *A Dead Priestess Speaks*, which includes: "A Dead Priestess Speaks," "Electra-Orestes," "Calypso," "In Our Town," "Delphi," "Dodona," "Sigil," "Priest," and "Master (Magician)." These poems point to the dominant themes of H. D.'s major poetry. As a significant representative of her middle period, *A Dead Priestess Speaks* "conveys its sense of resurrection by moving from Greek masks toward a personal voice, in a volume that moves at the same time from Greek to Christian themes."[2]

2. Louis L. Martz, Introduction, in *H. D. Collected Poems 1912–1944* (New York: New Directions, 1983), p. xxvi.

Sent to Norman Holmes Pearson in 1949, but partly published in 1932 and early 1933, *A Dead Priestess Speaks* begins with a monologue of the same title spoken by the dead priestess, Delia of Miletus, "whose voice," Martz notes, "has come alive in the form of a personal confession."[3] Martz also adds that in this first poem,

The Greek mask . . . is quite transparent: the prophetess is a modern woman speaking modern thoughts about herself and her psychic resurrection—presumably after the consultation with Freud (whom, she says in "The Master," she spoke with in "Miletus"—and "Delia" [Alton] was her favorite nom-de-plume.[4]

The other poems of this sequence, except for "The Magician (Master)," deal exclusively with Greek themes prevalent in the first poetry. Perversion of love and lapsed rituals are the themes in "Electra-Orestes"; the rejected goddess-lover is reiterated in "Calypso"; the power of the gods' divine work, their presence, mystery, and ecstasy dominate the two oracle-poems, "Delphi" and "Dodona." The symbol (seal or talisman) and its meaning in religion, ritual, myth, and poetry are encapsulated in "Sigil," also a powerful demonstration of a personal voice. "Priest," as Martz points out, is "the longest and most openly personal poem . . . cast in the form of a frank conversation with a lover of long ago. . . ."[5]

The sequence concludes with "Magician [Master]," a vision of the wise man who symbolizes perfect wisdom, truth, and beauty, and who foreshadows the spirit-master-magician Kaspar of *Trilogy*. Martz adds that the poem is "a long and subtle evocation of the spirit of Jesus as evidenced in his effect upon his followers and audiences."[6] Although it was published before H. D.'s sessions with Freud, Martz suggests that

3. Martz, p. xxv.   4. Martz, p. xxv.
5. Martz, p. xxvi.   6. Martz, p. xxvi.

the strength of the poem shows what Freud himself appears quickly to have understood: that H. D. needed chiefly the counsel that would bring forth in her the poems of the future.[7]

The "Magician," however, may be read as part of yet another group of poems: "The Master," "The Dancer," and "The Poet." In the "Introduction" to *H. D. Collected Poems 1912–1944*, Martz writes that the typescripts show that

H. D. had experimented with another arrangement of her uncollected and unpublished poems, in at least four groupings. Most significant of all is her suggestion for "Part IV": "The Priest," "The Master," "The Dancer," and "The Poet"—all four highly personal poems and all speaking in an open voice about another human being for whom the speaker feels a strong attachment.[8]

"The Dancer" addresses woman-as-artist and the supremacy of the goddess. "The Master" is a poem about Freud, one which H. D. resolutely withheld from publication because of her unresolved conflicts and differences with Freud, as Rachael Blau DuPlessis and Susan Stanford Friedman argue in "'Woman Is Perfect': H. D.'s Debate With Freud." If "The Master" pays tribute to Freud, then "The Poet" pays "a calm and measured tribute to the memory of D. H. Lawrence," writes Martz.[9] Moreover, the metonymic structure of "The Poet" places it at the very core of H. D.'s middle period, since it catalogs the poet's dominant images, syntactical phrases, and signs.

The last group of poems clearly points to the major poems. "Two Poems for Christmas, 1937," "Ancient Wisdom Speaks" (dated April 14, 1943), "Body and Soul," "R.A.F.," "May 1943," and "Christmas 1944" function as a prologue to the apocalypse-resurrection poem *Trilogy*. They also surface as "star-by-day" poems, illuminating many of the themes devel-

7. Martz, p. xxvi.   8. Martz, p. xxvii.
9. Martz, p. xxviii.

oped in *Helen in Egypt* and *Hermetic Definition*. "Saturn" and "Zeus-Provider" (fragments from *Temple of the Sun*), and *"Archer,"* while seeming "wildly dissimilar" ("Scribe" *CP* 476), are both hieroglyphs of transcendence. Finally, in "Erige Cor Tuum Ad Me in Caelum" (*CP* 479) and "Ecce Sponsus" (*CP* 480) H. D. goes beyond the horror of World War II. These poems envelop everyday reality with the verities of Christian mysteries, arrived at through authentic prayer.

In "Late Spring" (*CP* 309; 1916), the worshipers, overcome by too perfect a flowering, become transfixed by its beauty. As in "Orchard" and "Pear Tree," the worshipers in "Late Spring" cannot bear the divine beauty revealed in nature: "We can not weather all this gold"; "we can not hold our heads erect / Under this golden dust"; "We can not stand"; and "We can not see." Devoted as they are, their spiritual progression has not advanced to the level necessary for worshipers to "see" the cornucopia of "late spring," symbolizing divine gifts.

"Helios and Athene" (*CP* 326; 1920) is a catalog of prose epigrams that function as "carven hieroglyph[s]." For instance, in the exquisitely engraved shield, the serpent and the swan are found side by side, and it is Athena, the goddess of wisdom, who gives succor to the serpent. The goddess is also associated with Demeter and the Eleusinian mysteries. The goddess' other symbols, the "Nike" and "birds," symbolize liberty and the soul. Foreshadowing *Helen in Egypt*, the goddess admonishes Helios to consider his soul. Through the goddess' words, the poet defines her ars poetica.

Helios' statue, suggestive of youth and beauty, transfixes the beholder: "we gain from the statue the . . . glow of physical warmth and power" (p. 327). Since the statue acts as a go-between for the sculptor and the gods, "The human imagination is capable of no further expression of beauty than the carved owl of Athene, the archaic, marble serpent" (p. 327).

The aesthetic theory articulated in "Helios and Athene" directly echoes *Notes on Thoughts and Vision*. The sculpture, or the poem, is more than the "self-complacent admiration" (p. 327) of the perceiver or of the artist.[10]

The perceiver enters the art work as the priest (or worshiper) engages in a religious ritual. Participation leads to penetration and contemplation which, for H. D., further self-knowledge, or transcendence. Therefore, she writes: "the statue was like a ledge of rock, from which a great bird steps as he spreads his wings" (p. 328). Similarly, the perceiver "rests for a moment, in the contemplation or worship of that Beauty" (p. 328). In so doing, "The mind grips the statue as the bird grips the rock-ledge" (p. 328). By entering the work of art, one discovers "a new approach" to the world of art (p. 328). Through the perception of the shield, a new perception of the poem is attained. "Helios and Athene" is about more than a merging of female and male powers, as it is about the male-female attributes that constitute the kind of beauty found in Greek sculpture, myth, and literature. This prose poem, moreover, clearly establishes the dominant hieroglyphs of H. D.'s poetics.

Vestiges of divine beauty are also perceived in nature, where the worshiper-quester, as in many *Sea Garden* poems, discovers in "Projector" (*CP* 349; 1927) the "unrecorded grace" of divinity: "Light takes new attribute." The abandoned gods are intent on regaining their loss and those who seek them experience an "insidious fire" which "reasserts" their "power" and

> reclaims the lost;
> in a new blaze of splendour
> calls the host. . . .
>
> (25–27)

10. H. D., *Notes on Thought and Vision* (San Francisco: City Lights, 1982).

By tracing the gods' footsteps along the sea-path, the speaker escapes the evil of modern day and returns to worship among the ruins:

> I have returned
> though in an evil day
> you crouched despairingly
> who had no shrine[.]
>
> (83–86)

With her return, "vision returns" and "with new vision / fresh / hope / to the impotent" is given. Clearly in "Projector," the speaker validates and valorizes the *Sea Garden* experience.

In "Projector II (Chang)" (*CP* 353) light becomes insight, the gift bestowed by the gods upon the worshiper-questers. The voyage out brings with it a "vision of streams and pathways," one "that sears and breaks / us / from old doubts / and fears / and lassitudes." The perfect moment is often experienced when their "souls are merged with quietness." The worshipers' supreme recompense is to rest "beside the riverhead / and lap / waters / of holiness." The voyage out has rescued the worshipers "from old fears / and powers / and disenchantments." The suffering of the drifting self has brought the quester "into realms of magic," where she and others remain "spell-bound."

The light of the sun god draws the worshipers to his altar, a transcendent experience described by the speaker as a necessary rite of passage: "we pass into a space / of intermediate life." As if entering realms of gold, the speaker feels enveloped in "a ray of gilded light," sustained by the imagination — "man's inventiveness." Having discovered a "new approach" to her art of spiritual realism, "through the medium of the Mysteries and through the intercession of other Gods" (*CP* 329), she now is able to "create / form / from the formless dark," and having reached the "waters / of holiness," the poet is enveloped within a *mysterium tremendum et fascinans* which translates her into "pure ecstasy."

Yet the quester does not permanently remain "beside the river-head." In her pursuit of physical love, she once again experiences suffering and anguish which seem to be the outcomes of passionate love. "Amaranth," "Eros," and "Envy" are poems of betrayal. By the time of their composition and partial publication in 1924 in *Heliodora* H. D. had experienced "the infidelities of Richard Aldington (whom she had married in 1913, after her close relationship with Pound had faltered)," and these "created a sense of betrayal that became too strong for these modes of mythic or poetic control."[11] According to Martz, this story is told in "Amaranth," "Eros," and "Envy," "preserved in a carefully bound typescript containing only these poems and bearing on the flyleaf the inscription in H. D.'s hand: 'Corfe Castle — Dorset — summer 1917 — from the poems of *The Islands* series.'"[12] These poems "enact the anguish of a deserted woman."[13]

The purple flower that never fades in "Amaranth" (*CP* 310) is not a symbol of the male lover but of the goddess, whom the speaker had rejected for the lover. Now deserted, she stumbles toward "her altar-step,"

> though my flesh is scorched and rent,
> shattered, cut apart,
> and slashed open;
> though my heels press my own wet life
> black, dark to purple,
> on the smooth rose-streaked
> threshold of her pavement.
>
> (I, 37–44)

Part II describes the debilitating consequences of betrayal, causing the self to become blind and deaf (II, 1). Renouncing

11. Martz, p. xiv.   12. Martz, p. xiv.
13. Martz, p. xiv.

the dishonesty of the lover, the speaker returns to the goddess and discovers her unsurpassing beauty (III). Bitterness from betrayal diminishes as the speaker returns to the "Lady of all beauty" (III), to whom she brings the offering of "white myrrh-leaf / and sweet lentisk" (III).

"Eros" (*CP* 315) fully depicts the speaker's frailty and vulnerability under the spell of a false lover, reducing her to a petal "about to fall shattered" (VI). In "Eros" Martz points out, "the speaker calls to the love-god in agony: 'Where is he taking us / now that he has turned back?' And the 'fever' of her passion leads to the most intimate account of physical love to be found in H. D.'s early poetry."[14]

Betrayal, in "Envy" (*CP* 319), brings forth a kind of despair that makes death tolerable. Abandoned, she despairingly cries to the lover "What can death send me / that you have not?" (II), and what can be worse "than the memory of those first violets?" (II). The consequences of his betrayal have "rent" (III) her apart. Her suffering is rendered more acute because she feels that the goddess has also rejected her love and, therefore, has slain her.

Reading the poem from a different viewpoint, Martz notes that "Envy" impinges upon "the wartime threat of death to the lover: 'I envy your chance of death / how I envy you this'":

> what can death loose in me
> after your embrace?
> your touch,
> your limbs are more terrible
> to do me hurt.
>
> What can death mar in me
> that you have not?[15]
>   (I, 24–31)

14. Martz, pp. xvi–xvii.   15. Martz, p. xvii.

Martz also points out that "It is clear, from the original version of these three poems, that by 1916–17 H. D. was beginning to create a strongly personal voice, breaking out of the Imagist confines, breaking through the Greek mask."[16]

"I Said," written in 1919 but not published until 1982, could easily have been incorporated in *Red Roses For Bronze*, although it is more personal than many of the poems in that volume. The links to *Red Roses For Bronze* are perceived in the attempt to sustain a meaningful dialogue — about love and poetry — with a lover, and in the search for beauty among gods and goddesses, in their images and worship.

The search for beauty in "I Said" (*CP* 322) translates into the "need for beauty" (II) that leads the speaker to search for it in Greek poetry and art, where she finds the symbols that solidify it: in the "shield, helmet, light as fire —" (III), "wrought and hammered" by Hephaestos; and in "the lance and the shield, / the helmet that rested as light / as the silver under-side of the grape-leaf / that Bacchos strips / from the tough, warped wood-stem" (III). Contrasting with this beauty that brings forth "the gold in our hearts" is the harsh reality of a lover who does not share her view of art and love, who does not "understand" (III).

Harsh also is the awareness that modern poetry cannot be sustained by the Greek masks she has developed over the years. More importantly, she realizes that the modern world without divinity cannot perceive "unrecorded grace":

> how can we to-day in a crude tongue,
> in a strange land hope to say
> one word that can hint at the joy we had

16. Martz, pp. xviii–xix. He adds: "One suspects that this tendency toward greater openness was encouraged by her friendship with D. H. Lawrence, which began in 1914 and ended abruptly about 1918, after they had exchanged poems and letters for several years" (p. xix). Unfortunately, these letters were destroyed.

> when the rocks broke like sand under our heels
> and they fled?
>
> (III, 24–28)

The inability to experience love within a context of beauty, divinity, and ritual deflects from modern love poetry. Amid the wasteland, she therefore resolves, as she does in *Red Roses For Bronze,* to write a poetry that fulfills her ideals of beauty, love, art, and religion, since "to-day we are one in our need for beauty" (II). Her aim, then, as stated in "Gift" (*CP* 338), is

> to tempt a chisel
> as a sculptor, take
> this one,
> replacing this and this and this
> for some defect
> of point, of blade, of hilt[.]
>
> (4–9)

The pattern of her chiseled poetry resembles "a most gracious vase" in its being "formal-wise, / inset with stiff acanthus leaves and bays." Her poetry will be "marble wise," a permanent gift of incandescent beauty.

This view of poetry results from the bitterness of betrayal. Having discovered permanence in poetry, the poet resolves that poetry will be her gift to others. Unlike "Psyche" (*CP* 339; 1927) and other betrayed women and goddesses, she will not be driven to dwell in hell, but like them, especially "Eurydice," she has learned a great deal from her love-hell experience. Having been in hell, she has partaken of the "mysteries" and "eternity."

The dead priestess in "A Dead Priestess Speaks" (*CP* 369), the first poem of the proposed volume, shares the hopelessness and desolation of H. D.'s poems about betrayed women. Desertion brings forth isolation and sterility: Delia of Miletus retreats to the "wild-wood," surrounded by dry rock. Yet for Delia, seclusion brings forth insight by means of memory.

In remembering, the priestess reconstructs her shattered identity.

Before her city was sacked, she was a priestess; her role was to nourish her "secret thought," "secret song," and "secret way." While her city was sacked, the priestess was ravished. "Honour" returned only at her death.

The priestess' entrance into the "wild-wood" surrounded by "dry rock" is similar to the entry into the Hall of Truths in Egyptian myth. This ritual of seclusion and isolation functions as a cleansing of the soul. The poem "A Dead Priestess Speaks," where Delia of Miletus reveals her soul "circumspectly" (reiterated throughout the poem), shows the last phase of the ritual.

In the Egyptian ritual, Osiris, God of Being and Lord of Abydos ("Abydos," IV, 72), reigns in the Hall of Truths. Osiris and an additional forty-two judges are summoned to pronounce a sentence upon a particular sin or sinner.[17] In "A Dead Priestess Speaks," Delia, however, assumes the combined roles of Osiris and the judges in evaluating her past experiences and judging her own fate.

She begins by listing her imperfections in Part I, beginning the catalogue with "I was not pure." She acknowledges her weaknesses and her strengths (Parts II and III). She admits her culpability in a crime of passion (IV), and recounts its aftermath of shame, death, and burial (V–VII). In the Egyptian ritual one of the scribe gods — Horus, Anuris, or Thoth — writes down the proceedings, but in the priestess' case, she writes her own testament of truth, writing her own "epitaph" (II): "no one [else] could write . . . / [such] an epitaph of glory and of spears" (II).

In "Electra-Orestes," (*CP* 378), a translation-adaptation, and "Calypso" (*CP* 388), H. D. returns to the themes of be-

17. Thomas Bulfinch, *The Age of Fable* (Philadelphia: David McKay, 1898), pp. 361, 362, 363, 367, 368, 369–370.

trayal, loss of love, and perverted ritual. As a child, Electra had associated Clytemnestra with Aphrodite, the goddess of the "rhododendron," the "rose," and the "sea-wave and the salt-wave." To Electra and Orestes, Agamemnon was a manifestation of Zeus. The poignancy of the ensuing tragic events increases when contrasted to Electra's rejoinder: "No one knows, / the heart of a child."

The blood-bath that followed completely destroys all values espoused by Electra and Orestes. Electra accuses Orestes: "You loved this travesty / of love"; and he bitterly replies: "And you loved / love-for-man / and love-for-woman." Travesty of love equates in H. D.'s mind with travesty of religion and ritual. Another dark note is struck in the role of the priest, who had served as Electra and Orestes' spiritual advisor. After she has gained the painful knowledge from the tragic consequences, Electra perceives the priest as "the Pythian who was drunk-with-god like / wine — / . . . Unsexed / inhuman, / doomed" (pp. 387–88).

In "Calypso" the rejection and betrayal of the goddess-priestess of magic by Odysseus are reenacted. Two of H. D.'s most ironic monologues are "O you clouds," sung by Calypso "(on land)," and "She gave me fresh water / in an earth-jar," sung by Odysseus "(on the sea)." Although Calypso lures the famous hero, master of men, the opening lines of the poem foreshadow her tragic experience. Knowingly she says, "my beautiful peace has gone."

Susan Stanford Friedman, in *Psyche Reborn*, offers a brilliant reading of "Calypso." After the first two lines of address and redress, Calypso erupts like a volcano and tells her story "most probably for the first time in cultural history."[18] Angrily, she commands the "clouds" ("winds," "waves," and "skies") to punish Odysseus, as well as his men, for his crime:

18. Susan Stanford Friedman, *Psyche Reborn. The Emergence of H. D.* (Bloomington: Indiana University Press, 1981), p. 236.

"man is clumsy and evil / a devil." She wishes for his death: may he "suffocate" and "die of thirst." Her death-wish extends to his men and all men: "drown all men in slow, breathless / suffocation — ." Stanford Friedman writes, "The anger of Calypso's first speech is raw and stark — not masked by appeasing smiles, not even coded in natural image as H. D.'s poems about emotion so often are."[19]

Calypso, the wronged goddess, wants nature and the gods to witness Odysseus' betrayal, which symbolizes man's insensitivity and egoism:

> and witness, all earth and heaven,
> it was of my heart-blood
> his sails were woven;
>
> witness, river and sea and land;
> you, you must hear me —
> man is a devil,
> man will not understand.
>
> (II, 20–26)

Odysseus' "evil" nature prevents him from understanding the goddess' true nature. "A moral, even religious weight," according to Stanford Friedman, "appears in the final stanzas of Calypso's speech as Calypso justifies her curse. . . ."[20]

From Odysseus' monologue, it is clear that he does not understand Calypso. "With his desire turned entirely toward his own needs," Stanford Friedman writes, "Odysseus celebrates her power and gifts with complete insensitivity to her needs."[21] Betrayed and bereft, Calypso laments her loss:

> He has gone,
> he has forgotten;
> he took my lute and my shell of crystal —
> he never looked back[.]
>
> (II, 55–58)

19. Stanford Friedman, p. 237.   20. Stanford Friedman, p. 238.
21. Stanford Friedman, p. 239.

True to his real nature, Odysseus, as he and his men leave
Circe's island, remembers that Calypso gave him a great deal,
which he took, and, then he left. Her gifts ("she gave" reiter-
ated nine times) — "fresh water," "wine," "wool," "an ivory
comb," and above all "peace in her cave" — are taken as spoils
of a past adventure. When Odysseus speaks, nothing is new
to us, since, as Stanford Friedman writes, "We have all heard
Odysseus 'speak' — from Homer to Joyce, he has held center
stage and we have seen his adventures unfold in countless
ways, but all variations of the myth have focused on how his
trials related to his needs and desires."[22]

"In Our Town" functions as an idyll between the poems of
betrayal and the two oracle poems that follow in the sequence
A Dead Priestess Speaks. The epic strain of "True, the walls
fell" and "the hosts came," foreshadowing *Helen in Egypt*, sur-
faces in this dramatic monologue with the persona of Menex-
eus, as he addresses a chance acquaintance, laments the fall
of Troy, and describes his role in the epic event. His conver-
sation reveals the mariner: "I watch the cycle of the stars"
(III). "In Our Town" (*CP* 396; 1937) H. D. contemplates
not only what has taken place since the sack of Troy, but also
what might have been.

"Delphi" (*CP* 401; 1933) and "Dodona" (*CP* 406; 1935)
prepare the way for the later poetry. The god's word, his
presence, mystery, and ecstasy foreshadow *Trilogy*. Every
word in "Delphi" is charged with divine resonance. Although
the gods in general, and Apollo in particular, have disap-
peared from the world of men, their divine word is heard by
the worshipers:

> his word
> is withdrawn,
> hieratic,

22. Stanford Friedman, p. 236.

> authentic, a king's,
> yet all may receive it[.]
>> ("HIS SONG")

The god "one day . . . will speak"

> through a child or a thrush
> or a stray in the market;
> he will touch
> with the arm of a herdsman
> your arm,
> he will brush
> with the lips of a brother
> your lips;
> you will flame into song.
>> ("HIS SONG")

The disappearance of the gods and goddesses has not diminished the fervor of the worshipers, who know the power of their word and who feel their presence. To arrive at this state of consciousness, the initiate worshiper embraces books on "old magic":

> I read volume and tome
> of old magic,
> I made sign and cross-sign;
> he must answer old magic
> he must know the old symbol,
> I swear I will find him. . . .
>> ("HIS PRESENCE")

Having prepared for the god's presence, the initiate now understands his mystery, or "HIS RIDDLE," and participates in "HIS ECSTASY" "among prophets" ("HIS ECSTACY").

In "Dodona," the oracle of Zeus, communal worship attains centrality of focus; "THE PEOPLE INVOKE GOD" and accept his symbols and rituals of worship:

> the rod and the oak-bough,
> the fire and the altar,

> the bowl and the pillar,
> the oil-vat and its savour,
> the wine-jar and its flavour.

The speaker-worshiper is astounded by the large number of worshipers which has increased since she began her search of divinity in "The Gift" (1916). A communal voice is now heard:

> we come from afar,
> we await,
> we implore,
> we hide and attend,
> we are lost,
> without friend,
> loving your word the more;
>
> we fear while we wait,
> will you speak,
> will you heal?
> shall we creep,
> shall we kneel?
> shall we stand
> with palms spread?
>
> shall we bring white or red wine,
> shall we bake brown or white bread?
>   (2, 8–23)

Unlike many of the early poems, where the worshipers do not hear a god's response, the priests answer for the gods in "Dodona." Speaking for the god, they state that the worshipers not only should engage in rituals of purgation and of sacrifice, but should "sing and pray," to

> declare
> meaning and rhythm and grace
> in each daily act;
> defeat the tale of man fallen. . . .
>   (26–29)

In sections 4 and 5, THE HIGH PRIESTESS SPEAKS to celebrate the god's mysterious ways and to appease his wrath at men's wrongs. Hermes and other gods are invoked as manifestations of the godhead, and in lines that foreshadow *Trilogy*, she addresses the "eternal, / inscrutable, / . . . all-father" (5, 16–17; 19).

The poem culminates in sections 6 and 7 where ZEUS SPEAKS THROUGH THE ORACLE to command worship of the god and goddess (father and mother) and to praise the noteworthy role of the high-priestess. Through her rituals (in section 7), the priestess brings the worshipers closer to the god's divine presence, his "ineffable fragrance." The high priestess answers:

> I stand by your portal,
> a white pillar,
> luminous.
>
> (7, 8–10)

"Sigil," (*CP* 411) a sequence of short lyrics begun in *Red Roses For Bronze*, where the first seven appear, is now further developed. Written in the 1930s and published at later intervals, "Sigil" demonstrates "a personal voice speaking of love with great conviction, subtlety, and strength."[23] Talismans, or signs, are for H. D. signposts for meditation. The sigils are symbols of sacramental transformation and substantiation. Section X is built entirely on the sacred function of the seals which enable her to traverse between paganism and Christianity:

> Let me be
> a splinter in your side
> or a bride,
>
> eventually,
> I will go

23. Martz, p. xxvi.

> from the red,
> red,
> red fire-lily,
> back
> to the snow.
>   (X, 1–10)

The beautiful lyric XI, "If you take the moon in your hands / and turn it around" relies totally on the efficacy of ritual to arrive at the synthesis between naturalism and supernaturalism: "if you pull dry seaweed from the sand / and turn it round / and wonder at the undersides' bright amber, / your eyes" should recall "when my soul turned round, / perceiving the other-side of everything." The stance of poet-magician is achieved in lyric XII, "Are these ashes in my hand / or a wand / to conjure a butterfly / out of a nest. . . ?"

Lyric XIII returns to the poems in *Red Roses For Bronze* which have become part of her "inheritance." The red roses sculpted in "marble wise" have become hieroglyphs of transcendence, or of "waited eternity." The speaker simultaneously wishes to be swept by poetry (XIV) and love (XV), but to love man as god is seen as a curse (XVII). Passion has prevented her to "carry vision further" (XVIII) and to concentrate on the "horror / of finality" (XIX). Love, as Helen later suspects in *Helen in Egypt,* involves a greater loss, missing "the clue" (XVIII) — "the sense / of all the scrawled script. . ." (XVIII).

Love, however, has not blinded her to the portent of this "argument" (XV). Fortunately, her "signet" reveals to her that she is to write "marble wise" poetry that will transcend physical love. Her goal is to write a transcendent poetry: "God marked me to be his, / scrawled, 'I, I, I / alone can comprehend / this subtlety'" (XV). She now contemplates a different kind of poetry (XV) that in time will break through the barriers she has imposed upon herself as a poet (XVIII),

as well as those imposed by others, retaining only those hiero-
glyphs that have furthered her search for spiritual realism.

The role of the scribe as priestess is one of the thematic
structures that H. D. retains. In the long poem "Priest" (*CP*
419), the speaker wishes for the priest's "prescience" of the
divine mysteries. She wants to follow his path to eternal
truths but realizes that the journey is long:

> (O, long, long was my way,
> long, long was the path
> I took,
> many, many years,
> seasons, moons, noons,
> winter, summer
> all day
> with a song,
> a scimitar). . . .
>   (I, 25–33)

The priestess' role is also difficult. She is stubbornly deter-
mined to serve the goddess: she is "stubborn as moon-ray, /
stubborn as steel, / stubborn as that platinum-disc." In fact,
in this section, "stubborn" is reiterated twelve times, and
with each incremental repetition the priestess is associated
with the cosmos, cycles of nature, everyday reality, and love.

Although the priestess-poet may not have a valid function
in modern society ("She is dead" III), there is still need for
the power of the goddess as creatrix. The speaker's increas-
ing identification with the priestess in section III culminates
in sections IV–XIV, where a dialogue takes place with a
lover of long ago who did not share her opinions of love and
goddess-worship.

Her poetry seems to have repelled him, or at least, she
imagines that he thinks she is rather simple-minded in fol-
lowing this path. Her response is to believe that the lover had
followed God in his own way (V), yet he seems to have
broken all the Commandments (VI) and, therefore, she pities

him. Through his response, she foresees the "danger" (VII) of writing this kind of poetry, which may be read as "worship [of] beauty / that is dead" (VII).

Yet, his love and betrayal have made life "cold" (VIII), and "more terrible than death" (VIII), a reflection that comes to her with old age. Her inner poetic life has surpassed his coldness and his death-in-life existence; she can now boast, "I did not die" (IX). Her red roses endured, and she was able to survive his betrayal:

> "there is no measure to the thing I knew
> that took me out-of-time,"
> how measure the years?
> my hopes, my fears
> were measureless,
> five minutes?
> five days?
> (fifteen to be exact,
> exactly fifteen years, almost to the day).
>   (X, 12–20)

It is difficult to read such an intimate expression of betrayal, love, and poetry without finding here a reference to Aldington's infidelities (1916–1917), from which H. D. later derived the strength that had been shattered.

In "Magician [Master]" (*CP* 431) H. D. defines the nature of the priest-master-magician, who largely foreshadows Kaspar in *Trilogy*. In the "Magician" she puts forth the essential hieroglyphs of her poetry. In section 1, the need and the efficacy of prayer are established, the need to "pray constantly" to the manifestations — Artemis, Aphrodite — of the goddess. Offerings of flowers — "clematis," "delphinium," and "violet" — flourish, as does the "worship" of the "old gods," each separately according to his or her own mystery: "give us back the old gods. . . ."

The return to nature and the worshipers' affinity to the revelatory experiences that emanate from nature are seen, as a return "into the womb," as a *rite de passage* toward a tran-

scendent reality (sections 2–3). The suffering entailed in
true worship "we have dared too long to worship" (4) — its
"horrors" and "terror" find recompense in the ability to tran-
scend into "another world": she can now command the reader
to "consider the flower of the field" (5).

The complexity of the poem is reached in section 6, where
the speaker feels that the worshipers' submission, suffering
("we bled"), and propitiation deserve a response, a sign:

> we never heard the Magician
> we never, never heard what he said.
>
> (6, 21–22)

They expected some gesture:

> We expected some threat or some promise,
> some disclosure,
> we were not as these others. . . .
>
> (7, 9–11)

The miracles occur in section 8, beginning with

> A basket,
> a fish
> or fish net,
> . . .
> the grape,
> the grape-leaf,
> the half-opened tendril . . .
>
> (8, 1–3; 12–14)

and extending to section 9 with its clear reference to the New
Testament. Christ as the magician "would see worlds in a
crystal" and

> he would tell of the whorl of whorl of light
> that was infinity to be seen in a glass,
>
> or a shell
> or a bead
> or a pearl.
>
> (9, 12–16)

Clearly the "embers," the girl who "came where he sat," the "alabaster" box of "a rare scent," the "jewels," "crystal," and the "merchant," all foreshadow *Trilogy*.

Martz introduces "The Dancer" (*CP* 440; 1935) as a "tribute to the achievement and perfection of the female artist," which "prepares the way for an allusion to this poem in the middle of 'The Master,' recognizing by implication that the knowledge of herself brought about by Freud had made possible that intrepid assertion of feminine integrity."[24] In "The Dancer," the poet shows that she has traveled the paths of the priestess and has discovered the infinite ways of her magic.

In part I, the priest and priestess meet in their worship of nature and the goddess. In part II, she reaffirms her worship of "art." Her insight has deepened ("nothing is hidden / from me"); her experience has rendered her immune to future betrayals); and she has rejected the kind of poetry advocated by her previous lover:

> for you are abstract,
> making no mistake,
> slurring no word
> in the rhythm you make,
> the poem,
> writ in the air.
>   (II, 35–40)

In contrast, her poetry has a different rhythm. Strongly affected by dance, the poet now dances to a different tune and sings a different song: the "miracle, / miracle of beauty returned to us, / the sun / born in a woman" (III). She has discovered the source of her creative force: "we are more than we know" (IV). What she now seeks is the "strength to follow" (V) the steps of this new dance, "the power to hallow / beauty" of the goddess (sections VI–XII), and the freedom to pursue her hallowed dream.

---

24. Martz, p. xxvii.

"Priest," "Magician," and "The Dancer" relate to "The Master" (*CP* 451), a poem central in H. D.'s middle period, and one that breaks new ground. Ostensibly, "The Master" is a poem about Freud (as noted earlier, H. D. was Freud's analysand in 1933–1934), but the poem is also about the embodiment of truth, beauty, wisdom, and love.

Above all, the master is endowed with "measureless" gifts. She recognizes "that he was beyond all-men." Under the spell of Freud's tutelage, the poet learns that "'every gesture is wisdom'" and that "'nothing is lost.'" Naturally, she becomes "caught" in his revolutionary teachings:

> I caught the dream
> and rose dreaming,
> and we wrought philosophy on the dream content,
> I was content. . . .
>
> (I, 26–29)

Freud's "interpretations of dreams" fully substantiated for H. D. the concept that "God is all / and the dream is God" (I, 31–32).

Freud's knowledge of mythology (II) is as infinite as his knowledge of human passions, emotions, and feelings, and from Freud, she learns to isolate and identify her own passions, emotions, and feelings. Prior to her sessions with Freud, she states:

> I did not know how to differentiate
> between volcanic desire,
> anemones like embers
> and purple fire
> of violets
> like red heat,
> and the cold silver
> of her feet:
>
> I had two loves separate. . . .
>
> (II, 24–33)

The miraculous nature of the sessions with Freud was that he

understood the underlying themes of her poetic structures
and perceived them as the hieroglyphs of her psyche:

> but how could he have foreseen
> the impossible?
>
> how could he have known
> how each gesture of this dancer
> would be hieratic?
>
> (III, 17–21)

In section IV, however, part of H. D.'s conflict with Freud,
also delineated in *Tribute to Freud,* emerges. First, she had
wanted to know the "secret" (IV) behind the master. His
reply, that as "poet" (IV) she should know it, angers her:

> 'you cannot last forever,
> the fire of wisdom dies with you,
> I have travelled far to Miletus,
> you cannot stay long now with us,
> I came for an answer. . . .'
>
> (IV, 12–16)

Second, she could not agree with his views of male superi-
ority and that women attain knowledge only through love.
Delia of Miletus had traveled too far to seek the wise man
only to discover that Freud did not perceive woman as crea-
trix. Contrarily, H. D. argues that the woman artist

> . . . needs no man,
> herself
> is that dart and pulse of the male,
> hands, feet, thighs,
> herself perfect.
>
> (V, 39–43)

Progressively in the "Lady" in *Trilogy,* Helen in *Helen in
Egypt,* and the multiple manifestations of woman-as-creatrix
in *Hermetic Definition,* H. D. substantiates the truth of this
argument.

Although the quarrel with Freud was never resolved, she never doubted the permanent influence of his work and its effect on the human psyche. It is Freud

> who will bring a new world to birth . . .
> it is he,
> it is he
> who already has formed a new earth.
> (VI, 21–24)

Martz points out that "The Master" "reveals, with an intimacy and anguish beyond anything in her prose *Tribute*, how Freud taught her to accept and understand the ambivalent responses of her nature as a part of God's creation."[25] What follows is a more powerful and explicit tribute to Freud than her prose work but one which clearly expresses her break with the master:

> He will trouble the thoughts of men
> yet for many an aeon,
> they will travel far and wide,
> they will discuss all his written words,
> his pen will be sacred
> they will build a temple
> and keep all his sacred writings safe,
> and men will come
> and men will quarrel
> but he will be safe;
> they will found temples in his name,
> his fame
> will be so great
> that anyone who has known him
> will also be hailed as master,
> seer,
> interpreter;
>
> only I,
> I will escape.
> (VII, 1–19)

25. Martz, p. xxvii.

She will escape because Freud set her "free / to prophesy" (VIII).

She takes leave of the master and his objets d'art (IX), but she "does not forget him" (X), even if her poetry argues against his views of women. In her future poetry, "no man will be present in those mysteries" (XI), and "yet all men will feel / what it is to be a woman" (XI), a feat she eventually accomplishes in *Hermetic Definition*. Then, "men will see how long they have been blind" (XI), and they "shall see woman, / perfect" (XI). They will perceive the power of the goddess and will worship her: "'you are near beauty the sun, / you are that Lord become woman'" (XII).

In *Psyche Reborn*, Susan Stanford Friedman argues that H. D.'s novels *Her* and *Asphodel*, her letters to Bryher, written during her sessions with Freud, and "The Master" demonstrate that she had "brought both her lesbian and heterosexual loves to their discussions for explanation. Freud apparently told her that, as she wrote to Bryher, 'I am that all-but extinct phenomenon, the perfect bi-[sexual].'"[26] Stanford Friedman points to the line, "I had two loves separate . . ." (II) as "clear reference to her bisexuality."[27]

The conflict between Freud and H. D. partly brought to the foreground their different ideas about male and female creativity. In "'Woman Is Perfect': H. D.'s Debate With Freud," (1981) Rachael Blau DuPlessis and Susan Stanford Friedman further elaborate the differences between the master and the analysand. They argue that in "The Master" she reveals more about herself than she does in *Tribute*, since the poem "directly addresses the compelling questions of identity that H. D. brought to Freud, but that she did not reveal in her public accounts of analysis: her anger with Freud, her rejection of the prescriptive bias in his theories of female sexual-

26. Stanford Friedman, pp. 46–7.   27. Stanford Friedman, p. 47.

ity, her love for women, her bisexuality, and the relationship of her womanhood to her destiny as a poet-prophet."[28]

In the last poem of this triad, "The Poet" (*CP* 461; 1935), H. D.'s skillful metonymy comes into full view. "The Poet" catalogues her central images and gives a sample of the verbal magic that takes the speaker from the "tide-shelf" to "seaweed," and from "inland" to "water-lilies," and from a "translatable sound" to the song "of something intangible." The image of the snail (I) is developed in part II, where with other images and syntactical phrases ("I believe that I have failed, / because I got out of the husk that was my husk"), "butterfly," "snail," and "skull" H. D. moves closer to the verbal magic of *Trilogy*. Whereas the scattered "seed-pods" allude to the "sea garden" experience, the self-shell image (III) brings the reader closer to *Trilogy*, where the body, like the shell, "is a temple" (IV).

Part V reinforces Martz's idea that the poem is a tribute to D. H. Lawrence, since, at this point in time, she imaginatively converses with him but admits that she does not "grasp his philosophy" (V). In *Tribute to Freud*, H. D. refers to D. H. Lawrence's short novel *The Man Who Died*, which I think greatly influenced many sections of her long poem *Helen in Egypt*. In this light, part VI is elegiac, bidding the poet (perhaps Lawrence) "'hail,' / or 'farewell,'" thus moving closer to the world of *Vale Ave*.

The remaining poems, beginning with "Two Poems For Christmas, 1937" and ending with "Christmas 1944," also prepare us for the major poems. The first of the two Christmas poems, "Star By Day" (*CP* 469), foreshadows *Hermetic Definition* (the third part entitled "Star of Day"). The hermeticism that transpires in the later poem is here evinced in

---

28. Rachael Blau DuPlessis and Susan Stanford Friedman, "'Woman Is Perfect': H. D.'s Debate With Freud," *Feminist Studies*, 7 (Fall 1981), p. 419.

such lines as "I shot past heaven's centrifugal heaven, / to find / the ultimate Sun that makes our own sun, blind." "Star By Day" also foreshadows Christ, Kaspar, and the Holy Spirit of *Trilogy*, in such lines as "His wings, / the stars and ultimate suns / fall softly on our hands" and "O star-spun shroud." The star imagery of the second poem "Wooden Animal" moves even closer to the multiple manifestations of the all-father of *Trilogy*, here present as "Ra."

In "Ancient Wisdom Speaks" (*CP* 482, dated April 14, 1943), H. D. assumes the contemplative stance that she was to retain in the later poems. In this poem the efficacy of prayer is stressed. The lady in parts III and IV brings to mind the Lady in *Trilogy*, although the lines, "but she stood, / the sun on her hair" may also foreshadow Mary Magdalene's climactic meeting with Kaspar.

"R.A.F." (*CP* 485; 1941), a war-poem about shell-shocked people ("we were people who had crossed over, / we had already crashed, / we were already dead," (XI), also approximates both *Trilogy* and *Hermetic Definition*, especially "Sagesse." Here, too, the "emissary" (IV) is "branded for eternity" (IV). "May 1943" (*CP* 492) is memorable because of the personal experience it conveys. Visiting "William's orangery" (I) (this orangery is a building close to Kensington Palace, built for William III) at the age of fifty-six, H. D. on May 14, exactly at noon, imaginatively transcends time and space: "I mend a break in time." From Kensington to Venice and into "King William IVth's water-trough" and to "Dutch William's Dutch garden," the poet soars above war and travels to places where "humanity returns." She does, however, return to a war-shocked world, and "The reason is / rats leave the sinking ship / but we . . . / we . . . / didn't leave" (X).

"Christmas 1944" (*CP* 502) functions as a perfect prologue to *Trilogy*. The fires of destruction of World War II have affected men, earth, and sky: "the stratosphere was once where angels were," but now it is "where no angels are." Amid this desolation, the poet realizes that *"we have our journey now"* (I; emphasis mine) mapped before us. As the poet in "Christmas 1944" thinks of "Him" in "the Manger," she begins to map her vision of universal redemption as she journeys through the desert world.

5. Desert Quest: *Trilogy* (1944–1946)

The poems in *Trilogy*, published posthumously together for the first time in 1973, appeared separately during the war years: *The Walls Do Not Fall* (1944), *Tribute to the Angels* (1945), and *The Flowering of the Rod* (1946).[1] The war and its devastating effect on society and the individual are major concerns in *Trilogy*, although the poem is about much more than war. Ironically, the desolation of war brings forth a rich and more mature poetry. Desolation ushers in inspiration, and fragmentation gives rise to the imminent need for reconstruction of self and the world. Consequently, a new and significant development emerges in H. D.'s poetry: "through our desolation / thoughts stir, inspiration stalks us / through gloom" (*WDNF* 1). During World War II, she produces a sustained and unified vision of a new self in a redeemed world.

The richness and complexity of the new poetry in *Trilogy* result, first, from a nexus of symbols which reflect the poet's war experiences; and second, from the poet's mythmaking consciousness. The myriad symbols — drawn from Scripture, the Cabala, and Egyptian mythology — constitute the tropes

1. All quotations taken from *Trilogy* (New York: New Directions 1973). The following conventions are observed: numbers in parentheses refer first, to the number of the lyric within each section of the *Trilogy;* second, to the specific lines. The following abbreviations are used:

WDNF:	*The Walls Do Not Fall*
TA:	*Tribute to the Angels*
FR:	*The Flowering of the Rod*

of the quest in *Trilogy.* H. D.'s use of Egyptian mythology, with its bearing on mystery, the Word, and the Cabala, enables her to weave these crosscurrents into a unified vision. Prophecies embedded in Egyptian theogony are related to the messianism of the Old and New Testament and translated "in today's imagery" (*WDNF* 20).

The syncretism in *Trilogy* emphasizes the sacred nature of the poet's inner experiences and the revelatory nature of the poetic word. It is the importance of the poet's inner experience that, by analogy, elevates her role to that of the scribe in ancient Egyptian hierarchy. In H. D.'s case, the modern scribe's position "takes precedence of the priest, / stands second only to the Pharoah" (*WDNF* 8). Modern poets are the "bearers of the secret wisdom" (*WDNF* 8). Poets play a central role in transmitting "ancient wisdom" (*WDNF* 15). Speaking for modern poets who assume this responsibility, H. D. substantiates their contribution:

> we are the keepers of the secret,
> the carriers, the spinners
>
> of that rare intangible thread
> that binds all humanity
>
> to ancient wisdom,
> to antiquity[.]
> (WDNF, 15, 5–10)

Collectively, the poets' task is to record the human voyage toward the "spiritual realities" (*WDNF* 38): "*we are voyagers, discoverers / of the not-known, / the unrecorded; we have no map*" (*WDNF* 43). By mapping the quest, toward the "spiritual realities," "*possibly we will reach haven, / heaven*" (*WDNF* 43). In *Trilogy,* H. D. maps her own "search for historical parallels, / research into psychic affinities" (*WDNF* 38). Although the quest in *Trilogy* is to be seen as her "personal approach / to the eternal realities" (*WDNF* 38), it represents "the intellectual effort / of the whole race" (*WDNF* 38) as well.

H. D. also enhances the trope of the quest by creating her own version of traversing the desert with hope of entering the promised land, envisioned in a bundle of myrrh. The quest demonstrates her ability to transform fears and doubts into affirmation, love, and ecstasy. Kaspar's vision becomes an apt metaphor for this transformation from doubt to affirmation and from fear to love: "and what he saw made his heart so glad / that it was as if he suffered, / his heart laboured so / with his ecstasy" (*FR* 28). Throughout the quest she also evaluates the struggles that underlie the commitment to poetry as a viable path toward the search for spiritual reality.

The quest in *Trilogy* is initially localized in Karnak and London, Bethlehem and Philadelphia. Egypt's ruins reaffirm and renew her kinship with the spiritual past. *Trilogy* opens with the obvious parallel between the ruins of Karnak and London: the "rails gone (for guns) / from your (and my) old town square" (*WDNF* 1) and:

> there, as here, ruin opens
> the tomb, the temple; enter,
> there as here, there are no doors:
>
> the shrine lies open to the sky,
> the rain falls, here, there
> sand drifts; eternity endures. . . .
> (*WDNF*, 1, 10–15)

"Eternity endures" (*WDNF* 1) amid ruin and devastation. In *The Flowering of the Rod* the quest brings H. D. to Bethlehem, the biblical town of Jesus. In *Advent*, Bethlehem, Pennsylvania, is the source of her spirituality: "Church Street was our Street, the Church was our Church. It was founded by Count Zinzendorf [the Church's influential first leader in America], who named our town Bethlehem."[2] Philadelphia

2. *Advent* is taken directly from the 1933 Vienna notebooks and is written as a continuation of *Writing on the Wall*, written from memory. Both are

belongs to the Book of Revelation and to the vision of a New Jerusalem; it is also the city founded by William Penn and the Quakers, and where H. D. lived when the family moved there from Bethlehem. Karnak and London, Bethlehem and Philadelphia are a part of her personal history as well as of the history of the race.

The outbreak of World War II occasions the outcry of many civilian poets whose poetry protests the inhumanity of war: Pound in *Pisan Cantos,* Eliot in *Four Quartets,* and Sitwell in "Still Falls the Rain," for example. The war gives H. D. a new vision and voice. For her, living in London during the city's worst incendiary attacks, the war is "Apocryphal fire" (*WDNF* 1). Nonetheless, the individual poet ("the industrious worm," *WDNF* 6) persists and escapes the onslaught of the Gorgon. The renunciation of destruction gives rise to a strong denunciation in the pivotal lyric "In me (the worm)" (*WDNF* 6). It is clear that "persistence" underscores her quest.

> I escaped, I explored
> rose-thorn forest,
>
> was rain-swept
> down the valley of a leaf;
>
> was deposited on grass,
> where mast by jewelled mast
>
> bore separate ravellings
> of encrusted gem-stuff[.]
>   (*WDNF,* 6, 9–16)

The industrious and persistent poet profits "by every calam-

---

published as *Tribute to Freud* (Boston: David R. Godine, 1974), p. 122. The Moravians, led by Zinzendorf, settled in Bethlehem during the latter part of the seventeenth century, and it remains a Moravian stronghold to this day. H. D.'s father taught mathematics and astronomy at the University of Pennsylvania in Philadelphia, and it was in Philadelphia that she met Ezra Pound.

ity" (*WDNF* 6) and knows that "the Lord God / is about to manifest" (*WDNF* 6). After destruction there is resurrection.

Lyric 6 functions as an epiphany for the entire poem. The poet survives the calamity of war because she finds "nourishment" in the flowering of a tree in the charnel house. Throughout *The Walls Do Not Fall* the poet sees the warmongers as antithetical to herself. In their espousal of a war mentality, they epitomize the alienated self rooted in unreality. This theme is also expressed by Merton in *New Seeds of Contemplation*. False cultural standards create depersonalized individuals incapable of attaining authenticity. The poet pits herself in direct opposition to the perpetrators of war and perceives their actions as revealing what Merton calls a pantomime of the unreal.[3] The war enacts this pantomime.[4] The enigma of war, therefore, compels her to create a panoply of spiritual reality.

Divine inspiration informs the very first lyric in *The Walls Do Not Fall:* "unaware, Spirit announces the Presence" (*WDNF* 1). The Word is manifested in the divine presence of the Ancient of Days, the Holy Ghost, Mercury-Thoth-Hermes, Christ, Mary, or in one of the seven angels: Azrael, Raphael, Gabriel, Uriel, Annael, Michael, and Zadkiel. At this advanced level of mythmaking, Cassirer points out that divine inspiration (the Word) has a "fundamental function in the construction and development of spiritual reality."[5]

L. S. Dembo states, in *Conceptions of Reality in American Poetry*, that the trope of prophecy (revelation of the incarnate

3. Thomas Merton, *New Seeds of Contemplation* (Norfolk: New Directions, 1960), passim.

4. H. D., *End To Torment*, eds. Norman Holmes Pearson and Michael King (New York: New Directions, 1979), p. 56. This pantomime is dramatized in Pound's imprisonment. In *End to Torment* H. D. writes that "The prison actually of the Self was dramatized or materialized for our generation by Ezra's incarceration."

5. Ernst Cassirer, *Language and Myth*, tr. Susanne Langer (New York: Dover, 1946), p. 62.

Word) gives the modern poet a "mode for crystallizing the nameless, invisible world in the human consciousness."[6] In *Trilogy*, H. D. follows the Gospel of John. Reality lies in the Word: "*in the beginning / was the Word*" (*WDNF* 10). The Word is the begettor of Dream, Vision, and Sword (11) which would not exist without "the Word's mediation" (11). The poet survives through the poetic word/sword, her weapon against oppression and her mode of salvation. The image of word/sword is drawn from the Book of Revelation: "And he had in his right hand seven stars: and out of his mouth went a sharp twoedged sword: and his countenance was as the sun shineth in his strength" (Rev. 1:16); and "Repent; or else I will come unto thee quickly, and will fight against them with the sword of my mouth" (Rev. 2:16). The power of the Word redeems the quester from the wasteland and enables her to perceive that "other values were revealed to us, / other standards hallowed us" (12).

In *Trilogy*, ritual brings H. D. closer to her Moravian heritage, values and rituals. For example, a Moravian ritual of lasting influence is the Christmas Eve Candle Service. In *Trilogy* each of the seven angels is associated with a candle. Other Moravian rituals are echoed throughout *Trilogy*, such as the making of the "putz," or nativity scene; the washing of the feet on Maundy Thursday; the hour-by-hour participation in Christ's Passion; and participation in the Love Feast. The inclusion of Moravian ritual and angelology enables her to oscillate between a private and a world myth, so that prophetic urgency underscores both. Revelation becomes the incarnate Word, and personal salvation lies in the quest of the Word, directed toward a universal and individual reconstruction of self. The result is a liberating poetry, deeply interiorized, which gives birth to a new self:

6. L. S. Dembo, *Conceptions of Reality in Modern American Poetry* (Berkeley: University of California Press, 1966), p. 215.

> so that, living within,
> you beget, self-out-of-self,
>
> selfless,
> that pearl-of-great-price.
>   (*WDNF*, 4, 43–46)

H. D.'s Moravian beliefs are strongly influenced by Zinzendorf, especially by his focus on the Christian mysteries and mysticism.[7] Pearson best sums up Zinzendorf's influence on H. D.:

what impressed her most was the spirit of the "Unitas Fratrum" . . . which lay at the heart of the Moravian settlements throughout the world. Also, behind her was what Count Zinzendorf would refer to as the Mystery. It was a mystery that lay at the center of the world, a mystery that one tried to pierce through meditation and thought and, above all through love. And the Moravian love feast, which was part of their ritual, lay very much at the center of H. D.'s emphasis on love in her poetry throughout her entire career.[8]

This background brings forth the image of the new self in a redeemed world in *Trilogy*, an image analogous to Merton's in *The New Man*. The self creates a new identity in union with divinity, and this transforming union affects the entire quest in *Trilogy*.

The search for the Word; enactment of ritual; inclusion of cosmic and heroic themes; sustenance of form by its even texture (uniformity of diction and rhythm); synthesis of private and world myth; prophetic urgency; and the use of epiphany make *Trilogy* the quintessential modern long poem.[9]

The overall heady reiteration of images and talismanic phrases are also in perfect accord with the poet's role as hiero-

7. Frederick Klees, *The Pennsylvania Dutch* (New York: Macmillan, 1964), pp. 123–132; pp. 300–304.

8. Norman Holmes Pearson, "Interview," by L. S. Dembo *Contemporary Literature*, 10 (1969), p. 438.

9. *Trilogy* clearly illustrates a uniformity of prosody. A perfected two-line cadence places the poem at the center of the modern poetic tradition. In

phant. The highly charged sequence of hieroglyphs (carved images) evokes and creates a slow rhythm conducive to meditation, sustained by the repetition of words and phrases.

Words are healing and revelatory: "I know, I feel / the meaning that words hide; / they are anagrams, cryptograms, / little boxes, conditioned / to hatch butterflies . . ." (*WDNF* 39). Lyric 40, for example, demonstrates H. D.'s use of words to denote the prophetic nature of the Word. Osiris, the god of resurrection, is Sirius, the star, so that in the visualization and sound of a word, the entire Osirian cycle is condensed: Osiris is the One (the Sire) whose soul traverses the sky and is apotheosized as the star Sirius.

Similarly, lyric 8 (*Tribute to the Angels*), a sentence of fourteen short lines, brings together the associations of the name Mary. The Hebrew *"mar,"* meaning brine, and "mor," meaning "bitter," are associated with *"marah"* (bitterness) and the Latin "mare" (sea) and "mater" (mother). The bitterness of the sea is equated with the archetypal symbol of the sea as mother, derived from the sea-mother goddess (i.e., Aphrodite or Thetis) and her multiple attributes as seducer (Circe), love (Aphrodite), and so on. The associations result in "sea, brine, breaker, seducer, / giver of life, giver of tears" and to "mer, mere, mère, mater Maia, Mary." Maia is the mother of Hermes, the Greek logos.[10] St. Jerome's praise of the Virgin Mother as Stella Maris generates the association of Mary as

---

Trilogy, H. D. arrives at a prosody which suits the thematic content. The two-line cadence is used in all but two of the one hundred and twenty-nine lyrics where each part consists of forty-three lyrics. The only exceptions are the first lyric, in *The Walls Do Not Fall,* which is written in triads, and lyric 41, where a two-line cadence alternates with a quatrain.

10. Arthur Weigall, *The Paganism in Our Christianity* (London: 1928), p. 38. Weigall points out that "many gods and semi-divine heroes have mothers whose names are 'Mary': Adonis, son of Myrrha; Hermes, the Greek Logos, son of Maia; Cyrus, son of Mariana; Moses, the son of Miriam; Joshua, according to the Chronical of Tabarí, the son of Miriam; Buddha, the son of Maya; Krishna the son of Maritaea, and so on."

"Star of the Sea, / Mother," so that Mary is a star and a sorrowful mother. The bitter ("*mar*") brine ("*marah*") generates the image of myrrh, the gift the Magi bring to the star of Bethlehem, and relates it to Mary "of the Sea."[11]

At first, the search for spiritual realism may seem coded and esoteric, yet it does encompass and reveal a wide scope. H. D.'s concentrated images facilitate participation in a universal drama of destruction and reconstruction, death and rebirth. These pregnant moments elucidate the esoteric, while they substantiate the universal. The superimposition of the personal, esoteric, and universal demonstrates her unique "palimpsest" (*WDNF* 2) technique.

Trilogy also reveals elliptical allusions to its own ars poetica. Part of the difficulty in the composition of the poem is disclosed in lyric 32 of *The Walls Do Not Fall:* "Depth of the sub-conscious spews forth /too many incongruent monsters / and fixed indigestible matter / such as shell, pearl; imagery / done to death."

The first phase of the search in *The Walls Do Not Fall* deals with endurance and prophecy, although the landscape points to destruction caused by war. The carved hieroglyphs in the temples of Luxor and Karnak — the bee, chick, and hare — symbolize the fulfillment of divine promise in their pursuit of "unalterable purpose" (1). As they "continue to prophesy / from the stone papyrus" (1), they also symbolize the will to live, to endure, and to survive the holocaust of war. Unlike natural cataclysms, the horrors of World War II defy comparison, so that "Pompeii has nothing to teach us" (1). No

11. Robert Graves, *The White Goddess* (New York: Vintage, 1958), p. 156. Graves adds: "The Eleusinian mysteries celebrate the 'Advent' of Eleusis, the arrival and the birth of the Divine Child. The mother of Eleusis was 'Daeira,' daughter of Oceanus, 'the wise one of the sea,' and was identified with Aphrodite, the Minoan dove-goddess who rose from the sea at Paphos in Cyprus every year with her virginity renewed," p. 156. He also writes that Mary meant "of the sea" to the Gnostics (p. 156).

catastrophe is comparable to this "Apocryphal fire" (1). Even though humankind was not created to endure the horror and torture devised by the Nazis, humanity survived the holocaust. The skeleton is the first wall that does not fall: "the bone-frame was made for / no such shock knit within terror, / yet the skeleton stood up to it" (1). The quester's salvation lies in her search "for the nourishment, God" (2). She seeks this nourishment first in the sacred past.

The oppressors, governed by illusions and misconceptions of a war-mentality, pursue an "Ill promised adventure" (2). They reject the old gods (the triple goddess, Isis-Aset-Astarte is considered a harlot) and negate the reality of myth (perceiving it as "past misadventure," (2). They accuse the poet of following the devil's rhythm and of writing a diabolic script. Moreover, they view the poet's search as a futile attempt:

> your stylus is dipped in corrosive sublimate,
> how can you scratch out
>
> indelible ink of the palimpsest
> of past misadventure?
>
> (2, 25–28)

Since the poet knows that the "gods always face two-ways" (2), she searches the past in order to find the significant present: "let us search for the old highways / for the true-rune, the right-spell, / recover old values" (2).

The first recovery is that of the rod (or shaft), symbolic of spiritual authority and sovereignty. The "Sceptre" (3) is crowned with a lily bud and foreshadows "the flowering of the rod." Unlike the thorns associated with the Crucifixion, the lotus lily symbolizes the opening life of the spirit: its petals bend backward to reveal the rising god. The lotus also symbolizes the soul emergent, reborn.[12] Its petals signify the

---

12. R. T. Rundle Clark, *Myth and Symbol in Ancient Egypt* (London: Thames and Hudson, 1978), p. 239.

five stages of life encompassed in *Trilogy:* birth, initiation, fertility, repose, death.[13]

The staff is also a caduceus (3), a symbol of healing and eternity associated with the Egyptian Thoth whose wand heralds messages from the gods and heals souls. The caduceus is also associated with Hermes, the Greek version of Thoth. In Egyptian mythology, Thoth delivers the Word. R. T. Rundle Clark in *Myth and Symbol in Ancient Egypt* points to Pyramid Texts (par. II, 46) where Thoth is the universal scribe:

> I am the Scribe of the Divine Book
> which says what has been and effects what is yet to be.[14]

In the Coffin Texts (IV, Spell 321), the utterance comes from the mouth of the serpent who transmits the Word to the Divine Book carried by Thoth.[15]

The "rod of power" is also the symbolic tau cross, associated with Attis, Prometheus, and Osiris.[16] It is, of course, symbolic of Christ as "the flowering rod" of Jesse, the tree of new life. In early Christian iconography, Christ is depicted as a winged serpent.[17] In recovering the rod of power, the poet implies that this poetry, with its bearing on spiritual reality, has a healing effect. Like the caduceus, "it bears healing / . . . among the dying, / or evoking the dead, / it brings life to the living" (*WDNF*, 3).

The process of rebirth is recreated in the memorable lyric 4, "There is a spell," where the shell is equated with the body, the artist, and the imagination. The "house, / temple, fane, shrine" symbolize artistic imagination: the "craftsman" (or "master-mason") creates the shell of "stone marvel" — art (poetry).

The poet's survival is likened to Jonah's experience: "so I

13. Graves, p. 132 and p. 136.   14. Clark, p. 50.
15. Clark, pp. 51–52.   16. Weigall, pp. 79–83.
17. Graves, p. 145.

in my own way know / that the whale / can not digest me."
The war experience does not annihilate her; on the contrary,
she emerges with a strong conception of her inner self:

> be firm in your own small, static, limited
>
> orbit and the shark-jaws
> of outer circumstance
>
> will spit you forth:
> be indigestible, hard, ungiving.
>
> (4, 38–42)

This begetting opens a new stage in the poetry and a new
phase in the quest. The "self-out-of-self" process is the neces-
sary transformation for the pursuit of the transcendent self.
In *Seasons of Celebration*, Merton describes this process as
"compunction. . ." or "a liberation of ourselves which takes
place in the depths of our being, and lets us out of ourselves
from inside."[18]

The momentum of the quest is now directed toward Agape
embodied in "a new Master." In *Trilogy*, the Master is Christ
who manifests in the person of Kaspar, the Wise Man, or
"The Mage" who first brings myrrh to Jesus. He is "the Ge-
nius in the jar." This new level of spirituality inspires the poet
to write a new poetry.

The other spiritual guide is Thoth (Hermes-Mercury),
H. D.'s special god whom she sees as a prototype of the Holy
Ghost and Christ. In Egyptian mythology, Thoth is the bearer
of the Word and God's intermediary. His primary function is
to carry out the High God's instructions. "He is the 'reed pen
of the Universal Master,' the Lord of Law, who announces
Words of Wisdom and understanding."[19] In the Coffin Texts,
Thoth is an integral part of the Osirian myths and is at the
very center of the god's mysteries. He is also the genius of

18. Thomas Merton, *Seasons of Celebration* (New York: Farrar, Straus
and Giroux, 1964), p. 70.
19. Clark, pp. 172–173 and p. 174.

the moon, symbolic of illumination and inspiration; he is the master of powerful spells; and he is the patron of learning. The poet identifies herself with the Wisdom of Thoth, the ur-artist, the god who "invented the script, letters, palette" (10).

Kaspar and Thoth guide the quester through the desert, where a voice is heard and a presence is seen:

> The Presence was spectrum-blue,
> ultimate blue ray,
>
> rare as radium, as healing:
> my old self, wrapped round me,
>
> was shroud (I speak of myself individually
> but I was surrounded by companions
>
> in this mystery). . . .
>
> (13, 1–7)

In traversing the desert, the quester begins to fashion a new self. The dynamics of the quest urge this transformation, explained by Merton in *Seasons of Celebration* as follows: "man cannot enter into the deepest center of himself and pass through that center into God, unless he is able to pass entirely out of himself."[20] This shedding of the old self occurs in the act of attaining communion with a divine Being. In *Zen and the Birds of Appetite* and in *Faith and Violence* Merton also points out that this communion (or "consciousness of Being") is an immediate experience that goes beyond reflexive awareness. He states that it is not "'consciousness of' but 'pure consciousness,' in which the subject as such disappears."[21] Pure consciousness "is not an abstract objective idea but a fundamental concrete intuition directly apprehended in a personal experience."[22] H. D. discovers in the

20. Merton, *New Seeds of Contemplation* (Norfolk: New Directions), p. 64.

21. Merton, *Zen and the Birds of Appetite* (New York: New Directions, 1968) and *Faith and Violence* (Notre Dame, Indiana: University of Notre Dame Press, 1968), pp. 23–24.

22. *Zen and the Birds of Appetite*, p. 26.

desert of the holocaust that only the body of the old self remains, "the forlorn / husk of self," a "dead shell," and that a new self endowed with "pure consciousness" emerges, since "the new Sun dries off / the old body-humours" (14).

The nature of the desert quest in *Trilogy* also subsumes the reality of dreams and equates them with divine inspiration. Lyric 20 connects the individual's dream content with divine inspiration (i.e., the Holy Ghost) and recapitulates the motifs associated with the quest thus far.

> Now it appears very clear
> that the Holy Ghost,
>
> childhood's mysterious enigma,
> is the Dream;
>
> that way of inspiration
> is always open,
>
> and open to everyone;
> it acts as go-between, interpreter,
>
> it explains symbols of the past
> in to-day's imagery,
>
> it merges the distant future
> with most distant antiquity,
>
> states economically
> in a simple dream-equation
>
> the most profound philosophy,
> discloses the alchemist's secret
>
> and follows the Mage
> in the desert.
>
> (20)

H. D.'s interpretation of dream-content and dream-function largely derives from Freud, as is evident in *Tribute to Freud*, although it does show Jungian influence.

In lyric 20, H. D. stresses that racial memories are inherent in the human psyche and are enacted by the dreamer in his dreams. When fragments of these dreams (i.e., memories, visions, reveries) are brought to the conscious level, they function as constant reminders of "the shape and substance of the rituals of vanished civilizations" (*TF* 13). These dreams are "priceless broken fragments" which cannot be discarded as useless (*TF* 35). Their recovery bridges past, present, and future, enabling the dreamer to derive the present from the ancient past. The dream, therefore, acts as go-between and interpreter, as does the Holy Ghost. Dreams transfer meaning from generation to generation. The poet's task, in part, then, is to translate this meaning into her work. By equating the act of dreaming with the power of the Holy Ghost, H. D. reestablishes the sacred origins of dreams, a concept expressed in a *Tribute to Freud*, where she writes that dreams come "from the same source as the script or Scripture, the Holy Writ or Word" (*TF* 36).

The dream (or dream-vision), moreover, condenses centuries of thought into seconds, so that dreams function as illuminations (*TF* 92). The dream "states economically / in a simple dream-equation / the most profound philosophy." The dream symbol can be interpreted and translated in terms of both individual (private) and universal (collective) significance. *Trilogy*, then, is both a private and collective dream vision.

The dream vision of the Presence (lyrics 1, 12 and 13) is further developed in lyrics 16–22. The Egyptian sun god Ra and the resurrection god Osiris are manifestations of the Presence, the world-father, not to be confused with Jehovah. They appear "in a spacious, bare meeting-house," characteristic of "eighteenth-century / simplicity and grace" (16), thus recalling H. D.'s Moravian roots.

After the dream-vision, the quester awakens and asks, "but whose eyes are those eyes?" (16). The eyes "with amber / shining" (16) are the eyes of Christ of the apocalypse, whose eyes are "coals for the world's burning" (17). This image is drawn from the Book of Revelation where Christ has "eyes like unto a flame of fire" (Rev. 2:18).

Ra and Osiris are prototypes of Christ, the god of spiritual rebirth. The dream, in bringing forth this new perception in lyric 18 of the "Christos-image," enables the dreamer "to disentangle" Christ from pain and death worship. The dreamer has "deftly stage-managed the bare, clean / early colonial interior, / without stained-glass, picture, / image or colour," to remove the Christ-myth "from its art-craft junk-shop / paint-and-plaster medieval jumble." The image of the resurrected Christ (god of "regeneration") effects a different angle of vision: "the terror of those eyes" (19) has vanished from Velasquez's Christ: the "Splintered" self is made whole through Christ, the very "crystal of identity," and the "vessel of integrity" (21).

The dream also reveals that the desert quest is a return to sacred origins. This return is often interpreted as a star-voyage, "where stars blaze through clean air, / where we may greet individually, / Sirius, Vega, Arcturus." In lyric 24, the souls of the dead cross the sky as stars on their journey to the underworld, and then ascend again into the skies. Osiris and Isis, for example, are associated with Sirius, the dog star. In occult works, the stars symbolize the migration of human souls, and they are also the "living jewels in the Crown on God."[23]

Astrology is an important part of the magic associated with the Magi. The Magi considered astrology as supreme wisdom and the gate to the supernal world inhabited by planetary angels and other deities. Prophecy is revealed in the zodiac and horoscope. The ancient Egyptian scribe was familiar with the wisdom of the Magi revealed through Thoth, the scribe of the gods whose wisdom passed to Hermes Trismegistus, whose works are generally known as hermetic. In the Book of Revelation the stars are angels who guard God's

---

23. Paul Christian, *The History and Practice of Magic,* tr. James Kirkiup and Julian Show (New York: Citadel Press, 1969), p. 22.

throne; in Egyptian mythology and the Cabala the angels are
the geniuses and planets who rule the heavens.

The quester now perceives that "these separate entities /
are intimately concerned with us" and that each angel "with
its particular attribute, / may be invoked / with accurate
charm, spell, prayer." The stars-angels are jewels and "un-
guent" of the "absolute Healer, Apothecary," Christ-God
("the One, *Amen*, All-father"). Praying to the angels "will re-
veal unquestionably, / whatever healing or inspirational es-
sence / is necessary for whatever particular ill / the inquir-
ing soul is heir to." The stars are angels and jewels — "jasper,
beryl, sapphire," stones associated with God's temple in Reve-
lation. They are very precious boxes that hold "unguent,
myrrh, incense." Drawing nearer to them,

> by prayer, spell
> litany, incantation,
>
> will reveal their individual fragrance,
> personal magnetic influence,
>
> become, as they once were,
> personified messengers,
>   (24, 20–26)

from God to men and men to God. The angels are agents of
spiritual rebirth and salvation.

In lyric 25 efficacy of prayer is experienced when this com-
munion takes place. The "ultimate grain" lodges in "the heart-
core" and here takes "its nourishment." God opens the peti-
tioner's "heart-shell." This transformation is like that of the
phoenix, the "*bennu* bird" which "long ago" "dropped a grain /
as of scalding wax." In Egyptian mythology the phoenix (or
Benu Bird) is symbolic of the High God, and its appearance
signals a new life cycle.[24] The phoenix "embodies the original

24. Clark, p. 246. As a prophetic symbol in the sacred texts, it is usu-
ally pictured as perched in the water separating the abyss, as "It opens its

Logos, the Word or declaration of destiny which mediates between divine mind and created things. . . . It is the first and deepest manifestation of the 'soul' of the High God."[25] Its rebirth from its ashes is an apt symbol of the quester's spiritual rebirth amid the charnel house of war, but it also is a rebirth available to others. God sends the grain, "manna-beans" (2), as His nourishment: "To him that overcometh will I give to eat of the hidden manna, and will give him a white stone, and in the stone a new name written, which no man knoweth saving he that receiveth it" (Rev. 2:17).

The heart is pictured as a "small urn / of porphyry, agate, or cornelian" (28), semiprecious stones mentioned in Revelation. The grain lodges in the human heart, but the poet does not know "how it escaped tempest / of passion and malice, / nor why it was not washed away / in flood of sorrow, / or dried up in the bleak drought / of bitter thought." These lines fully reveal the effects of the war and the refusal to be destroyed by it. Following the miracle of the grail-stone, she prays for "strength to endure" (29), since the struggle is made more difficult by the "old-self" (29) which hankers after food and material comfort.

The grain foreshadows the flowering rod symbolic of Christ as the Tree of Life (Genesis [2:9] and Revelation [2:7]). She perceives that "the Kingdom is a Tree / whose roots bind the heart-husk / to earth" (25). But which flowering tree, fruit or flower "is our store[?] / . . . what particular healing-of-the-nations / is our leaf?" Is it "balsomodendron," "basil," "palm," "lotus," "pomegranate," "wild-almond, winter-cherry," "pine or fir," or "cypress"? (25–27). Which of these trees possesses the fruit of the hidden manna?

In the remaining lyrics in *The Walls Do Not Fall*, H. D. as-

beak and breaks the silence of the primeval night with the call of life and destiny, which 'determines what is and what is to be.'"
    25. Clark, p. 246.

sesses the spiritual quest. The war has brought the Age of Aquarius, one of agony and rebirth: "across the abyss / the Waterman waited, / this is the age of the new dimension, / dare, seek, seek further, dare more" (30). The quester has yet to delve deeper and await the reappearance of Christ: "O, for your Presence / among the fishing-nets / by the beached boats on the lake-edge" (29). To an extent, ritual has furthered the quest; however, lyric 31 sums up the poet's difficulties. The imaginative journey has been accompanied by "Wistfulness, exaltation, / a pure core of burning cerebration," and by constant "jottings on a margin, / indecipherable palimpsest scribbled over / with too many contradictory emotions."

Perhaps the most critical assessment of her own work is found here. Her research has resulted in "a riot of unpruned imagination, / jottings of psychic numerical equations, / runes, superstitions, evasions, / invasion of the oversoul into a cup / too brittle, a jar too circumscribed." H. D. may be warding off her detractors by stating in negative terms what she accomplishes and how she accomplishes it, not only in *The Walls Do Not Fall,* but throughout *Trilogy.*

To be sure, the poem is neither chaotic nor undisciplined. Her apology is directed toward the seemingly esoteric nature of her spiritual realism and toward her fears that her poetry may not reflect the themes she wishes to translate for others. The reference to the jar of myrrh suggests that her poetry may not be as sublime as its subject. It is Kaspar, the Magus, after all, who brings at Christ's birth the first jar; Mary Magdalene brings the other to anoint Christ before his death. Her poetry may not be dignified nor lofty enough to touch upon sacred matters. Perhaps it is "too porous to contain the out-flowing / of water-about-to-be-changed-to-wine / at the wedding" (31). To write about miracles may bring forth a "barren search" (31), grounded in "arrogance, over-confidence, pitiful reticence, / boasting, intrusion of strained / inappropriate allusion" (31) to pagan deities or dæmons. Most of all, she fears her audience may be unwilling to accept the poet's chosen role as a "gambler with eternity, / initiate of the secret wisdom, / bride of the kingdom" (31).

The poetics in *Trilogy*, however, negate this adverse criticism. Instead of "sterile invention" (32), *The Walls Do Not Fall* brings vision. From the dire consequences of war, the poet finds "the angle of incidence" (32) which best expresses her values and her myth. "The angle of incidence / equals the angle of reflection" (32), bringing forth a new perception: "Let us measure defeat / in terms of bread and meat"; "let us not teach / what we have learned badly / and not profited by" (33).

This assessment leads her to see that the search for the mother goddess also motivates her quest. At this point, it is Egyptian mythology that furthers this level of the search. She discovers that Osiris, as a prototype of the resurrected Christ, parallels the recovery of Isis as a prototype for Mary. Her effort, then, is to "correlate faith with faith, / recover the secret of Isis, / which is: there was One / in the beginning, Creator, / Fosterer, Begetter, the Same-forever / in the papyrus-swamp / in the Judean meadow" (40). Isis recovers Osiris' body in the Deltas and Mary attends to Jesus' wounds. The worship of Isis also points to the worship of Mary, as the lady of sorrows (the sorrow of Osiris) and as the divine mother (mother of Horus, the Redeemer).[26]

The role of sorrowful mother extends to other manifestations of the goddess. For example, Demeter's mourning for Persephone is at the center of the Eleusinian Mysteries, and Cybele exemplifies yet another version of the Mater Dolorosa in her mourning for Attis. Her shrine in Rome "stood on the Vatican hill where now stands St. Peter's, the centre of

26. Weigall, pp. 128–129.

the Church which worships the 'Mother of God' in just that capacity."[27] Fortuitously, the Assumption of Mary, cele-brated on August 15th, has replaced the festival of Diana (or Artemis) who as moon goddess is associated with Isis and Aphrodite (Venus). Artemis is also Selene, the moon goddess of the crescent moon, a symbol associated with Isis, Aphro-dite and Mary. Before the Christians, the Romans had as-similated Isis' mourning for the slain Osiris with the mourn-ing of Venus for the slain Adonis.[28] As a result, Isis is also identified with Astarte (known as Aset and by other similar names, such as Ashtoreth or Ashtaroth). And, "just as we learn from Jeremiah that the Hebrew women made offerings to her [as the Queen of Heaven], so, down right to modern times at Paphos in Cyprus, the women make offerings to the Virgin Mary as the Queen of Heaven in the ruins of the an-cient temple of Astarte."[29]

Therefore, H. D.'s allusion to the old shrines, such as "Mithra's tomb" (1) in *Tribute to the Angels*, and the associa-tion of "Venus, Aphrodite, Astarte" negate the poet's self-criticism of stylistic "intrusion of strained / inappropriate al-lusion" (*WDNF* 31). Isis, like Aphrodite-Venus, is a goddess of the sea and patron of seamen, as she is a prototype of Mary: "when the Madonna took the place of Isis she also took over the title *Stella Maris*, 'Star of the Sea,' by which she is so often called in Roman Catholic countries."[30] This very epithet is used in lyric 8, ("Now polish the crucible / and in the bowl distill / a word most bitter, 'marah'" [*TA*], dis-cussed above).

At this point also in *The Walls Do Not Fall*, the poet ad-dresses her prayers to Thoth, "the original Ancient-of-days, / Hermes-thrice-great." She entreats him by his symbolic "tau-cross" to invoke "true-magic," which will draw her nearer to

27. Weigall, p. 129.   28. Weigall, p. 132.
29. Weigall, p. 133.   30. Weigall, p. 132.

the Logos. She prays to Thoth to "illuminate" and "re-vivify the eternal verity" of her quest. The essence of her prayer is heard here:

> Let us substitute
> enchantment for sentiment,
>
> re-dedicate our gifts
> to spiritual realism.
>
> (35, 1–4)

Hermes-Thoth, god of the underworld and reincarnation, who in Greek mythology receives the wand of individuation from Apollo and the winged sandals from Perseus, is also given the name Trismegistus "'thrice-greatest Intelligencer' — because, so it is said, he was the [first] intelligence [angel] to communicate celestial knowledge to man."[31] It is interesting to note that Longfellow (admired by H. D.) had dedicated a poem to Hermes-Thoth, entitled "Hermes Trismegistus."[32]

The evaluation of her quest brings forth the revelation that the meaning of the Word "our secret hoard" (36) is found in the magic "talismans" and "parchments" that instruct each scribe of "*things new / and old*" (36). It is revealed that Osiris is a prototype of Christ, and, again, that the mystery of Osiris as a vegetation god is associated with Christ as the regenerative seed (the manna-grain) of the flowering rod in lyric 41. Parallels found in the Osirian legend and in the legends of other vegetation deities — Adonis, Attis, Mithra — in turn, are symbolic of the great human drama enacted in the union with nature in the hope of survival after death.

Osiris is simultaneously associated with the waste desert,

---

31. Gustav Davidson, *A Dictionary of Angels* (New York: Collier-Macmillan, 1969), p. 140.

32. Reference to "Hermes Trismegistus" in Davidson's *Dictionary of Angels*, p. 142. Longfellow's *The Golden Legend* may have influenced H. D.'s angelology.

the "seed" (41) that lies fallow, as he also represents the floods of the Nile that follow his drowning. As such, he is the inundation, the overflow, the sprouting, and harvest. He revives in the wasteland in the image of "white, little flowers."

The journey through "the waste" (42) leads the quester to the promised land. In *The Walls Do Not Fall* H. D. successfully "relates resurrection myth / and resurrection reality" (40); the latter is exemplified in Osiris and other gods, and the former is envisioned in the "Christos-image." The topography of the resurrection is graphic in both the "papyrus-swamp" and the "Judean meadow" (40). The journey has drawn closer to "the temple-gate" (42) and *"possibly we will reach haven, / heaven"* (43).

A brief respite from the bombings occasions *Tribute to the Angels*, H. D.'s most successful attempt at sustained meditation. *Tribute to the Angels* develops the thematic threads established in *The Walls Do Not Fall*, while focusing on salvation. Salvation is vision, and salvation gives direction to this phase of the quest which focuses on contemplative prayer or meditation of the angels.

H. D.'s angelology draws upon several sources and the angels have multiple functions. First, they are the angels who surround the throne of the Ancient of Days in Daniel's vision:

I beheld till the thrones were cast down, and the Ancient of Days did sit, whose garment was white as snow, and the hair of his head like the pure wool; His throne *was like* the fiery flame, *and* his wheels *as* burning fire.

(Daniel 7:9)

Second, they are the angels who guard God's throne in John's vision in the Book of Revelation. In his testimony, the seven angels are: lampsteads of gold; stars; spirits of the seven churches; spirits of God; and the bowls filled with God's wrath. The symbols for Jesus as star and a flowering rod are also found in John's vision: "I Jesus have sent mine angel to testify unto you these things in the churches. I am the root and the offspring of David, and the bright and morning star" (Rev. 22 : 16). H. D.'s angels possess all of these attributes, and in *Tribute to the Angels* they also are the Angels of Presence who direct the poet's meditation.

In his excellent *Dictionary of the Angels*, Gustav Davidson's exhaustive research leads him to the discovery that except for Michael, Gabriel, and Raphael, no other angel is named in Scripture, although an infinite number of angels are named in occult lore, cabalistic and apocryphal texts, such as the Book of Enoch. Davidson locates the reference to the seven angels in the Book of Tobit, where Raphael reveals himself to Tobit: "I am Raphael, one of the seven angels who enter and serve before the glory of God" (Tobit 12 : 15). Drawing upon canonical and noncanonical texts, H. D. names the seven angels who reign in her poem: Azrael, Raphael, Gabriel, Uriel, Annael, Michael, and Zadkiel. The angels are rulers, princes, geniuses of the heavens, tutelary spirits of the planets, and guardians of the sacred calendar.

The passage from the desert to the promised land of "spiritual realism" (*WDNF* 35) is also directed by "the original Ancient-of-days" — Thoth, "Hermes-thrice-great." Not only is he the scribe in the books of wisdom generally known as Hermeticism, but also in the history and practice of magic of the Magi Thoth receives God's wisdom through the angels who reveal to him the mysteries.

In Hermetic hierarchy the earth is at the center of ten circles of light which form the Crown of God.[33] These circles are governed by specific angels who preside over particular planets. The mystery involved in this divine plan of the cosmos is revealed by the Seven Spirits to Hermes-Thoth who transmits this knowledge to Hermes Trismegistus, the Great

33. Christian, p. 60.

Magus. Hermeticism stresses that the seven spirits "can be seen, according to the will of God, through the science of numbers and hierograms, or scattered letters, which are combined on the symbolic order attributed to each of the seven ministers of the changeless Providence."[34] Mystical numbers; sacred stones; the angelic script; signs of the zodiac; the magic circle; innumerable sigils, charts, and pacts; and sacred calendar — all fall within the mainstream of Hermeticism.

Hermetic symbols are equally numerous and complex. The Crown of Eternity, for example, contains the archangels, the order of spirits under Pi-Hermes or Thoth, the legendary father of Magism. In Talismanic Magic, an important part of Hermeticism, the seven archangels are: Zaphkiel, Zadkiel, Carmael, Raphael, Hamiel, Michael, and Gabriel.

According to Thoth, "'Fortunate is he who knows how to read the Signs of the Times.'"[35] In *Trilogy* the poet-scribe gives her own reading of the "signs of the times," her particular interpretation, a legacy from Hermes Trismegistus, which reveals the unity between the old and the new church through the seven angels. These spirits are the same "seven Devas of ancient India — the seven Amschaspards of Persia — the 'seven great angels' of Chaldea — the seven Sephiroths of the Hebrew Quabala — the seven angels who, in the Christian Apocalypse, are seen by John before the thrones of the Ancient of Days."[36] They are the angels in the Book of Revelation: "The mystery of the seven stars which thou sawest in my right hand, and the seven golden sticks / . . . are the angels of the seven churches: and the seven candlesticks which thou sawest are the seven churches" (Rev. 1 : 20).[37]

Thoth, whose "province is thought," also transmits the wisdom of the angels. Furthermore, his wisdom leads the poet to the original church, "the old church / found in Mithra's

---

34. Christian, p. 67.   35. Christian, p. 71.
36. Christian, p. 67.   37. Davidson, *passim*.

tomb" (*TA*, 1). In Persian mythology, the mysteries associated with Mithra's passion and resurrection are analogous to the mysteries of Christ. Consequently, it is Hermes Trismegistus who inspires the integration between the old church (Mithra) and the new church (Christ). It is the poet's task as scribe ("*for every scribe / which is instructed, / things new / and old*" *WDNF*, 36) to collect "candle and script and bell," rejected and shattered by the "new-church." By collecting "the fragments of the splintered glass," the poet furthers our spiritual quest. As the arch-alchemist, the poet is to:

> melt down and integrate
>
> re-invoke, re-create
> opal, onyx, obsidian,
>
> now scattered in the shards
> men tread upon.
>
> (1, 16–20)

Opal, onyx, obsidian, and other precious and semiprecious stones (symbols of stars, angels, and souls) are sacred and magical in Hermeticism. They also recur throughout Scripture: "And he that sat was to look upon like a jasper and a sardine stone; and there was a rainbow round about the throne, in sight like unto an emerald" (Rev. 4:3). The wall of the New Jerusalem is made of jasper: "Your walls do not fall, he said, / because your walls are made of jasper" (2).

The poet's vision of spiritual realism substantiates that of John in Revelation. John's testimony unequivocally asserts that promulgation of destruction is to be met by God's plagues and that our quest for salvation will inherit for us the kingdom of Christ. In H. D.'s poem, Christ states: "*I make all things new*, / said He of the seven stars, / he of the seventy-times-seven / passionate, bitter wrongs, / He of the seventy-times-seven / bitter, unending wars" (3). The poet's meditation is intended to postpone the eventual Armageddon. As such, *Tribute to the Angels* is a prayer for peace: "Not in our time, O Lord, / the plowshare for the sword, / not in our time, the knife, / sated with life-blood and life . . . / not in our time, O King, / the voices to quell the re-gathering, / thundering storm" (4). In her meditation the host of angels bring peace.

The catalog of angels intermittently extends from lyric 5 to lyric 43. A candle is lighted to each angel (star and planetary ruler). Our hearts share a "part of that same fire / that in a candle on a candle-stick / or in a star, / is known as one of seven, / is named among the seven Angels" (6). The angels reign over the sacred calendar: "Every hour, every moment / has its specific attendant Spirit; / the clock-hand, minute by minute, / ticks round its prescribed orbit" (24). More importantly, the angels relate life, "this temporary eclipse" (24), to eternity. A prayer to each of the seven angels follows.

Azrael (15 and 41) is the angel of resurrection — "the first who giveth life" (5) and his name means "'whom God helps.'" He is the angel of death, stationed in the third heaven. Raphael (15 and 41) symbolizes unswerving love for God and his Son. Raphael is the "lover of sand and shell" (5), "who withdraws the veil, / holds back the tide and shapes / shells to the wave-shapes" (5). The name Raphael means "'God has healed.'"[38] In Scripture and in angelology Raphael is one of the three greatest angels (the other two are Gabriel and Michael). In *Dictionary of Angels* Davidson traces Raphael's history to the Book of Tobit where he reveals himself as "'one of the seven holy angels' that attend the throne of God."[39] He

38. Davidson, p. 64 and p. 240.
39. Davidson, p. 240. In the apocryphal Book of Enoch, Raphael is "one of the watchers" (Enoch I, 20); he is a guide in the underworld (Enoch I, 22); and a healer (Enoch I, 40). In *Legends of the Jews*, I, Raphael is one of the angels who wrestles with Jacob at Peniel. In the Cabala, Raphael gives Noah, "after the flood," a "medical book." In occult lore, he is one of the seven angels of the Apocalypse and is numbered among the ten holy sefiroth.

is the regent of the sun who guards the Tree of Life. He is also the angel of repentance, prayer, love, joy, and light. Above all, he is the angel of healing and change.

Gabriel, on the other hand, is the angel of birth. "What is war," she asks, in contrast "to Birth, to Change, to Death?" Gabriel is, of course, the angel of annunciation (Luke 1: 19–25), resurrection, mercy, vengeance, death, and revelation.[40] He is the ruling prince of the first heaven and presides over paradise. He sits at the left side of God. The Cabala identifies Gabriel as the prince of justice and angel of cosmic war. He appears in Longfellow's *The Golden Legend* as the angel of the moon.[41] Lyric 28 recapitulates Gabriel's attributes:

> I had been thinking of Gabriel,
> of the moon-cycle, of the moon-shell,
>
> of the moon-crescent
> and the moon at full:
>
> I had been thinking of Gabriel,
> the moon-regent, the Angel,
>
> and I had intended to recall him
> in the sequence of candle and fire
>
> and the law of the seven;
> I had not forgotten
>
> his special attribute
> of annunciator; I had thought
>
> to address him as I had the others,
> Uriel, Annael. . . .

Uriel (lyric 5) is "red-fire"; "judgment and will of God, / God's very breath." Neither martyrs nor other worshipers realize that "the fire / of strength, endurance, anger / in their hearts" was instilled by Uriel (6). Yet no shrine (temple) is dedicated to him nor are there images in honor of the angel

---

40. Davidson, pp. 117–119.   41. Davidson, pp. 117–119.

who guides the questers toward the vision of the flowering rod:

> the lane is empty but the levelled wall
>
> is purple as with purple spread
> upon an altar,
>
> this is the flowering of the rood,
> this is the flowering of the reed,
>
> where, Uriel, we pause to give
> thanks that we rise again from death and live.
>
> (7, 6–12)

The flowering of the rood, the symbolic cross, alludes to Christ's resurrection prophesied by Isaiah: "And there shall come forth a rod out of the stem of Jesse, and a Branch shall grow out of his roots" (Isa. 11:1). In John's vision Christ is the root and offspring of David (Rev. 22:16). The war's fire of destruction is changed into the fire of Uriel, "God's very breath," which leads the quester to the vision of universal redemption: "*we rise again from death and live*" (43).

Uriel and Annael are hailed together as "two of the seven Spirits, / set before God / as lamps on the high-altar" (17). Each draws its beauty from the other, "as spring from winter, / and surely never, never / was a spring more bountiful / than this":

> tell me, in what other city
> will you find the may-tree
>
> so delicate, green-white, opalescent
> like our jewel in the crucible?
>
> (17, 17–20)

The jewel in the crucible refers first to the manna-grain lodged in the heart-core (*WDNF* 25); second, to the jewel of Mary — "now polish the crucible / and in the bowl distil / word most bitter, *marah*" (*TA* 8); and third, to the "Bitter,

bitter jewel / in the heart of the bowl" in lyric 9 of *Tribute to the Angels.*

Uriel, a guiding spirit, is fervently addressed (5–7, 16–18, and 28) as the "'fire of God.'"[42] As he is important in *Trilogy,* he is also the leading angel in noncanonical lore. Davidson lists him as the regent of the sun, flame of God, angel of the Presence, and archangel of salvation. In the writing of a prominent theologian, Uriel is "'the spirit who stood at the gate of the lost Eden with the fiery sword.'"[43] He is the one who warns Noah of the "impending deluge" in the Book of Enoch (Enoch I, 10:1–3).[44] Likewise, Uriel plays an important role in the Cabala, where he is said to have disclosed the mysteries of the heavenly arcana to Ezra, the Magus who "claims that alchemy 'which is of divine origin' was brought down to earth by Uriel, and that it was Uriel who gave the cabala to man."[45]

The angel Annael (15) is "another fire, another candle" and the "peace of God" (16). He complements Uriel's fire and also guides the quester toward the miracle of the flowering rod. The flowering of the rod directly relates to the mystery of "transubstantiation" (23): "not God merely in bread / but God in the other-half of the tree / that looked dead" (23). It flowers before her eyes — "*my eyes saw, / it was not a dream / yet it was a vision, / it was a sign, / it* was the *Angel which redeemed me*" (23, emphasis mine).[46]

42. Davidson, p. 298.   43. Davidson, p. 298.
44. Davidson, p. 298.
45. Davidson, p. 298–299. Alchemy is related to the Cabala in *Trilogy* through the presence of Uriel. In the Sibylline Oracles, Book II, Uriel is "one of the 'immortal angels'" of apocalypse, and it is perhaps this version of Uriel that influences lyric 6 where "Never in Rome, / so many martyrs fell" nor in Jerusalem or Thebes as during "the battle of the Titans" (6) where Zeus' thunderbolts shattered on earth. In the Sibylline Oracles the angel punishes the many ghosts of Titans and giants.
46. Davidson, p. 17. Annael is H. D.'s alternate spelling for Aniel or Annael also known as Haniel, Ariel, etc. According to Davidson, Annael

The angel Michael (33, 34, and 41) is associated with Hermes-Thoth (Hermes Trismegistus) and St. Michael who "casts the Old Dragon / into the abyss" (33). Hermes, the conductor of souls, takes this attribute "of Leader-of-the-dead from Thoth / and the T-cross becomes caduceus" (33). The angel, as St. Michael, is "the benevolent angel of death, in the sense of deliverance and immortality, and for leading the souls of the faithful 'into the eternal light.'"[47] He shares attributes with Hermes and Thoth. He also announces to Mary her approaching death: "the old-church makes its invocation / to Saint Michael and Our Lady / at the deathbed" (33). Hermes Trismegistus and St. Michael both slay ignorance, while Hermes Trismegistus

> spears, with Saint Michael,
> the darkness of ignorance,
>
> cast the Old Dragon
> into the abyss.
>
> (33, 7–10)

In mystic and occult lore, Michael is often equated with the Holy Ghost, the Logos, and God; therefore, he possesses an additional likeness to Hermes Trismegistus, to whom Hermes-Thoth transmitted his knowledge of the Word. Michael (34) is the regent of Mercury (Hermes). As the angel of final reckoning who balances the scales of justice, he is also related to Thoth who is the god of justice. Davidson re-

---

rules over Venus and is "concerned with human sexuality." "It is Annael who proclaims 'Open all ye gates' in Isaiah 26:2." In Longfellow's part III of *The Golden Legend* entitled "The Angels of the Seven Planets Bearing the Star of Bethlehem," Annael is the angel of the Star of Love, the Evening Star of Venus.

47. Davidson, p. 194. See also Robert Graves in *The White Goddess*, p. 152, where he states: the Druidic Essenes "evoked angels in their mysteries." They associate Hermes and Gabriel as conductors of souls. The hymn "The Hounds of Hermes the Hunter" is also known as "Gabriel's Hounds."

cords that Michael means he "'who is as God.'"[48] He is the prince of presence and the angel of repentance, righteousness, mercy, and sanctification.[49]

The seventh angel invoked is Zadkiel (42 and 43) who is "the righteousness of God."[50] He is the "regent of Jupiter" and is associated with the all-father figure:

> *Theus,* God; God-the-father, father-god
> or the Angel god-father,
>
> himself, heaven yet a home in a star
> whose colour is amethyst,
>
> whose candle burns deep-violet
> with the others.
>
> (42, 5–10)

Furthermore, the angels are associated with Mary (in lyrics 8 and 9) where the "crucible" and the "bowl" refer to the angels and Mary. In the Book of Revelation the angels are the seven bowls of God's wrath (Rev. 15:1–8; 16:1–21), and in Christian lore, Mary is the vessel of rebirth, the "crucible." Likewise, H. D. associates the angels with Venus as a star and as wisdom. The Gnostics identify the Holy Spirit with Sophia, wisdom, and wisdom is female.[51] In lyric 1 "the

48. Davidson, p. 193.

49. Davidson, pp. 194–195. In Islamic writing he is the Redeemer. He is the most important angel in the Old Testament: he stayed the hand of Abraham when Abraham was at the point of sacrificing Isaac; he is the fire of the burning bush; he assists in the burial of Moses; and he is one of the three angels Abraham entertained unawares. In *Tribute to Freud* (Boston: David Godine, 1974), p. 106, H. D. states: "The Angel Michael of the old dispensation, the archangel Michael of the Revelation, is regent of the planet still called Mercury. And in Renaissance paintings, we are not surprised to see Saint Michael wearing the winged sandals and sometimes the winged helmet of the classic messenger of the Gods."

50. Davidson, p. 324. According to Davidson, Zadkiel also holds back Abraham's arm at the point of sacrifice. He is one of the angels that stand in the presence of God. In rabbinic writings he is the angel of "benevolence, mercy and memory."

51. Graves, p. 159.

splintered glass" (an image for the old church) reflects the star Hesperus, Venus-Aphrodite-Astarte. In the Cabala, Venus is an angel of love who presides over human love and sexuality.[52] As a moon goddess, Venus is a manifestation of Astarte, the chief female star-deity of the Phoenicians, Syrians, and Carthaginians. The Greeks borrowed their Aphrodite from this moon fertility goddess.[53]

The "flame" and "substance" in the bowl (11) reveal that the name of Venus has been desecrated: an "impious wrong" has been leveled against the spirit of the goddess-angel whose name has become synonymous with lascivious desire and with the very root of the mandrake. Instead of reverence (veneration), Venus is subjected to sexual indulgence (venery). The poet undoes this wrong by invoking her as the angel of love, exclaiming "Swiftly re-light the flame" (12). Her prayer establishes Venus's rightful place among the planetary angels:

> return, O holiest one,
> Venus whose name is kin
>
> to venerate,
> venerator.
>
> (12, 7–10)

The Star of Love also guides the poet and others to the "charred tree":

> we crossed the charred portico,
> passed through a frame — doorless —

52. Davidson, p. 17. In some legends, the angel "Annael exercises dominion over the planet Venus." As one of the seven angels of creation, he rules the second heaven and is in charge of prayer from the first Heaven. In Longfellow's *The Golden Legend*, Annael is specifically the Star of Love. This angel is the Evening Star or Venus-Aphrodite.

53. Davidson, p. 59. As a moon goddess, Venus emerged from Astarte, the chief female deity of the ancient Phoenicians, Syrians and Carthaginians. "The Greeks borrowed their Aphrodite" from this moon fertility goddess. Astarte was worshipped by the Jews, and Davidson writes that Jeremiah called Astarte the "'queen of heaven.'"

entered a shrine; like a ghost,
we entered a house through a wall;

then still not knowing
whether (like the wall)

we were there or not-there,
we saw a tree flowering;

it was an ordinary tree
in an old garden-square.

(20, 5–14)

No words, according to the quester, can express the impact of this vision ("what I mean is — it is so simple / yet no trick of the pen or brush / could capture that impression" (21). The vision of the flowering tree creates a "new sensation" (22) totally affecting the consciousness of the quester: "there is no escape from the spear / that pierces the heart" (22). It is the Angel of Love who redeems the quester ("*it was the Angel which redeemed me*" [23, 11]), and it is the power of the Holy Ghost that enables her and the others to partake in the mystery of "transubstantiation" (23).

Meditation of the angels ushers the dream-vision of the Lady (25–32 and 35–41). The dreamer sees the Lady in an outer hall and doorless area, standing "at the turn of the stair" (25). The Lady "in some very subtle way . . . / had miraculously / related herself to time here" (27). Thinking of Gabriel, she wonders "how could I imagine / the Lady herself would come instead?" (28). (Gabriel is, we remember, the regent of the moon and the angel of annunciation). The Lady is enigmatic but "something of her cool beneficence" (31) approximates "the gracious friendliness / of the marble sea-maids in Venice, / who climb the altar-stair / at *Santa Maria dei Miracoli*" (31). She also resembles the Viennese sculpture "*Maria von dem Schnee* / Our Lady of the Snow" (31), for "her veils were white as snow" (32). She wore no "*golden girdle*"; "she bore / none of her visual attributes; / the Child was not with her" (32). This angel of love comes as annunciator to show that she is content with the poet, who had not forgotten the power of the goddess. Consequently, she concludes that the Lady "must have been pleased with us, / who did not forego our heritage / at the grave-edge; / she must have been pleased / with the straggling company of the brush and quill / who did not deny their birthright" (35).

The Lady is not to be confused with Santa Sophia nor with Eve (36). She is not a symbol of beauty (37), not the original for a sculpture "flanked by Corinthian capitals" (37) nor "the veiled Goddess" (37). In fact, she represents womanhood:

> she is the Vestal
> from the days of Numa,
>
> she carries over the cult
> of the *Bona Dea*,
>
> . . .
>
> she is Psyche, the butterfly,
> out of the cocoon.
> (38, 5–8; 19–20)

Significantly, Susan Stanford Friedman in *Psyche Reborn* points to the Lady's "protean" nature. She is ever-different but eternally the same. Like Christ, she is an incarnation of both time and eternal reality.[54] The Lady symbolizes the unchanging importance of the goddess. The Lady possesses a "dove's symbolic purity" and her veils resemble the "Lamb's Bride" (39). Yet neither the Lamb nor the Child is with her: "her attention is undivided, / we are her bridegroom and lamb" (39). The vision of the Lady (woman and muse) concludes this phase of the quest. The poet reaches "the point in the spectrum / where all lights become one" (43), where the "flames mingle" and the "wings meet" at the "arc of perfection" (43). The Lady carries the "Book of Life" (36). The

---

54. Susan Stanford Friedman, *Psyche Reborn* (Bloomington: Indiana University Press, 1981), pp. 111ff.

"book is our book" (39), and its "pages will reveal / a tale of a Fisherman" (39), and "a tale of a jar or jars" (39).

In *The Flowering of the Rod* H. D. fills in the blank pages of the "Book" with her vision of resurrection, enveloped in the mystery of Christ's Incarnation and Resurrection. Lyrics 1–10 focus on the necessary preparation for resurrection and redemption, while lyrics 11–39 depict her vision of resurrection in the tale of the two jars of myrrh. Kaspar, the Magus, brings myrrh as a gift of love to the infant Christ, and Mary Magdalene, through her love for Christ, anoints him with a jar of myrrh.

H. D. had originally entitled this section "We Rise Again," but just before publication changed it to the present title.[55] The quester "rises again" because God's presence lodges at the heart of her being (*The Walls Do Not Fall*) and she prepared the way for His presence ("the new Sun / of regeneration" [*TA*, 17, 14–15]) through meditation of the angels (*Tribute to the Angels*).

In *The Flowering of the Rod* H. D. achieves a transformation of consciousness. This "new consciousness" is a result of the "transcendent experience" the poet has undergone in the previous parts of the poem.[56] It is this transformation of consciousness which brings about the poet's vision of resurrection. Merton perceives it as a "transcendent experience" which "is metaphysically distinct from the Self of God and yet perfectly identified with that Self by love and freedom, so that there appears to be but one Self."[57]

55. TS. Z Doolittle, Hilda Doolittle Collection, Beinecke Rare Book and Manuscript Library, Yale University. The original title for *The Flowering of the Rod* in the typescript of the poem.

56. *Zen and the Birds of Appetite*, pp. 1–88 and *passim*.

57. *Zen and the Birds of Appetite*, pp. 71–72. John J. Higgins, S. J., *Thomas Merton on Prayer* (New York: Doubleday, 1973), p. 56–57. John J. Higgins further explains the dynamics of this transformation as follows:

The individual is no longer conscious of himself as an isolated ego but sees himself in his inmost ground of being as dependent on Another or

Having "withstood . . . / [the] bitter fire of destruction,"
the quester now feels compelled to "leave the smoldering cities
below" and to "mount higher / to love — resurrection" (1).
She has witnessed the Presence of a higher reality: "O the
beautiful garment, / the beautiful raiment" (1). These lines
refer to Matthew's description of the Angel of the Lord who
appears to the women at the tomb: "His countenance was like
lightning, and his raiment white as snow" (Matt. 28:3). Now,
she wants to go beyond the vision of the crucified Christ: "do
not think of His face / or even His hands, / do not think how
we will stand / before Him" (1).

Realizing that there is compensation only in knowing that
"(we could have done all we could)" (1), she is prepared
to climb yet another mountain — "remember the snow / on
Hermon" (1). Exuberance now underscores the quest: "I go
where I love and where I am loved, / into the snow" (2), leav-
ing "The place-of-a skull / to those who have fashioned it"
(2). Jubilantly, she cries, "I go to the things I love / with no
thought of duty or pity; / I go where I belong, inexorably"
(2). Instead of "confusion" (3), there is "affirmation" (3):
"seeking what we once knew, / we know ultimately we will
find / happiness; *today shalt thou be / with me in Paradise*" (3).
Christ promises the kingdom of heaven (Luke 23:43).

Yet, there is sadness in abandoning the evanescent beauty

---

as being formed through relationships, particularly his relationship with
God. By forgetting himself both as a subject and as an object of reflec-
tion, man finds his real self hidden with Christ in God. And so, as his
self-consciousness changes, the individual is transformed; his self is no
longer its own center; it is now centered on God. There is a death of the
self-centered and self-sufficient ego and in its place appears a new and
liberated self who loves and acts in the Spirit. Man is now empty of all
ego-consciousness; he is a Transcendent Self. . . . Hence, it is through
this dynamic process of inner transformation or transformation of con-
sciousness that man empties himself and transcends himself and ulti-
mately becomes his true self in Christ.

of the earth for the permanence of spiritual reality. She is aware of this "duality, this double nostalgia" (4):

> I know the insatiable longing
> in winter, for palm-shadow
>
> and sand and burnt sea-drift[.]
> (4, 3–5)

It is this "duality" that defines our human condition: "this is the eternal urge, / this is the despair, the desire to equilibrate / the eternal variant" (5). There is agony in the overwhelming desire to give oneself to natural inclination ("that demand of a given moment") and the simultaneous willingness to be drawn by the memory of another "desperate urge" of "what once was" — "the hunger / for Paradise" (5). The quester "would rather drown, remembering — / than bask on tropic atolls / in the coral-seas" (6). Ultimately drawn to the flight of the "mythical birds" (5), she expresses her vision: "I am seeking heaven" (6). In contrast the flight of those who circle the earth is seen as a "foolish circling," a "senseless wheeling" around "the pyramid of skulls" — their flight "has no vision" (6). There is but one reality for the quester: "only love is holy and love's ecstasy / that turns and turns and turns about one centre" (6).

"Yet resurrection is a sense of direction" (7): this cognition epitomizes the entire quest in *Trilogy*. It is at the heart of spiritual realism. "Resurrection is remuneration": it is the "food" and "shelter" of our transcendental existence in paradise — the self's spiritual home. Lyrics 8–10 fully demonstrate the quester's joy in reaching this stage of spiritual progression. Ecstasy lies in the quester's hypostatization of the Word: "I am the first or the last" (8), as is written in the prophecy — "I am he; I am the first, I also am the last" (Isa. 48:12; 43:10); or again, "*I am full of new wine*" — Christ as the new wine, the wine of the transubstantiation in the Gospels. She now enters this other reality, or "infectious — ecstasy" (9), the source of her identity: "I am an entity . . . / I live; I am alive" (9).

Clearly, then, the movement in *Trilogy* is from fragmentation to integration, from non-identity to identity, and from thought to vision. She now perceives that the smallest grain of the myrrh-tree, *"the least of all seeds"* (10), flowers miraculously as a symbol of redemption. Myrrh is *"the greatest among herbs / and becometh a tree"* (10). Resurrection is evident in this flowering tree, since myrrh is symbolic of Christ's birth and resurrection.

Lyrics 11–43 focus on the tale of jars of myrrh, which culminates with the birth of Christ. These lyrics further divide into two sub-groups: lyrics 12, 21–23, 25, 26 tell of the anointment at Bethany by Mary of Magdala, while lyrics 13, 20, 24, 27–41 describe the meeting between Magdalene and Kaspar, from whom she obtains the jar of myrrh. The concluding lyrics 42 and 43 celebrate the nativity.

Christ, coming to earth from heaven, is our first "heavenly pointer" (11), the star of Bethlehem. He is a divine messenger, as Hermes and Thoth were before him. Christ "not content to leave / the scattered flock / . . . journeys back and forth / between the poles of heaven and earth forever" (11). He is the bird of paradise, who rests on "the Tree of Life" and removes the Tree of Death: "He was the first to wing / from that sad Tree, / but having flown, the Tree of Life / bears rose from thorn / and fragrant vine, / from barren wood" (11). The agony of the Crucifixion brings the everlasting joy of the Resurrection. From the barren wood of the cross flower the vine and the branches: "I AM the true vine, and my Father is the husbandman. . . . I am the vine, ye are the branches" (John 15:1; 5).

On earth, Christ walked among the oppressed in body and spirit. Consequently, the first to receive the promise of heaven was the thief on the cross, an "outcast and a vagabond" (11).

At this point, the focus shifts to another outcast, Magdalene. The scene also shifts to Simon's house where the guests speculate how Magdalene obtained the jar of myrrh. Judas, in particular, reasons that she used the money designated for the poor to purchase this costly alabaster jar. "Then said Jesus, 'Let her alone: against the day of my burying hath she kept this. For the poor always ye have with you; but me ye have not always'" (John 12:7–8). Prophetically, it is Magdalene who is first among the women at the tomb.[58] Six days before Passover, Christ comes to Bethany to the house of Simon the leper, where the anointing takes place: "Then took Mary a pound of ointment of spikenard, very costly, and anointed the feet of Jesus, and wiped his feet with her hair: and the house was filled with the odour of the ointment" (John 12:3). In lyric 21, H. D. writes: "Anyhow, it is exactly written, / *the house was filled with the odour of the ointment*" (21).

While Judas questions Magdalene's actions, "she was deftly unweaving / the long, carefully-braided tresses / of her extraordinary hair" (21). Simon, perplexed, thinks of her as someone "in a heathen picture / or a carved stone-portal entrance / to a forbidden sea-temple" (22), or a siren whose song is fatal; anyway, she had not been invited. He becomes overwrought with anger when he sees her kiss Christ's feet. But, he "does not understand . . . [:] / *this man if he were a prophet, would have known / who and what manner of woman this is*" (23). Simon might have heard that this was the woman from whom Jesus had cast out seven demons (25); but, of course, this is not Simon Peter, but Simon the leper, "healed of body" (26), while "the un-maidenly mermaid, Mary of Magdala / was healed of soul" (26).

H. D. suggests that this version of the legend exists in the Cabala, although no mention of it is found there. According

58. Matthew 28:1–8; Luke 24:1–11, Mark 16:1–8; John 20:11–19.

to H. D., Magdalene obtains her jar from a merchant in a bazaar. Some say he is an Arab, but to the poet he is Kaspar, who brings myrrh on his way to a "double ceremony" — "a coronation and a funeral" (13). Later, Magdalene wishes to purchase a jar of myrrh, but Kaspar bluntly informs her that "his was not ordinary myrrh and incense / and anyway, it is not for sale, he said." Unaffected by his nobility and indignation, she persists undaunted: "she had seen nobility herself at first hand" (13) and what were insults to stoning?

She is, after all, one of the Marys associated with bitter experiences, yet another "Mother of Mutilations" (16) in the line of the sorrowful mothers of "Attis-Adonis-Tammuz" (16). "I am Mary, she said, of a tower-town . . . / for Magdala is a tower":

> I am Mary, she said, of Magdala,
> I am Mary, a great tower;
>
> through my will and my power,
> Mary shall be myrrh;
>
> . . .
>
> (though I am Mara, bitter) I shall be Mary-myrrh.
>   (16, 5–8; 9–10)

She, too, "will weep bitterly" (16) at Christ's Crucifixion. As she stands, a light reflects upon her hair "as of moon-light on a lost river" (17), and, as Kaspar stoops to pick up her scarf, he becomes lost in the light reflected in her "disordered, dishevelled" (18) hair. Before she slips out of the door, she repeats the prophecy:

> *I am Mary, the incense-flower of the incense-tree,*
> *myself worshipping, weeping, shall be changed to myrrh;*
>
> *I am Mary, though melted away,*
> *I shall be a tower. . . .*
>   (19, 1–4)

Some say that Kaspar, the Magus, had "arranged this meeting / to conform to the predicted pattern / which he . . . / had computed exactly from the stars; / . . . some say he was masquerading, / was an Angel in disguise"; others say that "he was Abraham" or "God" (20). He may have been one of her old lovers, or there may have been no meeting between them; but it was recorded that Mary anoints Jesus at Bethany.

Simon, the leper, wished to avoid the scene of the anointment, "but Kaspar knew the scene was unavoidable / and already written in a star / or a configuration of stars / that rarely happens, perhaps once / in a little over two thousand years" (24). Simon might have heard that Christ had cast out demons from this woman; but Kaspar, himself a heathen, knew that the demons' names were those attributed to the goddess (Isis, Astarte, Venus); and he knew that the goddess prefigured as a prototype of Mary. Kaspar, therefore, knew that the demons "were now unalterably part of the picture":

> they had entered separately or together
> the fair maid, perhaps not wantonly,
>
> but crossing the threshold
> of this not un-lovely temple,
>
> they intend perhaps to pay homage,
> even as Kaspar had done,
>
> and Melchior
> and Balthasar.
>
> (26, 18–26)

Kaspar did not know Mary Magdalene at first, nor did he recognize her until her scarf fell to the floor and he stooped to pick it up (27):

> And Kaspar heard
> an echo of an echo in a shell,
> *in her were forgiven*

the sins of the seven
dæmons cast out of her [.]
(28, 1–5)

Kaspar discovers that sin is vanquished through her. At this point, he envisions a "circlet of square-cut stones on the head of a lady" (28). Lost in the ecstasy of the "discovery" (29) brought forth through "the most painful application" and "rigorous sessions of concentration / and the study of the theme and law / of time-relation and retention of memory," (29) Kaspar unravels the "whole secret of the mystery" (30). As the grain unfolds, Kaspar steps "out-of-time completely" (31) and enters into a prelapsarian existence embracing "the whole scope and plan / of our and his civilization on this, / his and our earth, before Adam" (31).

In perceiving "Paradise / before Eve" (32), he discovers that Magdalene is a goddess, a pre-Christian dæmon in the line of Lilith, Isis, Demeter, Venus, Astarte, and Eve. Kaspar "understood and his brain translated":

Lilith born before Eve
and one born before Lilith,
and Eve; we three are forgiven,
we are three of the seven
dæmons cast out of her.
(33, 20–25)

He also discovers Magdalene's relation to Mary. Knowing this, Kaspar therefore also knows that Magdalene's appearance signifies "the last inner defence / of a citadel, now lost" (34) and that "it was all so very soon over, / the feasting, the laughter" (35).

Magdalene foreshadows the "Transfiguration" (36) of Christ on Mount Hermon (Matthew 17:1–8; Mark 9:18). Lyrics 36 to 41 explore the prophetic significance of the miracle on the mountain "and he was transfigured before them. And his raiment became shining, exceeding white as snow . . ." (Mark 9:2–3). Pivotal is the fact that the snow fell on "Hermon," "Hebron," and "on the slopes of Lebanon" (36). The desert quest through the charnel house has led the quester to "the place of the Transfiguration" (36) where *snow falls on the desert* and "the desert blossomed as it had always done" (37).

Kaspar also remembers the jar he placed before the infant Christ. With deference toward the other Magi, Kaspar "placed his gift / a little apart from the rest, / to show by inference / its unimportance in comparison" (42). Although enveloped in mystery, Mary knew that this was "the most beautiful fragrance, / as of all flowering things together" even though "the seal of the jar was unbroken" (43). They both knew that "the fragrance came from the bundle of myrrh / she held in her arms" (43). By following the Magus in the desert, the quester discovers the path towards personal salvation and universal redemption.

6. Invariance and Transformation:
Helen in Egypt (1951 – 1954)

In *Helen in Egypt,* written between 1951 and 1954 but not published until 1961, structure, form, theme, personae, and tropes all converge to sustain concurrently a palingenesis and invariance of self. The dynamics of palingenesis and invariance emerge from H. D.'s subtle transformation of the traditional Homeric version of the Helen of Troy myth, and adoption of the reconverted myth of Helen in Egypt, first invented by Stesichorus and later expanded by Euripides.

In his famous "Pallinode," a fifty-line extant fragment, Stesichorus (reputed for having raised lyric verse to the stature of the epic) recants his vilification of Helen as the destroyer of men, cities, and ships. In his earlier work, now lost, he blamed Helen as the sole cause of the Trojan War, and, according to legend, Stesichorus was blinded by the Dioscuri, Helen's twin-god brothers. In the "Pallinode," Stesichorus recants his defamation of Helen by inventing a reconverted version of the traditional myth: a phantom Helen leaves for Troy with Paris, while the real and virtuous Helen is summoned to Egypt. Because Stesichorus retracts his calumny against Helen, the Dioscuri restore his sight.

Euripides expands Stesichorus' invention in his play *Helen* by placing Helen in Egypt, where she awaits Menelaus' return from the war. In Euripides' play, the audience confronts a noble character who defends herself by denouncing the wrong done to her by rivalry and misalliance among men and gods.

In the work of both Stesichorus and Euripides, H. D. discovers that the blame for the war is not Helen's but the Trojans' and Greeks.'[1] This discovery enables her to recreate the myth from a new angle of vision by juxtaposing the traditional and reconverted versions of the myth and by superimposing on these levels her own version of the tale. Her version of the Helen myth forcibly revises our concept of war in the western world. She regards war as "the epitome of the forces that shattered the intersecting personal and public domains of history," writes Susan Stanford Friedman in "'I Go where I Love.'"[2] The recurrent intermingling of private and public realities is further explored by Albert Gelpi in "H. D.: Hilda in Egypt," where at the outset of this illuminating essay he states: "H. D. always wrote her own personal and psychological dilemma against and within the political turmoil of the twentieth century, the toils of love enmeshed in the convulsions of war."[3]

By transforming the traditional tale, H. D. arrives at newly developed implications, attitudes, and assumptions. These variations, moreover, reflect her revisionist mythmaking, as well as her own myth. In *Structure and History in Greek Myth-*

1. MSS. Za Doolittle 17-1, 2 and Za Doolittle 14, Beinecke Rare Book and Manuscript Library, Yale University. MS. 17-1 is a typescript of *Helen in Egypt* with corrections and changes made by H. D. MS 17-2, collected together with MS 17-1. "Notes" on the poem addressed to Norman Holmes Pearson. In the "Notes" she refers to Euripides' version of the reconverted myth. MS 14 is a lengthy typescript which she calls the "Red Notebook" and which is collected with the typescript to the poem and the "Notes." In the "Red Notebook" are found copious notes on Robert Graves' *The White Goddess* and on all of Euripides' plays.

2. Susan Stanford Friedman, "'I Go where I Love': An Intertextual Study of H. D. and Adrienne Rich," *Coming to Light: American Poets in the Twentieth Century* (Ann Arbor: University of Michigan Press, 1986, p. 236.

3. Albert Gelpi, "H. D.: Hilda in Egypt." *Coming to Light: American Poets in the Twentieth Century*, p. 74.

ology and Ritual, Walter Burkert states that any transforma-
tion of a traditional myth is a revelation of the user of the
particular myth, since it reveals the user's underlying struc-
tures of thinking.[4]

In the very first prose-link of the poem, H. D. clearly dem-
onstrates both her use of the traditional myth and her adop-
tion of the reconverted myth put forth by Stesichorus and
Euripides. In the first argument of *Helen in Egypt,* she writes:
*"We all know the story of Helen of Troy but few of us have followed
her to Egypt. How did she get there? Stesichorus of Sicily in his* Pal-
linode, *was the first to tell us. Some centuries later, Euripides re-
peats the story."*[5] In the traditional version of the tale, Helen is,
as we all know, the cause of the Trojan War, but in the recon-
verted myth adopted by H. D., *"Helen was never in Troy. She
had been transposed or translated from Greece into Egypt. Helen of
Troy was a phantom, substituted for the real Helen, by jealous
deities. The Greeks and the Trojans alike fought for an illusion"*
(p. 1). Adoption of the reconverted myth provides H. D.
with a pattern for her own mutations of the Helen-myth and
creation of the H. D. myth.

Palingenesis and invariance of self are mirrored in the

4. Walter Burkert, *Structure and History in Greek Mythology and Ritual*
(Berkeley: University of California Press, 1979). Burkert discusses the de-
veloping implications of myths and the transformations that occur in their
users. The study supports the theory of "traditional tales applied" and
offers a plausible view of "mythical thinking." The development of the
Heracles myth supports his thesis.

5. The following conventions are observed. Letters and numbers in pa-
renthesis refer to the following·

P:	"Pallinode"
L:	"Leuké"
E:	"Eidolon"
Roman Numerals:	Books
First arabic number:	Cantos
Second arabic number:	Lines
p.:	pagination for prose-links

The first quote refers to (*P,* I, 1, p. 1).

structure and prosody of this long poem consisting of one hundred sixty-eight cantos. The classical three-part structure, for instance, gives symmetry, balance, and stability to the poem: the "Pallinode," the first part of the poem, consists of seven books and each book contains eight cantos; Part II, "Leuké," (L'Isle blanche), consists of seven books, each book having eight cantos; and Part III, "Eidolon" (image) consists of six books, each of eight cantos. Moreover, the constant use of prose-links to introduce the cantos and of triads as the suitable stanza-form adds stability to constantly shifting scenes.[6]

The narrative line sustained in the prose-links is surpassed only by the subtle fusion of epic strain and lyrical impulse of the triads, which render *Helen in Egypt* a supreme example of prosodic achievement. The triads not only allow for an elaboration and variation of theme that the two-line cadences of *Trilogy* cannot support, but also are perfectly suited to the expansion of the ever-recurring "eternal moment" into a book-length poem. The overlaying of the five voices (of the personae of Helen, Achilles, Paris, Theseus, and Thetis) is supported by the triads: their open lines carry the reader from one perception to another.

6. Denise Levertov, "H. D.: An Appreciation," *The Poet in the World* (New York: New Directions, 1973), p. 248. Levertov states that the alterations in *Helen* of prose and poetry create "contrasted tone, as in a Bach cantata . . . and each illumines and complements the other." Horace Gregory, Introduction, *Helen in Egypt* (New York: New Directions, 1961, vii–xi), states that the prose-links, or "arguments" show the sort of experimentation with prose-poetry begun during the early Imagist period. They "act as a release from the scenes of highly emotional temper" in the lyrics. Linda Welshimer Wagner, "Helen in Egypt: A Culmination," *Contemporary Literature*, (1969), p. 534, disagrees with Thomas Swann, who states that the prose-links fail as meditative poetry. Wagner states that this technique is "an effective way to avoid 'telling' the story." More importantly, the prose-links put into effect what Harold Bloom calls the "phenomenology of literary allusion"; the complete internalization of the myth results in reiteration or self-reference, *Poetry and Repression* (New Haven: Yale University Press, 1976).

The structure of the entire poem, as she says in *End to Torment*, her memoir of Pound, is influenced by Pound's *Cantos*. At one point in the memoir, she writes: "Thinking of Ezra's work, I recall my long *Helen* sequence. . . . It all began with the Greek fragments — and living in seclusion in Lugano and Lausanne (and here, too) [Küsnacht] I finished, 1952, 1953, 1954, the long epic sequence, my 'cantos' as Norman [Holmes Pearson] called them."[7] She associates the reality of the two world wars and Pound's struggle with her work, but notes the difference: "Mine was a WAR, too, transposed to the heroic, retaining sea-enchantment."[8]

Perhaps the most dominant invariant in this poem is the search for identity. The psychological dynamics of this aspect of the search are put forth by Norman N. Holland in *Poems in Persons* (1973).[9] Holland posits that Helen's (H. D's) search for identity is a search for the mother. For Helen, the search is for the mother-goddess who takes several forms. Similarly, the quest for the mother underlies all H. D.'s work and is fused with the search for the muse and the goddess. Both dream of attaining unity and, therefore, identity with the mother principle. Referring to *Helen in Egypt* in *End to Torment*, she explicitly states: "the mother is the Muse, the Creator, and in my case especially, as my mother's name was Helen."[10]

The destructive "analysis of patriarchal violence and the

7. H. D., *End to Torment*, eds. Norman Holmes Pearson and Michael King (New York: New Directions, 1979), p. 41.

8. H. D., *End to Torment*, p. 58.

9. Norman H. Holland, *Poems in Persons* (New York: Norton, 1973). In his discussion, Holland refers to the following sources: Robert Walden, "The Principle of Multiple Function," *Psychoanalytic Quarterly*, V (1936), pp. 45–62; Heinz Lichtenstein, "The Role of Narcissism in the Emergence and Maintenance of a Primary Identity," *International Journal of Psycho-Analysis*, XLV (1964), pp. 49–56; and Heinz Lichtenstein, "Towards a Metapsychological Definition of the Concept of Self, XLVI (1965), pp. 117–128.

10. H. D., *End to Torment*, p. 41.

symbolic primacy of the mother," as Susan Stanford Fried-
man writes in "'I Go where I Love,'" are fully explored in
"H. D.'s profoundly antifascist epic *Helen in Egypt*. . . ." She
adds the insight that "the exploration of violence and the vi-
sion of love embodied in the avatars of female divinity form
the motivating purpose and symbolic center of both H. D.'s
modernist epics of war, *Trilogy* and *Helen in Egypt*."[11] In the
poem, the triple aspects of mother-muse-goddess are embod-
ied in the Isis figure and are enacted in Helen's search for Isis
(Venus, Thetis, and Demeter). In *End to Torment*, H. D.
states that *Helen in Egypt* is a culmination of her "life-long Isis
search."[12]

Central to the poem is the persona of Helen as an arche-
type of both Isis in search of Osiris and Thetis in search of
Achilles. Moreover, Helen-Achilles-Paris are viewed in rela-
tion to Isis-Osiris-Horus and Aphrodite-Adonis-Eros. Be-
cause the myth of Isis is inextricably connected to the Osi-
rian cycle, H. D. deftly manages to interrelate Helen with
Isis, and Osiris, Horus, and Typhon to Achilles and Paris.

Another constant in *Helen* is the search for love, this form-
ing a group of closely related themes. Love is life over death
(*E* VI). Love is rebirth and transcendence, and love is the
prime mover of the heavens, earth, and society. It is the
rhythm of the universe, the climate of the poem, and the land-
scape of the heart — "the seasons revolve around / a pause in
the infinite rhythm / of the heart and of heaven" (*E* VI).
Love shapes, defines, and informs the essentially human and
divine aspects of H. D.'s self-myth.

H. D.'s search for different kinds of love leads her to
the concept of the Absolute Lover, here culminating in her
unique creation of Achilles. Pearson explains that the idea of

---

11. Susan Stanford Friedman, "'I Go where I Love,'" pp. 234–236.
12. H. D., *End to Torment*, p. 32. Unlike *Trilogy*, *End to Torment* presents
the search for the father as subservient to the search for the mother-muse-
goddess.

a supreme lover may be variously interpreted: "This could be a physical lover; it could be God the Father, or Father the God as lover, or Father the God as lover within her own family, or even Freud the lover—the almost Neoplatonic sense of love."[13] Pearson sheds further light on this complicated supreme lover-complex centralized in the enigmatic Achilles persona:

There were other men whom she knew and liked, some of whom she simply endowed with these qualities in a poetic way even when the other people might not have suspected that person to have them. These kept on to the very end of her life. She was, to repeat, a very womanly woman, and her way of symbolizing what she was searching for was through males, not the man or the flesh. I mean the principle of malehood and womanhood combined into a wholeness.[14]

The search for manifestations of this male-female wholeness through the perfect lover forms an important part of the poem.

13. Pearson, p. 445. In many of the early poems, the lover is Richard Aldington (whom she married and later divorced). Pearson states that Aldington is a "kind of early figure of this lover." Pound, Lawrence, and others (some of whom she never met or knew personally) form the composite of this lover archetype. Apt are H. D.'s description and interpretation of her dream of both Aldington and Lawrence recorded in *Tribute to Freud:*

In the dream we [H. D., Aldington, Lawrence] wander along the Nile in Egypt or the Lehigh or the Delaware Rivers in Pennsylvania, or we find some portion of the "lost" home or the "lost" love by the Danube, the Thames, or Tiber. The dream in that sense is itself Osiris, the world beyond, death or the world across the threshold of waking life, sleep. We do not always know when we are dreaming (153).

The dynamics of the dream data and interpretation fully crystallize H. D.'s unique mode of commingling reality, dream, and myth to formulate her own myth or vision of life—life as she perceives and understands it. In her autobiographical novels—*Palimpsest* (1926), *Hedylus* (1928), *Bid Me to Live* (1960), *The Gift* (1982)—Aldington, Lawrence, and other men in her life are all fictionalized aspects of this lifelong evolution of the sublime lover.

14. Pearson, p. 445.

Another leitmotiv in H. D.'s search for the lover and the centrality of love is the enduring psychological impact of the experience of first love. *End to Torment* documents this life-long influence:

The significance of "first love" can not be overestimated. If "first love" is an uncoordinated entity, Angel-Devil — or Angel-Daemon or Daimon, Séraphitus-Séraphita — what then? Find a coordinated convention, Man-Hero who will compensate, complete the picture. By what miracle does the *mariage du ciel et de la terre* find consummation? It filled my fantasies and dreams, my prose and poetry for ten years.[15]

A frustrated first love, then, may often result in a formulation of the supreme man-hero, culminating in the poem in the persona of Achilles, Helen's "'spirit love.'"[16] From this union is born the child Eros-Euphorion, the legendary child born to Helen and Achilles on the island of Leuké.

H. D.'s myth of Achilles emphasizes the centrality and complexity of love. Her view of love grows from Moravian roots, is deepened by Freud's interpretation of love, and is expanded by the western attitude of love presented in Denis de Rougemont's *Love in the Western World*.[17]

Her concept of love is influenced by Zinzendorf's emphasis on the mystery of love:

It was a mystery that lay at the center of the world, a mystery that one had to pierce through meditation and thought and, above all through love. And the Moravian love feast, which was part of their ritual, lay very much at the center of H. D.'s emphasis on love in her poetry and throughout her entire career.[18]

---

15. H. D., *End to Torment*, p. 19.   16. H. D., *End to Torment*, p. 58.

17. Denis de Rougemont, *Love in the Western World* (New York: Doubleday/Anchor Books, 1957). Thomas Quinn states in *Hilda Doolittle* (New York: Twayne Publishers, 1967), TUSA, 126, p. 155: "H. D. regarded this book highly."

18. Pearson, pp. 437–438.

According to Pearson, *Helen in Egypt* is an essentially Moravian poem. Pearson writes, she "was brought up as a Moravian and this was always a great influence on her way of thinking. . . . *Helen in Egypt* is certainly Moravian."[19]

This emphasis on love lends itself to Freud's insistence that love is man's "eternal preoccupation" (*TF* 103). H. D. writes that it is Freud who "proclaimed the Herculian power of Eros and we know that it was written from the beginning that Love is stronger than Death" (*TF* 103).

These views harmonize with those expressed in *Love in the Western World*, a study of erotic passion, where de Rougemont traces the roots of this passion to mystical doctrines. The world that lovers create partakes in spiritual reality. Lovers "imagine themselves to operate in a kind of transcendental state outside ordinary human experience."[20] The power of love acts as a divinizing force, allowing "infinite transcendence, man's rise into his god. And this rise is without return."[21] For H. D., de Rougemont verifies the mystical dimension of love. Helen's love for Achilles cancels all Achilles' wrongs and goes beyond the good and evil consequences brought forth by the Trojan War, by its Trojan and Greek warlords, and by its bipartisan gods. It is the transcendental power of this love that acts as the agent in Helen's palingenesis and final apotheosis.

H. D.'s search for identity and love finds its closest analogue in D. H. Lawrence's *The Man Who Died* (1927). Ostensibly, the poem borrows nothing from this brief novel, but there are, nonetheless, several striking thematic similarities.[22]

19. Pearson, p. 437 and p. 438.   20. de Rougemont, p. 39.
21. de Rougemont, p. 62.
22. H. D.'s relationship (noted in her fiction and non-fiction) with Lawrence is, at best, ambiguous. In *Tribute to Freud*, p. 134, she acknowledges that although she had not come "to terms with . . . the Lawrence of *Women in Love* and *Lady Chatterley*," she greatly admires *The Man Who Died*. Stephen Guest (*TF* 134) suggests that this book was written for H. D.

In *The Man Who Died*, Christ's death symbolizes a rebirth into life governed by the mystery of love, enacted in the rituals associated with the Osirian-Isis cycle. Similarly, in *Helen in Egypt*, Achilles's death is a rebirth of devotion to the sacred rituals of love professed by Helen, a representative Isis. The woman in the novel who guides the man's rebirth is dedicated to the Temple of Isis. Lawrence sees her, as H. D. sees Helen, as "Isis in Search." [23]

Helen's search for Achilles repeats Isis's search for Osiris. Achilles's wrath, his fatal wound, and his hatred for Helen (the Hecate of the world) have to be transformed to accommodate the supremacy of love. The woman in the novel helps the "man who died" to perceive his previous life as an "overwhelming illusion" (169), as Helen helps Achilles to see that "*the Greeks and Trojans alike fought for an illusion*" (p. 1).

Rebirth from death-in-life is for the man, as it is for Helen and Achilles, an enlightening and transcending experience: "the doom of death was a shadow compared to the raging destiny of love" (172). Spiritual realism demands a rejection of this world's illusions, seeing them as "a vast complexity of entanglements and allurements" (183). By mining her racial memory, Helen moves beyond the "vast complexity of entanglements and allurements" of the Trojan War and strives to effect a transformation of consciousness within herself and Achilles. The "Lady Isis" (187) helps the man by showing him the way to the temple of love, dedicated to Isis; she withdraws into the temple "to muse, to go away in the dreams of the goddess" (188). In the "Pallinode," Helen withdraws within the carved walls of the Amen-temple to dream her own myth of the goddess in search of love.

As the woman waits for the man, Helen waits for Achilles —

23. D. H. Lawrence, *St. Mawr and the Man Who Died* (New York: Random House/Vintage Books, 1953), p. 190. All quotations are from this edition.

"rare women wait for the re-born Man" (189). In the final part of the poem, a transformed Achilles masters the rituals of love. Helen, again as the woman in the novel, is "a woman entangled in her own dream" (191). She, too, as the woman, "wrapped her dream around her, and went to the temple" (193) where the man joined her. When Achilles finally joins Helen, he is "re-born . . . in the other life, the greater day of the human consciousness" (194). Achilles realizes that it has been Helen who has helped him to attain a new level of existence.

This new existence is, in effect, defines H. D.'s concept of spiritual realism. Joseph N. Riddel states that *Helen in Egypt* is in "itself an act of willing one's existence, which is to say, affirming one's place at the creative source of all history, the 'eternal moment,' which is also La Mort."[24] Helen wills her own existence by engaging in contemplative prayer, thus reaching the deepest level of spirituality typified by sustained meditation. The hieroglyphs carved on the walls of the Amen-temple serve as her *meditatio scripturarum* to recollection and revelation.[25]

Meditation is sustained by the tropes of dream and memory. Dream data play an important role, and *Helen* may be read as a dream sequence. Dreams are visions: a waking dream is "a symbol of prophecy, prophetic utterance or occult or hidden knowledge" (*TF* 51). Freud helps H. D. to discover "that there are interchangeable parts in dreams, and that there is a relationship between the individual and the myth as the dream of the tribe.[26]

In *Helen,* memory becomes a metaphor for the creative

24. Joseph N. Riddel, "H. D. and the Poetics of 'Spiritual Realism,'" *Contemporary Literature*, X, No. 4 (1969), p. 472.

25. Thomas Merton, *Contemplative Prayer* (New York: Herder and Herder, 1969), p. 21.

26. Pearson, p. 438.

process, as it is a key aspect in H. D.'s mythmaking. Helen envisions the future by repeatedly turning to the past. These memory-traces are "revised belatedly so as to adjust to either a new experience or to a new vision of experience."[27] Memory, explained by Freud, is a "'process of stratification: the material present in the form of memory-traces being subjected from time to time to a re-arrangement in accordance with fresh circumstances—to a re-transcription.'"[28] In a similar fashion, Helen's memories constantly undergo rearrangement, transformation, or re-transcription when juxtaposed to new insight. In *Helen,* experiences are "graven in memory" (*P* V).

Symbols in *Helen in Egypt* are the hieroglyphs carved not only in the Amen-temple, but they are carved in Helen's mind. H. D.'s focus on hieroglyphs is, from Holland's point of view, a definite aspect of the self-myth. In *Poems in Persons* Holland puts forth a convincing definition of the H. D. myth. He supposes her to think along these lines: "'When I concretize the spiritual or mythologize the everyday, I create a perfect, timeless hieroglyph-world which I can be and be in.' Or, 'I want to close the gap with signs.'"[29] The hieroglyphs reduce the gap between unconsciousness and consciousness, individual and collective, concrete and abstract, mundane and spiritual, substantial and unsubstantial, absolute and relative, permanent and temporal.[30] Using *Tribute,* Holland substantiates his findings and concludes that "'to close the gap with signs'—this is H. D.'s 'myth' or her 'ego identity' or character or 'identity theme,' the style with which the ego mediates among forces acting on it."[31]

Another important aspect of the self-myth focuses on the role of the woman writer, strongly suggested when Helen

27. Bloom, p. 269.   28. Bloom, p. 288.
29. Holland, p. 30.   30. Holland, pp. 30–45.
31. Holland, pp. 51–52.

states that *"She herself is the writing"* (*P* II, emphasis mine).
H. D., like Helen, "must put herself into the text — as into
the world and into history — by her own movement. . . .
Woman must write her self."[32] Hélène Cixous' essay "The
Laugh of the Medusa" sheds much light here. In the persona
of Helen, H. D.'s "personal history blends together with the
history of all women, as well as national and world history":
in this sense, the Helen myth and the Trojan War belong
to the history of the Greeks and the western world. H. D.
transforms the myth of anti-love logic (Helen as a cause of
the war) into a myth of love as transcendence.[33]

At first a profusion of meaning seems to attack preconcep-
tions as the traditional myth explodes before us. It is as if the
poet wants the reader to perceive new meanings all at once.
H. D. changes our conceptions of the traditional myth by
effecting three dominant transformations. In the "Pallinode,"
the first sequence, Helen is *"translated to a transcendental plane,
the Amen-temple in Egypt"*; the Helen of the *"second sequence,"*
["Leuké"], is divinized; and *"our third Helen* ["Eidolon"],
*having realized 'all myth, the one reality,' is concerned with the hu-
man content of the drama"* (p. 255).

In the "Pallinode" H. D. adopts the mask of Stesichorus
but also begins to reconstruct her version of the myth. The
"Pallinode" has several functions. First it is *"a defence, expla-*

32. Hélène Cixous, "The Laugh of the Medusa," *Signs*, tr. Keith Cohen
and Paula Cohen, 1, No. 4 (Summer, 1976), p. 875. This same concern is
found in the autobiographical novel *Bid Me To Live* (1960), where H. D.
writes: "The writing creates myself . . . ; the story must write me, the
story must create me." See also p. 882 and *passim*.

33. Cixous, p. 887. From Cixous' point of view the woman writer is
forced to do this: "If woman has always functioned 'within' the discourse
of man, a signifier that always referred back to the opposite signifier which
annihilates its specific energy and diminishes it or stifles its very different
sounds, it is time for her to dislocate this 'within,' to explode it, turn it
around, and seize it . . . to invent for herself a language to get inside of."

nation or apology" (p. 1) for the invectives leveled against Helen. Second, it establishes the dialectic of the real versus the phantom Helen and the major theme that "*the Greeks and Trojans alike fought for an illusion*" (p. 1). Third, it expresses H. D.'s antiwar sentiments. H. D. exposes the futility of war, its ensuing suffering and guilt. She finds in Euripides' plays a coherent dramatization of war psychology. Although it is the Peloponnesian War that incites his fervor against war, for H. D. the world wars enact a pantomime of the unreal.

Against this background of war, survival is seen in terms of transcendence, or the ability of the individual to prepare for her own transcendence. Riddel aptly expresses this significant point: "Helen in her temple, then, is an analogue of the poet reentering the sanctuary of her own consciousness, the dark mysterious recesses of the self which holds the secrets" of life, death, and transcendence.[34] In Egypt, Helen retreats within the sanctuary of the Amen-Temple. Her tone sets the mood for the "Pallinode" and sets the stage for the transformations to take place.

> Do not despair, the hosts
> surging beneath the Walls,
> (no more than I) are ghosts;
>
> do not bewail the Fall,
> the scene is empty and I am alone,
> yet in this Amen-temple,
>
> I hear their voices,
> there is no veil between us,
> only space and leisure,
>
> and long corridors of lotus-bud
> furled on the pillars,
> and the lotus-flower unfurled,
>
> with reed of papyrus[.]
>
> (*P,* I, 1–13)

34. Riddel, p. 472.

At this point, Helen is the archetypal *"anathema or curse"* (p. 5). Although cursed through history, Helen forgives those *"who died imprecating her, beneath the Walls"* (p. 5). This act of atonement ensures the salvation of the host of thousands, those who died damning her. Salvation transforms these war-heroes. To atone for their evildoing, they conspire, with the aid of other divinities, to unite Helen with Achilles and to profess their dedication to love, not war. *"It is the lost legions that have conditioned their encounter"* (p. 7), as it is Thetis [Achilles' "sea-mother" (4), the very "sea-enchantment in his eyes" (4)], who wishes that they should meet.

Darkly, Helen perceives that she has been summoned to Egypt by Zeus and that the phantom-Helen has caused the *"'holocaust of the Greeks'"* as part of God's plan *"that two souls or two soul-mates should meet"* (p. 5). In Egypt, Helen forgives those who have defiled her name and character. "You are forgiven . . . / and God for his own purpose / wills it so" (*P* I).

> Alas, my brothers,
> Helen did not walk
> upon the ramparts,
>
> she whom you cursed
> was but the phantom and the shadow thrown
> of a reflection.
>
> (*P,* I, 3, 1–6)

In the opening cantos, H. D. establishes that there is "a magic greater than the trial of arms" (*P* I). Zeus wills that Helen meet Achilles to further his transformation from the "invincible, unchallenged Sire . . . / King of Myrmidons" (*P* I) to a priest of love. Similarly, Thetis aims at reclaiming her son whom she has lost to the war struggle and directs Helen's efforts toward eradicating "the fury of the tempest in his eyes" (*P* I).

They meet "among the shades" not as "shadows" (*P* I). Their meeting creates the "eternal moment" which is central to the poem:

the harpers will sing forever
of how Achilles met Helen
among the shades.
                    (*P*, I, 3, 22–24)

The harpers will sing of a new Helen and Achilles, *"But this
Helen is not to be recognized by earthly splendour nor this Achilles by
accoutrements of valour"* (p. 7). They are new creations, new
types in a new vision of the world where *"values are reversed, a
mortal after death may have immortality conferred upon him"* (p. 9).

Like the man who died, Achilles has to participate in the
human experience. Achilles' heel is the key to the rediscov-
ery of his humanity, or "mortality" (*P* I) when his "immor-
tality and victory / were dissolved" (*P* I). Achilles' quest be-
gins with this cognition:

> *I am no more immortal,*
> *I am a man among the millions,*
> *no hero-god among the Myrmidons.*
>   (*P*, I, 5, 4–6)

The fatal arrow is instrumental in Achilles' transformation,
since "it was Love's arrow" (*P* I). Prior to his death, Achilles
is symbolic of a soul enclosed in "an iron casement" (*P* I) or
trapped in an "icy fortress" (*P* I), but "it was God's plan / to
melt the icy fortress of the soul, / and free the man" (*P* I).

While contemplating Achilles' situation, Helen sees God's
mystery less darkly:

> I did not know why
> (in dream or in trance)
>
> God has summoned me hither,
> until I saw the dim outline
> grown clearer,
>
> as the new Mortal,
> shedding his glory,
> limped slowly across the sand.
>   (*P*, I, 5, 17–24)

Within the temple, Helen contemplates the significance of this vision; *"for the moment, she wants to assess her treasure, realize the transcendental in material terms"* (p. 11). Helen, like an excavator in Egypt, withdraws only to prepare for her eventual palingenesis.

It is Riddel's opinion that at this point in the evolution of the self-myth the real-phantom dichotomy becomes an "analogue of history and consciousness . . . expanded into a complex mythical exploration of the modern self's relation to the eternal mysteries."[35] What motivates this spiritual dig, Riddel perceptively points out, is the "separation of self from its source, both father and mother, the breakdown of unity of love before passion, the division of history into idea and action, as a 'mésalliance' of mortals and gods, and above all, the urgency to rediscover and redefine oneself in relation to the original mysteries."[36]

Instead of drinking from Lethe, Helen chooses a potion of "everlasting memory" (*P* I). Remembering "the glory and the beauty of the ships" (*P* I), she begins to contemplate her fate: "here in this Amen-temple, / I have all-time to remember" (*P* I).

At this point, Achilles sees Helen as "'a woman of pleasure,'" and in his blindness he laments his fate. As he is about to evoke Greece, Helen prays to Amen-Zeus:

> *let him forget,*
> *Amen, All-father,*
> *let him forget.*
> (*P*, I, 6, 28–30)

The efficacy of prayer cannot be denied. The gods answer her prayers in several ways. She is both consciously and unconsciously instructed by them, and under their tutelage she attains *"intuitive or emotional knowledge, rather than intellectual"*

35. Riddel, p. 472.   36. Riddel, p. 472.

(p. 13). They enable her to perceive her task in the Amen-temple as *"the difficult task of translating a symbol in time, into timeless-time or hieroglyph or ancient Egyptian time"* (p. 13).

The first important symbol is that of the host flying above Helen and Achilles in the form of an S-shaped bird. Helen associates this shape with Achilles' "carrion creature" (*P* I), symbolizing the carnage of the war.

She also reads another meaning: *"from the depth of her racial inheritance, she invokes (as the perceptive visitor to Egypt must always do) the symbol or the 'letter' that represents or recalls the protective mother-goddess. This is no death-symbol but a life-symbol, it is Isis or her Greek counterpart, Thetis, the mother of Achilles"* (p. 13). The role of the mother-goddess surfaces to consciousness and Helen begins to understand her task:

> I said, 'there is mystery in this place,
> I am instructed, I know the script,
> the shape of this bird is a letter,
>
> they call it the hieroglyph;
> strive not, it is dedicate[d]
> to the goddess here, she is Isis.'
>
> (*P*, I, 7, 7–12)

Helen pauses to pray to Zeus so that Achilles may forget Greece and the Trojan War:

> *flame,* I prayed, *flame forget,*
> *forgive and forget the other,*
> *let my heart be filled with peace,*
>
> *let me love him, as Thetis, his mother*
> *for I knew him, I saw in his eyes*
> *the sea-enchantment, but he*
>
> knew yet not, Helen of Sparta,
> knew not Helen of Troy,
> knew not Helena, hated of Greece.
>
> (*P*, I, 7, 16–24)

History wrongs her by labeling her the "femme noire *of antiquity*" (*P* I), Hecate.[37] To call Helen Hecate is to perceive her as a demonic agent, cause of the carnage of war, lover of the dead, and practitioner of black magic (*P* I), as does Achilles who attacks her:

> 'Helena, cursed of Greece,
> I have seen you upon the ramparts,
> no art is beneath your power,
>
> you stole the chosen, the flower
> of all-time, of all-history,
> my children, my legions'[.]
>
> (*P,* I, 8, 19–24)

Then he clutches her throat "with his fingers' remorseless steel" (*P* I), and both are struck by this awesome moment which ultimately leads to Achilles' metamorphosis and Helen's apotheosis.

Illumination leads her to pray to Thetis ("'*O Thetis, O sea-mother,* / I prayed as he clutched my throat'") either to forget the violence of this moment or to seek death — "*let me go out, let me forget,* / *let me be lost.* . . ." [35–36]; she also prays for everlasting memory and immortality:

> *O Thetis, O sea-mother,* I prayed under his cloak,
> *let me remember, let me remember,*
> *forever, this Star in the night.*
>
> (*P,* I, 8, 37–39)

37. Thomas Bulfinch, *The Age of Fable,* ed. J. D. Scott (Philadelphia: David McKay, 1898), p. 480. In Greek mythology, Hecate possesses extensive powers. She is said to have been Selene (Luna), Artemis (Diana) and Persephone (Proserpina), as it were a triple-goddess, described as having three bodies or three heads. Because she aids Demeter in the search for Persephone, she is a figure of the underworld. As a mighty and formidable underworld divinity, "She was supposed to send at night all kinds of demons and terrible phantoms from the lower world." She waits by the tombs to drink the blood of the dead and to wander with their souls. Hecate is one of the most powerful infernal deities (the others are Persephone and the Furies).

To Helen, his violence symbolizes *"defiance not only of Achilles, but of the whole powerful war-faction"* (p. 18). The warlords defied and defiled the gods, symbolic in Agamemnon's defilement of Cassandra. She wants to annihilate the horrors of war, but ultimately she wants to reconstruct them to understand Achilles' "unforgettable anger," (*P* II) toward herself and his mother:

> I do not want to forget his anger,
> not only because it brought Helen
> to sleep in his arms,
>
> but because he was, in any case,
> defeated; if he strangled her
> and flung her to the vultures,
>
> still he had lost
> and they had lost —
> the war-Lords of Greece.
>   (*P*, II, 1, 13–21)

These heroes are now engraved in her memory as "the thousand-petalled lily" (*P* II). Both the lotus and the swooping bird represent the host.

In sharp contrast to Achilles' sense of loss, Helen gauges her attainment:

> I feel the lure of the invisible,
> I am happier here alone
> in this great temple,
>
> with this great temple's
> indecipherable hieroglyph;
> I have "read" the lily,
>
> I can not "read" the hare, the chick, the bee,
> I would study and decipher
> the indecipherable Amen-script.
>   (*P*, II, 2, 25–34)

She measures her success by the ability to decipher to "Amen-script," especially the interpretation of those hieroglyphs which pertain to her story. At this point, symbols drawn from Egyptian myth are clearly interpolated into Greek myth. Even if Helen's interpretation of the hieroglyphs is deficient of dogma, she is nearer to the significance of the hieroglyphs "*than the instructed scribe; for her, the secret of the stone-writing is repeated in natural or human symbols*" (p. 22). In Sparta, Helen had cursory knowledge of Egyptian hieroglyphs; "stone-writing" to her was "crude, primeval lettering" (*P* II). In Egypt, however, the "stone-writing" is full of meaning.

She now focuses on the "caravel" — the boat of the sun-god Osiris and his death ship. The caravel, or solar barque, is an important symbol in the poem, especially in the "Pallinode." Sacred literature of the Pyramid and Coffin Texts is replete with allusions to the solar barque. The caravel epitomizes a mythology of the soul's journey and its palingenesis. Fundamentally, the solar barque is a symbol of immortality: "God sailed across the sky in his boat . . . [and] at death, the Egyptians hoped . . . to reach the divine barque."[38] The boat is also a symbol of judgment and divine law.

More importantly, the barque carries the soul across the horizon, the dwelling place of the ancestral gods, and there the souls join the Sun-Osiris. The caravel, an image of Osiris' death and resurrection, is assimilated to the Achilles myth. Achilles, too, is ferried to Egypt; here he is on the threshold of entering sacred space and time. His soul's journey, like Osiris', begins by embarking on the death barque.

The assimilation of Osiris-Achilles is further developed when Helen recalls Osiris' passion. In the struggle for sovereign rule of the universe, Osiris' jealous twin-brother Seth (or Typhon) kills him. Seth, the archetype of potential anger and destruction of the universe, symbolizes terror and

---

38. R. T. Rundle Clark, *Myth and Symbol in Ancient Egypt* (London: Thames and Hudson, 1978), p. 71.

strife, serving as a prototype for Achilles as warlord. In Plutarch's version of the myth, Osiris' mutilated body is placed in a chest on the Nile. The chest is washed ashore and reclaimed by Isis in the delta. Similarly, it is Helen who reclaims Achilles from a death-in-life existence. Osiris is temporarily the passive, helpless god, while Horus, his son, attains supremacy over Seth. Horus, the redeemer, sojourns in the underworld to bring back Osiris and thus frees and awakens Osiris from the underworld and sets his soul in motion.

Helen sees Achilles as the twin-god Osiris-Seth, and, as Isis, she strives to heal the wounded Achilles. She also attempts to make him perceive the mystery of his dual nature, symbolic in the Twin Sanctuaries of Egyptian temples. "When Horus resuscitated his father, he gave him the power of 'knowing,' which included comprehension of Seth's real nature."[39] Achilles' task is to understand and reconcile this duality within him. He must subdue his Seth-like nature and become Osiris.

With the help of the gods, especially Thetis, Helen directs Achilles toward this transformation, which entails the release of his soul from "the iron-casement / of the Whirlwind, War" (*P* II). Helen's task, at this point, is explicit: *"As Isis seeks to reclaim Osiris with the help of their Child, the son-god Horus, so Helen, with the aid of 'the unnumbered host' . . . would gain spiritual recognition and ascendency over 'Typhon, the Destroyer'"* (p. 28).

In the last canto, H. D. interpolates the myth of Horus, the son-god and assimilates it to the myth of Eros. Helen's love for Achilles is likened to rebirth, symbolized by the Child, a composite of both Horus (Helen as Isis) and Eros (Helen as Aphrodite): Eros with "flaming wings" (*P* II) and Horus with "golden feathers" (*P* II).

39. Clark, p. 114.

Helen's spiritual progression does not exclude periods of anguish and doubt. *"She seems to doubt her power, or the magic of the goddess Isis (Aphrodite, Thetis). . . . She seems to doubt her power to lure Achilles. . . ."* (p. 30). She is anxious about Achilles' remembrance of the war:

> does he dare remember
> the unreality of war,
> in this enchanted place?
> (*P*, II, 7, 4–6)

And she questions her understanding of the "written stone" (*P* II).

Helen's anguish expresses itself in her prayer to Zeus. It resounds with uncertainty. Will Achilles forget "the arrow / that stole Immortality / and made him a Mortal" (*P* II); will he challenge the will of the gods or Fate itself as did Orpheus, Phaethon, and Prometheus; will his arrogance imperil her task and frustrate her search; and will he not "let Helen's imperious quest / through this temple . . . solve the riddle / written upon the Walls" (*P* II)? She also asks Zeus to forgive Achilles' participation in the pantomime of the unreal, since she has learned that it was Zeus-Amen who had dreamed the whole war: "'it was he, Amen who dreamed of all this / phantasmagoria of Troy, / it was a dream and a phantasy'" (*P* I). Her prayer concludes the canto (*P* II).

In Books III of the "Pallinode," Helen recreates the scene of their meeting, focusing on Achilles' attack. First she defines her name of Helena, a "deathless name, / for deathless it must remain" (*P* III):

> I must fight for Helena,
> lest the lure of his sea-eyes
> endanger my memory[.]
> (*P*, III, 2, 13–15)

Second, she realizes that the host (the Holocaust, cloud, or veil) had sheltered her from his attack. Third, she intuits that

Aphrodite had sent this protective host to her (*P* III). Without divine intervention, both would have suffered extinction, "would have burnt out in a flash, / as Semele when Zeus / revealed himself" (*P* III).

Rapt in prayer and meditation, "*She knows that her name was Helen, in Sparta, in Greece. But she wants to know*" the phantom. She knows that her quest will involve "*Fate, Death, Reintegration, Resurrection*" (p. 47). She questions Achilles, who remembers her upon the ramparts as a "'mist / or a fountain of water / in that desert'" (*P* III). The seeds of his transformation are latent in this remembrance.

Book IV (cantos 1–8) is Achilles' version of the tale. He and the Greeks saw her as an enchantress, casting an evil spell on them "with a dream of daring, of peril, / as yet unwrit in the scrolls of history, / unsung as yet by the poets?" (*P* IV). Hating Helen and mistrusting the "iron-ring" of the elect, Achilles plans to consult the oracle, but before doing so, he stoops "to fasten a greave" (*P* IV), and he looks at Helen upon the ramparts; "all things would change but never / the glance she exchanged with me" (*P* IV). The arrow pierces his heel. It is at this point that he is brought to Egypt.

He then recounts his journey from the field of battle to Egypt. Following the classical journey, the old man ferries Achilles, and he makes his voyage in a strange ship, "a caravel." During the voyage, Achilles notes that the mast is not the usual one but a "flaming host / of the familiar stars" (*P* IV). The sail is like Helen's scarf, a veil. Stranded on a desolate beach, he meets Helena. Now he asks, "was it a trivial thing / to have bartered the world / for a glance?" (*P* IV).

In Egypt, he realizes that the phantom and the real Helen are the same yet separate. Achilles, the archetype of the active life, is not given to reflection and meditation as is Helen ("rapt apart / . . . in [the] Amen-temple"). His meeting with Helen enlightens him of his task in Egypt: "I work to reclaim the coast / with the Pharos, the light-house." His task is to reconstruct the sacred past and reinstitute the mystery of love.

Helen realizes that their meeting is part of God's mysterious plan — the *"Greater Mystery,"* (p. 64) and that theirs is the lesser, personal mystery. She accepts divine providence and does not challenge Fate. She sees herself as a "neophyte" (*P* V) devoted to the "Mystery" (*P* V) and momentarily returns to the hieroglyph of the caravel and to the caravel that ferried Achilles so as "to relate the graven line / to a fact, graven in memory" (*P* V) revealed in the "Book of Thoth" (*P* V). She also perceives that Achilles' final glance saves him from total destruction, and that it is Amen-Thoth (Fate and Destiny) who brings Achilles to her.

Her reflections also clarify the role the Dioscuri play in her rescue, but she wonders if her sister, Clytaemnestra, is also involved: "is she Nemesis or Astarte, / or Nepenthe, forgetfulness" (*P* V) — an avenging-moon-death goddess? The family tragedy plagues her:

> has it ever happened,
> or is it yet to come?
> do I myself invent
>
> this tale of my sister's fate?
> Hermione, my child,
> and Iphigenia, her child, are one.
> (*P,* V, 3, 19–24)

Clearly in her world of meditation, *"Time values have altered, present is past, past is future. The whole heroic sequence is over, forgotten, re-lived, forgotten again"* (p. 57). In this remembrance of the family saga, Pylades marries Electra and Orestes marries Hermione. She also discovers that the root of tragedy lies in the sisters' divine-human nature:

> half of our life was given
> to another hierarchy;
> our children were children

of the Lords of the world and Troy,
but our birthright bound us to another dynasty,
other than Trojans and Greeks.
(*P*, V, 4, 19–24)

She recalls Iphigenia's tragedy, because she sees herself in
Iphigenia as a pledge of death rescued at the last moment by
a goddess.[40] Under the pretext of marriage to Achilles ("the
greatest hero in Greece") Iphigenia is commanded to Aulis
by Agamemnon "'as a bridal pledge at the altar'"; in actu-
ality, she is summoned to Aulis as "a pledge to Death, / to
War and the armies of Greece" (*P* V). Artemis snatches
Iphigenia at the altar, but Clytaemnestra "could never for-
get / the glint of steel at the throat . . . / but not even Ar-
temis could veil / that terrible moment, / could make Cly-
taemnestra forget / the lure, the deception, the lie / that had
brought her to Aulis" (*P* V).

Clytaemnestra's revenge begins here. *"It is as if Helen were
re-living her own story and visualizing her own fate in terms of that
of her twin-sister"* (p. 74). Her sister's murder of Agamemnon
is a crime comparable to her desertion of Menelaus and flight
with Paris. "Do they share Nemesis together?" (p. 75). She
envisions a singularly beautiful image of Clytaemnestra and
Iphigenia as "one swan and one cygnet" and reflects that "the
wings of an angry swan / can compass the earth, / can drive
the demons / back to Tartarus, / can measure heaven in their
span" (*P* V). As children of Zeus, they are more powerful
than all of the Greek armies and ships.

Her meditation brings forth this re-assessment of new af-
firmation and awareness. First, Helen renews her acceptance
of a supreme divinity: "He is One, yet the many / manifest
separately" (*P* VI). She also realizes that she belongs and
participates in a divine scheme of things: "'*God does not weave
a loose web*'" (p. 82). And, she sees herself as an initiate of the

40. MS. Za Doolittle, 14. H. D.'s sources for this part of the family
tragedy is Euripides' *Iphigenia in Aulis* and *Iphigenia in Tauris*.

Great Mystery but does not presume to possess omniscience: "you may ask forever, you may penetrate / every shrine, an initiate, / and remain unenlightened at last" (*P* VI).

In Book VII, the voice of Thetis, or the Image (Eidolon) of the goddess speaks and substantiates the validity of Helen's perceptions. Thetis suggests that Helen try to reconcile her Greek past with her present existence in Egypt, and that this reconciliation will bring about Achilles' transformation. Although Helen considers herself a Child of Egypt, she constantly returns to the Greek past, *"For it is through her Greek identity that she understands"* (p. 80). She yearns to reconcile Achilles' warlike nature and crimes to her concept of spiritual reality, and she intuits that this reconciliation will be worked out through contemplation and prayer. Now she prays to the twin-gods: "yet I conjure the Dioscuri, / those Saviours of men and of ships, / guide Achilles" (*P* VI). She cannot accept that Achilles is "the false bridegroom" who failed to impede the sacrifice (*P* VI). She concludes that his sanctioning "his bride to Death" (*P* VI) was a communal crime of the warlords, the iron-men. By meditating, she strives to save Achilles and to destroy the "iron casement" enclosing his soul.

"A memory or race-memory prompts her" (p. 87) to recall Calchas, the soothsayer. It is Calchas who commands Iphigenia's sacrifice, and had Achilles refused, he *"would have been stoned to death by the 'elect'"* (p. 87). She hears Calchas' death sentence — *"the ships shall never leave Aulis, / until a virgin is offered / to Artemis"* (*P* VI). This message reaches Helen's consciousness as she reflects and contemplates the past: "How does the Message reach me? / do thoughts fly like the Word / of the goddess? a whisper —" (*P* VI). She wonders which goddess sends this message (who is "this Presence, this Voice,"; "is it Nemesis? is it Astarte)?" (*P* VI).

The goddess corrects Helen's misguided musings on Clytaemnestra, who did not accept Fate. Her sister's error was in trying to hoodwink fate. Unlike Helen, she "struck with her mind, / with the Will-to-Power" (*P* VII). Perhaps, Astarte, in time, will recall Clytaemnestra, but Helen, Thetis warns, is not to interfere with the divine plan of things: *"Clytaemnestra's problem or Clytaemnestra's 'war' was not Helen's, but her Lord Agamemnon and Achilles have the iron-ring of the war or the death-cult in common"* (p. 99).

Her urge is to share this absolution with Achilles so that he can eradicate his overwhelming guilt. *"She would share her happiness, she would proclaim the miracle, she would reestablish the Egyptian Mysteries in Greece, she would pledge herself anew to Achilles' work"* (p. 89).

It is in Egypt, however, that Helen profits from "the wisdom of Amen and Thoth," a treasure which she can take to Greece so "that enchantment may find a place / where desolation ruled" (*P* VI) under the iron men. This realization prompts a return to Greece to establish a new reality. She would re-create the whole scene. *"Helen is the Greek drama. Again,* she herself is the writing" (p. 91).

Thetis now enters Helen's meditation, *"It is Thetis (Isis, Aphrodite) who tells us this, at last in complete harmony with Helen"* (p. 93). In the first canto of Book VII, Thetis says that "A woman's wiles are a net" which would catch "the stars / or a grasshopper in its mesh" and would dare a million other things to find their match. Helen finds hers in her love for Achilles; and, because of Achilles, she vanquishes the Sphinx, the ancient enemy of the Phoenix. The essence of Thetis' message is, after all, that *"Helen with her brothers shall be deified"* (p. 95). The host decrees, because Zeus-Amen decrees, that Helen shall be deified, worshiped, and enshrined forever. Men shall honor her in "the name of Love, / begot of the Ships and of War" (*P* VII). Incense will be offered to her "upon the altars of Greece" (*P* VII). All Greece shall worship her:

> from Argos, from distant Scythia,
> from Delos, from Arcady,
> the harp-strings will answer
>
> the chant, the rhythm, the metre,
> the syllables H-E-L-E-N-A.
>   (*P*, VII, 2, 7–11)

Helen is to be "Mistress of Fate," Proteus reveals to Thetis. This revelation brings forth a new transcription (a new evaluation) of "the tale of Troy, / [her] legend, [her] history" (*P* VII). Zeus decrees that she shall be worshiped along with the Dioscuri, the twin stars and the star-host. Her name shall remain inseparable from the Dioscuri "who are not two but many, / as you read the writing, the script, / the thousand-petalled lily," Helen fully accepts "*the decree of the Absolute, the King of Egypt, Proteus or Amen, 'the Nameless-of-many-Names'*" (p. 105).

Enlightenment moves her toward the next stage of the journey. The script is clear, "the sail is set, / the ship waits in the harbour" (*P* VII). Thetis' last words reassure Helen that her meditation has been effective. She reaffirms Helen's findings that hieroglyphs, "*timeless, hieratic symbols can be paralleled with symbols in-time*" (p. 107). Helen, now, is ready to decipher the "*Greek symbols of a Greek sea-goddess*" (p. 107). Thetis tells her that she is ready to journey home.

> dare the uncharted seas,
> Achilles waits, and life;
> beyond these pylons and these gates[.]
>   (*P*, VII, 8, 10–12)

Thetis inspires and urges Helen to return to a new Greece, divine nature, symbolized in the sea shell. Thetis reminds Helen that "a simple spiral-shell may tell / a tale more ancient / than these mysteries." There is more magic in the beauty of the fair islands than on the walls of the Amen-temple. The magic and mystery of nature, "the mystery of a forest-tree, / whispering its secrets upon Cithaeron," (*P* VII) are more significant than the hieroglyphs: the actual "holds subtler meaning" (*P* VII) than its representation on stone.

In the second part of the poem, Helen journeys to Leuké, ("L'isle blanche)." According to legend, Achilles and Helen were married in Leuké and their son, Euphorion, was born there. However, Helen meets Paris and Theseus in Leuké, not Achilles. (She is not reunited with Achilles until the third part, "Eidolon.") In "Leuké," Helen's mode of understanding spiritual realism is through memory and her task is to translate timeless symbols into human terms.

Whereas in the "Pallinode" Helen depicts her psychic projections, in "Leuké" she unleashes her repressed memories and confronts the buried past. "Helen's epiphany in Egypt" (*L*, I) has prepared her for this task. She reassesses the illusory past in contrast to the spiritual realism she encountered in Egypt: "I remember a dream that was real" (*L* I). She realizes that in Greece, the phantom Helen outlives the goddess:

> and Helen, half of earth,
> out-lived the goddess Helen
> and Helen's epiphany in Egypt.
> (*L*, I, 2, 13–15)

In Leuké, Helen re-evaluates the significance of the human experience ("Helen, half of earth"). In the process, Helen accepts the invariances of self, her divinity.

Leuké externalizes the kind of spiritual realism H. D. associates with divinity. It is Greece of her imagination. It is nature, sensuous and mysterious. Helen's perceptions are attuned to this landscape. She says, "I woke to familiar fragrance, / late roses, bruised apples; / reality opened before me, / I had come back; / I retraced the thorny path" (*L* I). Leuké is the island of *"forest trees, involuted sea-shells, snow"* (p. 112). The imagery of snow recurs throughout Leuké and its reiteration suggests the tempering of Helen's passionate nature: "*her overwhelming experience in Egypt must be tempered or moderated, if, 'in life,' she is to progress at all*" (p. 117).

Spiritual progress is evident in Helen's contemplation of the goddess, since it is Thetis who recalls Helen from Egypt "to a Greek union, marriage or mystery" (p. 117). It is Thetis who guides her toward new revelations and interpretations. The host, for instance, is now likened to the shell and its priceless pearl:

> O the tomb, delicate sea-shell,
> rock-cut but frail,
> the thousand, thousand Greeks
>
> fallen before the Walls,
> were as one soul, one pearl[.]
>   (*L,* I, 4, 1–6)

Helen is aware of Thetis' influence and that Leuké is the island of the sea-goddess, but, at the same time, she is anxious about the goddess' role in her affairs:

> And Thetis? she of the many forms
> had manifested as Choragus,
> Thetis, lure-of-the-sea;
>
> will she champion?
> will she reject me?
>   (*L,* I, 7, 1–5)

During her meditation her thoughts shift to the scene of her "first rebellion" (*L* I), the flight with Paris. Was he responsible for the war, as Hecuba dreamed?[41] She concludes that he is not to blame. The gods are guilty. Aphrodite instigates Paris' rape of Helen; therefore, the war ensues because

---

41. In the dream, Hecuba gives birth to a burning log of wood, which sets fire to the entire city. Because the child Paris would bring trouble upon the city, Priam and Hecuba delegated their parental roles to a shepherd-couple on Mt. Ida. This precaution, however, did not prevent Paris' eventual abduction of Helen and the subsequent war.

she wills it. Eris, the "uninvited guest" at Thetis and Peleus'
wedding, is also to blame: "surely, the gods knew / that
Thetis was fairer than Helen" (*L* I). Because of Aphrodite's
wiles and Eris' discord, Paris tragically chooses Helen as the
fairest. For the first time, this new Helen transfers her mis-
placed guilt to the misalliance of the gods and their "petty
strife" (*L* I).

In viewing the past with new insight, Helen realizes it was
Paris' arrow (love's arrow) that fatally wounded Achilles; "*it
was Paris who was the agent, medium or intermediary of Love and of
Troy's great patron, Apollo, the god of Song*" (p. 112). She is now
no longer beguiled by Paris or Apollo. In Leuké, Helen hears
the same whisper that had lured her from Sparta. He is no
longer a lover but a go-between for her and Achilles: "so it
was his arrow that had given me Achilles — / it was his ar-
row that set me free" (*L* I).

In the last canto of Books I, II and III, Paris desperately
strives to regain Helen. Unlike Achilles, he does not attack
nor blame her. His primary aim is to expose Achilles as
leader of a death-cult. In so doing, Paris wishes to convince
Helen that he (like the Dioscuri) is her savior who comes to
defend and protect her, whereas Achilles is the destroyer-
slayer who sees her as another potential sacrificial victim to
be dedicated to his goddess. In canto 8 of Book I, Paris be-
gins his appeal by recalling his early days on Mt. Ida.

In cantos 3–8 of Book II and cantos 1–8 of Book III,
Paris reenacts his involvement in the Trojan War and ex-
presses his own interpretation. Oenone, with magical skills,
was unable to save him from Hercules' poisoned arrow. Not
only the destruction of Troy but also the Greeks' "*unforgivable
sin of attacking a Trojan princess who has sought sanctuary at the
altar*" (p. 121) precipitate additional tragedy. To these Pallas
is pitiless, although Helen's prayers in Egypt help to expiate
these war-driven men.

The scene shifts to Priam's palace and "*we are with Paris who*

in his delirium sees Helen as he saw her for the last time" (p. 123).
He sees her fleeing down a corridor. As insults are hurled at
her, she falls, turns at the stairs, and disappears, escaping
from the sentry's spear. In Leuké, Paris asks her, "what
hand / stayed your death? / what hand smothered your cry /
and dragged you back? / what arm, stronger than Hercu-
les, / sustained you?" (*L* II). He cannot forget that Helen
"'flashed as a star . . .'" (*L* II). The harpers tell the story that
Helen "'*was rapt away by Hermes, at Zeus' command,*'" and
Paris adds, "'*the harpers never touch their strings to name Helena
and Death*'" (p. 129). For Paris, Helen never dies and his last
vision of her is that of a "flowering pomegranate" (*L* II). She
goes somewhere other than Hades, and he knows that "when
she finds fulfillment, / . . . she will come back" (*L* III).

It is Aphrodite who saves Paris and brings him to Leuké.
For a second time, Aphrodite favors Paris. "*It is as if she were
again offering Paris the most beautiful woman in the world — only
this time, it is* l'isle blanche" (p. 136). In H. D.'s version, Paris
is "*the dying King, the Adonis of legend*" (p. 136), and Helen is
Aphrodite. Under the influence of the goddess, Paris tries to
convince Helen that Achilles' love is destructive and that he
is her true lover. Leuké could be their haven, their place
of solace as lovers in the lineage of Adonis and Cytheraea.
He also knows that Helen is a goddess, to be deified and
worshiped as "*Dentritis*" in "Rhodes, / Helena of the trees"
(*L* III). He sees her as a "*partial manifestation of the vision*"
(p. 145), but the goddess Helena leaves him and continues
her search for Achilles.

In Book IV, Helen meets Theseus who, before Paris, had
stolen her from Sparta when she was but a child.[42] Theseus,
like Thetis, welcomes her as a goddess and recounts his past
adventures to her. "*The love-stories, he tells us, have grown dim*

---

42. Theseus leaves Helen with his mother when he is summoned by his
friend, Pirithous, to help him steal Persephone from Pluto: "we had sworn,
each, to wed only / God's daughters, Swan-Helen / and Eleusinian Per-

and distant, but the memory of the heroes, the Quest and the Argo is still vivid and inspiring" (p. 149). To Theseus, Helen is a manifestation of Athene. He informs her that "all myth, the one reality / dwells here" (*L*, IV) in Leuké, governed by the law "that only Love, the Immortal, / brings back love to old-love, / kindles a spark from the past" (*L* IV).

Because Theseus is aware of Helen's divinity, he says of her visit: *"A goddess speaks;* so throned / before an altar-fire (my brazier here), / *a goddess dares reveal her soul"* (*L* IV, emphasis mine). Helen tells Theseus of her search: "'in all my search' (she says), / 'the shadow followed the star,'" or Achilles. "Love is insensate and insatiable, / I found perfection in the Mysteries" (*L* IV). She adds that she does not feel that her rejection of Paris is a loss: "I lost the Lover, Paris, / but to find the Son," Euphorion (Eros or Horus) (*L* IV). She also reveals that her heart "had been frozen, melted, / re-moulded, re-crystallized / in the fires of Egypt" (*L* IV), thus renewing the cycle of the phoenix. She concludes that "in the fire of Death, / the funeral-pyre of the Greek heroes; / they, the many, the One / were born of myself and Achilles, / our Son" (*L* IV). Love is born from death.

Theseus, "'*weary of War,*'" stresses that "'*only the Quest remains*'" (p. 157). He "*would recall, re-vitalize and re-awaken Helen*" (p. 160); "*Helen must be re-born, that is, her soul must return wholly to her body*" (p. 162). She must think neither of Troy nor of Egypt, and he says, "you are neither there nor here, / but wavering / like a Psyche / with half-dried wings" (*L* V). To assuage Helen's primordial fear of the Trojan War, Theseus tells her of his conquest of terror, symbolized by the Minotaur. His function is to ensure Helen's divinity, "*so as if to reassure, to strengthen this Psyche, this revenant*" (p. 167).

---

sephone" (*L*, IV, 1, 20–22). In his absence the Dioscuri rescue Helen. After this incident, his first departure from Helen, Theseus becomes involved in many adventures (the Minotaur) and with many lovers—Ariadne, Hippolyta, and Phaedra.

Theseus' labyrinthine self-myth mirrors the psychological wanderings experienced by Helen, and, from this parallel, Helen draws several insights.

She perceives the pattern of her own search and meditation:

> so we were drawn back,
> back to the past,
> and beyond, to the blessèd isles,
>
> and beyond them to Lethe,
> and beyond forgetfulness
> to new remembrance,
>
> and beyond the new remembrance
> to the opiate of non-remembrance,
> when the spark of thought goes out[.]
> (*L*, V, 3, 19–27)

Theseus informs Helen that perhaps the Minotaur had been an invention of Daedalus, or had been a fiction or myth of Theseus; it, nonetheless, symbolized the victory of Greece over Egypt. Theseus argues that in slaying the monster, he "slew Egypt" (*L* V). Similarly, Helen must destroy the past. He calls her "my butterfly, / my Psyche" and urges her to "disappear into the web, / the shell, re-integrate, / nor fear to recall / the shock of the iron-Ram, / the break in the Wall, / the flaming Towers" (*L* V).

His instruction to the goddess includes a cautionary tale of the women sacrificed to Achilles — Chryseis, Deidamia, Briseis, Polyxena, and Iphigenia: "they were all sacrificed in one way or another" (*L* V). When Helen offers her interpretation, Theseus asks "can you read the past / like a scroll?" (*L* V) Helen replies, "there is a voice within me, / listen — let it speak for me" (*L* V). She, now a goddess, speaks in the heroic voice of Helen of Sparta. She now perceives that war (death) offers the necessary release into another level of existence. War brings about love, atonement, and affinity with divinity.

When she assumes this other voice, "*It is a lyric voice, this time, a song rather than a challenge. It takes us back to Egypt but in a Greek mode*" (p. 178). Love, "Amor" (*L* VI), is the major theme. Aphrodite (Cypris) now speaks as Thetis who calls her "*O Helen, loved of War*" (*L* VI). From Achilles (war) and Helen (love) springs Amor, the love-child, Paris-Eros, born "in the temple, in the dark, / in the fragrance of the incense, / without touch, without word, / by thought, Amen begot Amor" (*L* VI).

It is clear now that Theseus and Helen experience success in their respective quests: "*Theseus had been successful in his Quest of the symbolic Golden Fleece, Helen in her Quest of Love*" (p. 181). Helen has only to reconcile "the magnetic, steel-clad Achilles" (*L* VI) with her goddess-self. She knows, however, that part of her task has been accomplished when she tells Theseus, "but I passed the frontier, / the very threshold you crossed / when you sought out the Minotaur":

> was Achilles my Minotaur?
> a dream? a dream within a dream?
> a dream beyond Lethe?
>
> Crete? magic, you say,
> and Crete inherited the Labyrinth,
> and Crete-Egypt must be slain,
>
> conquered or overthrown — and then?
> the way out, the way back,
> the way home.
>
> (*L*, VI, 2, 13–21)

The way home for Helen-Helena is to retrace the past. Paris and Helen were cursed: he by Hecuba's devastating dream-prophecy, and she by Eris, the Goddess of Discord. Para-doxically, she concludes that "he, my first lover / was created by my last" (*L* VI). Paris, like Oedipus, slays his father, Achilles, who is made "incarnate, manifest Egypt" (*L* VI). Paris, "the fire-brand" is born while Helen, under Achilles' cloak, prays to Thetis: "*O Thetis, O sea-mother . . . / let me remember, let me remember, / forever, this Star in the night*" (*L* VI).

She, then, proceeds to compare Theseus with Achilles and asks "how have the arcs crossed? / how have the paths met?" (*L* VI). Achilles's ship and the Trojan War parallel Theseus' Argo and the Quest, complementing each other and meeting finally in Helen in Sparta, Helen in Egypt, and Helen in Hellas:

> Helen in Egypt,
> Helen at home,
> Helen in Hellas forever.
> (*L*, VI, 7, 13–15)

Consequently, Helen is able to reconcile her contradictory nature: her humanity [("Tyndareus, my earth-father") (*L* VI, 8, 8)] and her divinity [("Zeus-Amen in heaven") (*L* VI, 8, 9)]. Death (her earthly nature) gives birth to life (love, or her heavenly nature), so that Isis (Cypris) is the goddess of the "Tomb of Love" (*L* VI). She perceives herself as a daughter-goddess, not a mother-wife-goddess: "and I am only a daughter; / no, no, I am not a mother, / let Cypris have Amor, / let Isis have Horus, / let Leda have Zeus, / and Hecuba, Priam" (*L* VI). Finally, vision is achieved: *"she has found the answer, she will rest"* (p. 193).

As a daughter-goddess, she perceives an affinity to Persephone. She is found by Dis-Achilles. She says, "I reflect, I re-act, I re-live," and the "Dark Absolute" claims her who has met Death, found Dis, and embraced Hades. She wishes to remain under Thetis' protection: ". . . only let Thetis, / the goddess hold me for a while / in this her island, her egg-shell," adding, "I must have time to remember / Dis, Hades, Achilles" (*L* VII).

In Leuké, Helen encompasses *"infinity by intense concentration on the moment. She has finished her cycle in time"* (p. 200). Although she participates within sacred time (Egypt, for instance, is *"time with its widening star-circles,"* and Leuké is *"time with its moon-shape"*), Helen refuses to relinquish her humanity (*L* VII). She vows, "I will not be flung out / with wild wings, / I will bring the Hyperboreans to me" (*L* VII). Everlasting bliss must incorporate the human experience: "I will encompass the infinite / in time, in the crystal, / in my thought here" (*L* VII). In meditation she traces the search of her identity — the star-cycle of a goddess:

> but the Vision is not Protean,
> it is actual, unwavering,
> each station separate, each line drawn,
>
> each pillar erect,
> each porch level with the rocks,
> and rock-steps leading to a throne
>
> or down to a pool, a mirror
> and a reflection . . .
> that is the star-way.
>
> (*L*, VII, 4, 19–27)

Helen's meditation includes reflection of "*Time-in-time (personal time)*" and "*star-time (the eternal)*" (p. 202). If she cannot suffuse time with the timeless, she wills to remain within time, at least until Achilles accomplishes his task and completes his transformation. Once Achilles finishes his work, she will resume her voyage toward eternity, reading "*the star-script*" and re-living "'*picture by picture*'" (p. 204) the visions of her meditation.

To find Achilles, Helen "would renew the Quest." Her quest "*is possible only through reflection and meditation* (p. 206; emphasis mine). Significantly and appropriately, Leuké concludes with Helen's prayer to Theseus:

> There is one prayer,
> may he find the way;
> O god-father, draw nearer,
>
> help me to speed the ship,
> he must sail far, far;
> help me, you Master of Argo,

> to re-assemble the host,
> so that none of the heroes be lost,
> teach me to remember,
>
> (there is one prayer,
> may he find the way),
> teach me not to remember.
>
> (*L,* VII, 8)

The choice between what to remember and what to forget defines the level of Helen's spiritual ascendency. Contemplation of selected experience indicates her advancement of meditation and contemplative prayer.

Helen's spiritual progression is evident in "Eidolon." In cantos 1 through 3 in Book I Achilles speaks. Theseus commands him to say that his transformation is effected through the power of "Formalhaut," a manifestation of the High God, described by Achilles to Helen as "the Initiator, royal, sacred / High Priest of love-rites, / more ancient than Troy citadel" (*E* I). Formalhaut commands Achilles to seek Helen in Egypt, not in Troy. Instead of being subservient to the war lords of death, Achilles now serves the "'*High Priest of love-rites*'" — love feasts (p. 210). He also discloses that although they are in Egypt, this Egypt is similar to Eleusis. Finally, Achilles tells Helen that she "is Persephone, / Achilles is Dis, / (the Greek Isis-Osiris)" (*E* I). Achilles' transformation is complete, when he prays before Helen on the catafalque.

A discordant note sounds in this almost perfect scene of reconciliation. This enclosed circle of "*the innermost mystery of 'life-in-death'*" (p. 213) is shattered by the reappearance of Paris (cantos 4–7 of Book I). His aim is to dishonor Achilles, since he fears that Helen is trapped within Achilles' death-cult. He exposes Achilles' cowardice, but, once again, Paris fails to convince Helen. She does not see Paris as an intruder but as the necessary completion of the circle.

He belongs to Helen's new mythical construct: Helen is

Persephone, Achilles is Pluto, and Paris is Dionysus. Paris
will accept his role in the new myth and accept Achilles as
"*father-symbol, if Helen will take the place of his mother, Hecuba,
the Trojan Queen*" (p. 216). If Paris accepts Achilles as a father
and Helen resumes her role as lover, there would be, how-
ever, a repetition of the old, tragic story: "Jocasta, Oedipus?
Hecuba, Paris? / this is the old story, / no new Euphorion"
(*E* I).

Paris unsuccessfully attempts to release Helen from Achil-
les' clutches. He sees Achilles as Pluto-Achilles, leader of
the "death-cult" (*E* I) and admonishes her to "leave him to
the sea-ways, / let him re-assemble new Myrmidons / rather
than call by stealth, / ghosts, phantoms of old legions" (*E* I).
Paris alludes to the catalog of women sacrificed in one way or
another to Achilles. "*It is however especially with the sacrifice of
his sister, Polyxena, that Paris is concerned*" (p. 218). He sug-
gests that her plight is similar to Helen's, since "*Polyxena was
slain to propitiate a ghost. . . . But Polyxena's sacrifice was to one
already dead, and so by implication, Paris seems to say that Helen's
might be*" (p. 218). Pyrrhus, Achilles' son, "slew her" "by
the altar," and Paris laments, "where did she wander? / O
golden sister, / are you still subjugated? enchanted? / are all
the slain / bound to this Master?" (*E* I). Paris also reminds
Helen of the others — Iphigenia, Briseis, and Chryseis (priest-
ess of Apollo).[43]

As the image of Paris vanishes, Helen awakens to new yet
familiar surroundings. She perceives new and old images: "a
catafalque, a bier, / a temple again" (*E* I). Her catalog of im-
ages and symbols is drawn from her experiences in Troy,
Egypt, and Leuké: ring, band, crystal, tomb, small room,
taper, candle, flame, brazier, and snow. The catalog extends

43. Briseis, Chryseis, and Deidamia, in addition to Iphigenia and Poly-
xena, are all sacrificed in one way or another to Achilles. (See Bulfinch,
p. 269 and p. 472).

throughout "Eidolon," and in Book II, canto 7, the image of "shells, / whiter than bone, / on the ledge of a desolate beach" is added. "Eidolon" suggests a high degree of fulfillment and peace. Throughout "Eidolon," H. D. writes, *"We feel that there is a balanced perfection in her surroundings, her state of mind"* (p. 222), as she relinquishes Troy, Egypt, and Leuké by accepting transcendence, befitting a goddess well-versed in human ways.

From Egypt, Helen is translated to Sparta. She reviews the past in light of her experiences in Egypt and Leuké. Her past before Troy is one of ecstasy ("but O the ecstasy — familiar fragrance, / late roses, bruised apples"). She remembers what she has repressed and revises it with the insight gained from her search:

> now I remember, I remember
> Paris before Egypt, Paris after;
> I remember all that went before,
>
> Sparta. . . .
>
> (*E*, II, 3, 7–10)

In Sparta, she had all that she lost because of Troy: "I had all that, everything, / my Lord's devotion, my child" (*E* II).

Against her loss, Helen attains identity as a goddess and adds a new myth to the cycle — a poem sung to a "rhythm as yet un-heard" (*E* II), a song the harpers will sing forever. This song will include *"the unrecorded . . . her first meeting with Achilles 'on the ledge of a desolate beach'"* (p. 234; emphasis mine).

Was it Aphrodite who, once more, set the scene, whose snare lured the players? Or was it Thetis, who dominated Achilles' memories — "a wooden image, / a mermaid, Thetis upon the prow" (*E* III), Helen wonders. She knows the depth of *"the dedication of the 'child of Thetis' to the Sea"* (p. 243). Is she, after all, another offering to Thetis, another promised "white throat to a goddess?" (*E* III). There is only one image that dominates Achilles' soul — Thetis.

> I say there is one image,
>
> and slaves and princesses
> and the town itself are nothing
> beside a picture, an image, an idol
>
> or eidolon. . . .
>
> (*E*, III, 3, 15–19)

Helen is willing to be another sacrificial victim, "*at least for the immolation of herself before this greatest love of Achilles . . .*" (p. 245). Consequently, she recreates the enchantment of the goddess' eidolon on Achilles' ship, the image of "'*Thetis upon the prow*'" (p. 245). In so doing, Helen's imagination becomes entangled with the magic of the eidolon:

> Did her eyes slant in the old way?
> was she Greek or Egyptian?
> had some Phoenician sailor wrought her?
>
> . . .
>
> did the blue afterwards wear away?
> did they re-touch her arms, her shoulders?
> did anyone touch her ever?
>
> had she other zealot and lover,
> or did he alone worship her?
> did she wear a girdle of sea-weed
>
> or a painted crown? how often
> did her high breasts meet the spray,
> how often dive down?
>
> (*E*, III, 4, 1–3; 13–21)

Achilles' prowess and wrath are rooted in his childhood relationship to Thetis. Although reared by Chiron, the Centaur who trained most of the Greek heroes, Thetis' child is controlled by his obsessive love for his mother. "*So Helen recalls the scene of his boyhood and childhood's secret idol, the first Thetis-eidolon*" (p. 284). Thetis' fierce devotion reciprocates his love for her. She aids him in all difficulties and watches over his interests from birth to death and life-in-death. His every wish or lament reaches her in the depths of the sea. As a child, "He could thunder, entreat and command, / and she would obey . . ." (*E* V). Her magic superseded Chiron's powers, nor did the Centaur interfere in the sacred bond between the child and the goddess. The charmed eidolon "worked magic, always answering, / always granting his wish or whim" (*E* V). He built an altar for her; when praying to her, his eyes would reflect sea-enchantment, and "fire of battle," and "desire" (*E* V).

She consoles Achilles in his overwhelming grief at Patroclus' death. During the war, Achilles secretly goes to his ship to seek solace; "so he went to the prow / of his love, his beloved, / feeling her flanks, / tearing loose weed from her stern, / brushing sand from her beams, / not speaking, but praying" (*E* III). He will rejoin the Greek army and wage victory against the Trojans by slaying Hector, if Thetis promises a swift return to Greece. Thetis procures his armor. Filled with rage and vengeance and armed in full splendor, Achilles seems invincible. "He was the tempest-self . . . / [in] his unspeakable grief, / for his friend is dead" (*E* III).

It is at this point in the poem that Helen realizes that she cannot subvert Thetis' sway over Achilles: "*It is not granted human or superhuman intelligence and ingenuity to escape the 'lure of the sea'*" (p. 253). Enlightened, Helen sees Achilles' "ecstasy of desolation, / a desire to return to the old / thunder and roar of the sea . . ." (*E* IV). She is devastated when she discovers that all meaning for Achilles is entangled with Thetis:

> So it was nothing, nothing at all,
> the loss, the gain; it was nothing,
> the victory, the shouting
>
> and Hector slain; it was nothing.
> (*E*, IV, 1, 1–4)

It was nothing — their meeting, the Amen-temple, the Amen-script, her prayers, Theseus, Paris, the star-script, "the Writing, the star-space, / the Wheel and the Mystery; / it was all nothing" (*E* IV). In reliving Achilles' memories (p. 260), she discovers his potent love for his mother. Helen "knew he loved . . . [that] / the ecstasy of desire had smitten him, / burnt him; touched with the Phoenix-fire, / the invincible armour / melted him quite away, / till he knew his mother" (*E* IV).

Helen's "*arduous, preliminary training or instruction of the Amen-script*" (p. 262) enables her to unravel this complicated web of passion. In the process of reliving and recreating every scene in Achilles' history, a pattern unfolds: "so it seemed to me / that I had watched, / as a careful craftsman, / the pattern shape, / Achilles' history" (*E* IV), revealed in "the very scenes / on his famous shield, / outlined with the graver's gold" (*E* IV).

Now, she prays to Thetis: "I cried to one Daemon only, / the goddess I knew from his eyes, / was his mother, the sea-enchantment" (*E* V). Was it Thetis who had sent the host to protect her and who had harbored them "in the caves of the Mysteries, / when they wheeled and fell from heaven?" (*E* V). The host was designated by Thetis as Helen's divine guide, since "*To each adept of darkness, it seems, she appoints a companion 'from the circles of heaven'*"(p. 275).

It is clear that *Helen in Egypt* is a poem dedicated to Thetis — her power, magic, and enchantment (*E*, V, 4–5). But her worship is far less auspicious and significantly smaller than Aphrodite's. No priestess is devoted to Thetis; only a simple servant-girl sweeps the temple floor; "Oh, yes, the world knows her name" (*E* V), but the offerings are mean — "a fili-gree ring of no worth, / a broken oar, / a snapped anchor-chain" (*E* V), whereas sea chests of priceless treasures are offered to Aphrodite.

Helen, however, now knows the infinite and far-reaching powers of the goddess. Thetis loses Achilles to war but de-votes her energies in regaining him. Because of the glory of war, Achilles forgot the Thetis-idol, *"and that is where her power lay. Was not his own mother more desirable than the 'wooden doll' he had made to represent her?"* (p. 295). His transformation is directed toward his reunion with his mother. This new knowledge of the goddess [whose "wings are folded about her / and her wings only un-furl / at the cry of the *New Mortal*, / or the child's pitiful call" (*E* VI)] becomes part of her vision of Achilles as the *New Mortal* (*E* IV, 15, emphasis mine).

Helen's meditation concludes with the *"Message"* (p. 303) of H. D.'s reconverted myth. In Helen's labyrinthine meditation on Egypt, she slays the Sphinx (her minotaur and phantom self), thus allowing the rebirth of the Phoenix. Her contemplation "reveals the innermost / key or clue to the rest / of the mystery" (*E* VI): a goddess reveals her soul and discovers her place within the *"eternal moment"* (p. 277) where "the seasons revolve around / a pause in the infinite rhythm / of the heart and of heaven"(*E* VI).

Helen in Egypt is a poem of perpetual movement toward spiritual perfection, taking into account earthly and divine passion and love. *Helen* is a search for spiritual reality fashioned by human love as it is also a journey of exploration and recompense guided by divine knowledge. It is an initiation into a new cycle of existence, a "divine milieu." Helen undergoes initiation as she enters the threshold of a new existence, governed by intricately intimate human and divine laws and mysterious ways ordained by a divine will but transformed by human consciousness. *Helen in Egypt* defines an existence of magic and enchantment, where a balanced perfection exists between the natural and the supernatural, the real and the spiritual. H. D.'s poetic vision shows the supernatural in the natural, the spiritual in the real, and the divine in the human psyche. From the panoply of the Trojan War springs her version of the saga and the myth of Helen as a new song which the harpers will sing forever.

Helen, in Egypt and Leuké, must first understand her role in the traditional myth, in Sparta and Troy, before she can alter it and create a new one. By contemplating the past and revising it, she transforms it and herself. In *Helen in Egypt*, Helen's search for spiritual realism finds recompense in *"apotheosis"* (p. 160). Had H. D. not revised the Helen-myth, Helen would have remained a victim of *"Time-in-time"* (p. 202), *"a memory forgotten"* (*E* VI). In revising it, however, H. D. creates a new song, a *"star-script"* (p. 204), with "a rhythm as yet un-heard" (*E* II), but a song that "the harpers will sing forever" (*P* I).

7. Portent, Mystery, and Epiphany: *Vale Ave* (1957) and *Hermetic Definition* (1957–1961)

In *Helen in Egypt*, H. D. writes that Helen has been successful *"in her Quest of Love"* and has *"received immortality."* [1] Helen's ultimate transformation has been brought forth by her search and cognition of the role of *"the protective mother-goddess,"* not as a death but as a *"life-symbol"* (p. 13). Through her worship of the goddess (and her manifold manifestations as Isis, Thesis, Aphrodite, Diana, and others), she has achieved *"the difficult task of translating a symbol in time, into time-less or hieroglyph,"* of learning *"the script"* (p. 13), and of realizing that "She herself is the writing" (p. 22), the creatrix of her own transcendent myth.

In *Vale Ave* (1957) H. D. unabashedly reveals that she "herself is the writing" and creatrix of her own authentic myth. Throughout the seventy-four lyrics of *Vale Ave,* she provides unveiled and uncoded references to the evolution of this self-myth in *Trilogy, Helen in Egypt,* and *Vale Ave* itself.

"Pharaoh"; "alabaster"; "there was no time to dream till it was over"; "there was no time / in which to read the pictures, / the messages and the writing on the wall" clearly re-

1. H. D.: *Helen in Egypt* (New York: New Directions, 1961), p. 181; p. 187. All quotations from this poem are taken from this edition.

fer to the creative impulse and the disaster of World War II. The desert quest in "Trilogy" (XLVII) recapitulates the time when "the dark angels fell, / and the Apocalypse was clear to read," but "not then in din and furor, but long after" (LIII, 14–16).[2] The regenerative experience in *Trilogy* begets the poet's "self-out-of-self" (*WDNF*, 4, 44) and transforms the "wavering . . . / Psyche / with half-dried wings" in *Helen in Egypt* (Leuké, V, 2, 22–24) into a creatrix in the lineage of the goddess.

The Dioscuri; ark; "an image in the sacred lotus pool"; "brazier"; eagles; legions; death; war; "I transcribed the scroll"; and "palimpsest" certainly recreate Helen "in Egypt, in a sort of trance" (XLV). Breaking through the masks in lyric XLVII, H. D. reveals that she wrote *Helen in Egypt* "to break all barriers, to surpass myself / with Helen and Achilles." Was *Helen in Egypt* "an epic poem? unquestionably that."

Additional references to *Trilogy* and *Helen in Egypt*, moreover, substantiate her explosion in *Vale Ave* of the myth that the role of woman's creativity, knowledge, and wisdom is subservient to man's. From the fragments of this myth, H. D. recreates "a new mythology" (LXXIII) which vanquishes "*from the depth of her racial inheritance*" (*HE*, p. 13) the conception that the role of the woman artist is inferior to that of her male counterpart.

H. D.'s "new mythology" in actuality begins in the *Collected Poems* with poems like "Eurydice" and "Demeter" where the poet knowingly shifts the viewpoint of these familiar myths and focuses on the self-transforming powers within woman and goddess. *Red Roses For Bronze, Trilogy,* and *Helen in Egypt* fully develop her revisionist mythmaking which looms large as Alicia Ostriker suggests, once we learn to read H. D.

2. H. D., *Vale Ave,* in *New Directions 44* (New York: New Directions, 1982), p. 51; p. 55. All quotations from this poem are taken from this anthology.

within the context of women writers. In "The Poet as Hero-
ine. Learning to Read H. D.," Ostriker forcibly sums up her
deliberate evolution as a revisionary mythmaker.

By persistence H. D. became the first poet in our history to create
poetic myths centered on a feminine principle, in which male fig-
ures play the kinds of roles females have always played in male
myths. To the heroine, man is desired, and feared; he is father,
lover, brother, infant; she herself must define his nature while she
defines her own. What the female principle meant to H. D., above
all, was love and unity: 'chasm, schism in consciousness / must be
bridged over'; division, fragmentation must be healed. She is the
single one among the Moderns who begins poems with death and
ends them with birth. It is appropriate that H. D. is our first poet
to imagine a female being in whom a biological life, a life of feeling,
and a life of dedicated spirituality and artistic creation are not di-
vided but one.[3]

Ostriker's comments in regard to H. D.'s revisionist myth-
making in "The Thieves of Language: Women Poets and Re-
visionist Mythmaking," where she focuses on the poet's radi-
cal transformation of ancient Greek and Egyptian mythology
which challenges our concepts of gender and reality, directly
bear upon Vale Ave.[4] In Vale Ave, she is a "thief" of knowledge
derived from canonical texts and "occult books" (LXI) tradi-
tionally guarded by patriarchs. Retrieval and transformation
of thought and vision of Hermetic texts bring forth a new
knowledge previously hidden from women.

Once privy to this secret knowledge, H. D. repudiates two
major patriarchal myths: (1) the myth of the male-father as
the sole source of creativity; and (2) the myth of the male as

    3. Alicia Ostriker, "The Poet as Heroine; Learning to Read H. D."
Writing Like a Woman (Ann Arbor: University of Michigan Press, 1983),
p. 40.
    4. Ostriker, "The Thieves of Language: Women Poets and Revisionist
Mythmaking," Coming to Light: American Poets in the Twentieth Century, eds.
Diane Wood Middlebrook and Marilyn Yalom (Ann Arbor: University of
Michigan Press, 1985), pp. 19–22.

the sole quester. In *Vale Ave,* no man has access to knowledge, power, love, or any activity that is unavailable to woman. Moreover, "No god is set in an alcove, no god upon a plinth, / no plain Adonis, no slain Hyacinth" (XXXIV). Wisdom is sought in the goddess whether she is Thetis, Circe, Demeter, Aphrodite, the "Lady" in *Trilogy,* Helen in *Helen in Egypt,* "the unjustly desecrated Lilith" in *Vale Ave,* or Isis in *Hermetic Definition.* As Susan Stanford Friedman points out, the goddess is "the prototype of the woman-spirit incarnated throughout . . . history" who cannot be "weighted down by patriarchal wisdom."[5] Although "her name changes throughout the poems as H. D. fuses protean forms of ancient goddesses," Stanford Friedman continues, "her core meaning remains essentially the same. She is the female spirit embodying the power of regenerative Love in the midst of a fragmented, death-centered modern world."[6]

In *Vale Ave,* H. D. redresses patriarchal interpretations of the goddess and of the woman artist. The goddess' incarnations "in myth, dream, and religious experience transform the misogyny of patriarchal tradition and validate H. D. as a woman, as a poet," affirms Stanford Friedman.[7] Stubbornly following this transformation, H. D. in the prose-poetry prologue of *Vale Ave* asserts that "mystery and a portent" inextricably affirm that "there is Resurrection and the hope of Paradise" (p. 19). In *Vale Ave,* H. D. now asserts "the Vision is not Protean, / it is actual, unwavering" (*HE,* p. 201).

By demonstrating Lilith and Elizabeth ("Lizzie") as questers, instead of objects of quests, H. D. in *Vale Ave* shatters the myth of the male as the sole quester. Woman, writes Susan Stanford Friedman, is "the seeker and doer instead of the angelic or evil object of the male quest."[8] Not surprisingly,

5. Susan Stanford Friedman, *Psyche Reborn. The Emergence of H. D.* (Bloomington: Indiana University Press, 1981), p. 230; p. 229.
6. Stanford Friedman, p. 230.   7. Stanford Friedman, p. 230.
8. Stanford Friedman, p. 11.

therefore, H. D.'s women-questers, identifying themselves with the ancient goddesses, transform the concept of quest literature and myth. In *Vale Ave*, she ultimately displaces the last "Dragon-lover of mythology" (LXXIII) of numerous mythological and historical incarnations, like "Hannibal" and "Caesar," (LXXIII), who "ploughed the earth inexorably, / and the sea" (LXXIII).

Only when "the last *Dragon volant* sought the sky" (LXXIII), did women, as H. D. writes in *Vale Ave*, give credence to the voice, "the Voice within the Tree" (II) that they heard in their dreams. Rejecting centuries of stony silence, she allows Lilith to invoke her "inexorable destiny" (II). As the ultimate poem of women's artistic creativity, *Vale Ave* encourages women to resume their inheritance from Lilith, to seek meaning in their "long dreams before, long daydreams after" (IV), thereby refuting "the stone-story of Creation and the Fall" (V) that woman gave up her creativity through Eve's seduction and the consequent loss of Paradise. Contrary to received tradition, H. D. insists that mystery, portent, and ancient wisdom derived from the goddess "spell one story, / and only one, Love is the altar that we burn upon" (XXII). In the penultimate lyric of *Vale Ave*, the "last *Dragon volant*" seeks the sky "to inaugurate a new age and a new mythology" (LXXIII).

This new mythology demands a revisionist perspective, a new perception of questers — "a new Circe, Helen, and Lilith" (LXXIII) — a new mythic formula, and a new authentic prayer that delivers women "from all iniquity, questioning, and distrust" (LXXIV). As Susan Stanford Friedman forcibly puts it, H. D. in *Vale Ave* personally calls for the negation of lapsed myth, the victimization of women.[9]

Mystery and portent, H. D. writes, have "revealed infinite secrets" (LXVIII) that hitherto have been prohibited to

9. Stanford Friedman, pp. 10–11.

women. The Cabala, for instance, has informed the poet that "the secrets kept were greater / than we dreamed of or dared dream" (LXVIII). Moreover, her "dabbling in psychic matters" (LIV) has led to the discovery of the "secret key" (LX) which can open doors that for centuries seemed to have been "shut inexorably" (LXVI). Opening these doors, as she does in *Vale Ave*, requires a revision of patriarchal myths that have maligned Lilith, Circe, Helen, Guinevere (LXV), and others.

Vale Ave is also a liberation poem. Who, H. D. asks, can "Keep Lilith in a cage, curse Lilith in a Tree?" (IX). Women need no longer suppress the validity of their racial memories, the efficacy of their prayers, nor the significance of their dreams. Throughout her poetry and specifically in *Vale Ave*, she stresses the value of memory by stating, "remembrance brings us to this hour / in which I strive to save identity" (LIX). Prayers ("a prayer within a prayer" [XLI]) and their efficacy—"and then there came as answer to a prayer" (LVI)—are recurrent in *Vale Ave*. H. D. prays to "deliver us / from all iniquity" (LXXIV). As a "dream-sequence" (LXVIII), *Vale Ave* takes us from the beginnings of Lilith's dream in primordial time to a *"near extension of our own common time"* (LXIV).

H. D. accomplishes these difficult tasks by using the same meditative-mythical structure that enabled Helen in *Helen in Egypt* to attain *"immortality"* (p. 187) and partake in the *"'eternal moment'"* (p. 277). In bringing *"the moment and infinity together 'in time . . .'"* (p. 200), H. D. encompasses *"infinity by intense concentration on the moment,"* and *"she brings the moment and infinity together 'in time, in the crystal, in my thought here'"* (p. 200). In *Vale Ave*, she labels this pattern (formula) a *"processus"* (p. 18).

By transcending ordinary time and space and simultaneously partaking in sacred time and space, H. D. recreates the meetings and partings of Lucifer-Lilith and of Elizabeth ("Lizzie") Dyer ("the niece of the Elizabethan poet and alchemist Sir Edward Dyer") and Sir Walter Raleigh (as seen "during the last months of his life in the Tower of London") (p. 18). Specifically, they meet in "late Rome, dynastic Egypt, legendary Provence, early seventeenth-century England, and contemporary London" (p. 18). In stressing the universality of her mythic *"processus,"* H. D. insists that these archetypal pairs of lovers "bring the moment and infinity together," a concept of myth that Mircea Eliade describes as "sacred history": "an event that took place in primordial Time."[10] Susan Stanford Friedman writes that in *Vale Ave,* "Time is a paradox: simultaneously unique and universal."[11] *Vale Ave,* Stanford Friedman adds, is a portrait "of love between archetypal pairs" which furthers "H. D.'s notion of time as protean incarnation."[12]

Significantly, then, in *Vale Ave* H. D. prepares the reader for the heightened level of meditation sustained in *Hermetic Definition.* Its dense symbols, images, fragments of myths, prayers, and other metonymies produce a level of poetic discourse that is simultaneously interiorized, meditative, and communicative. In *Vale Ave,* as in *Hermetic Definition,* the mythical-meditative level of discourse is sustained, in part, by her knowledge of the Cabala, alchemy, astrology, hermeticism, as well as her use of apocrypha. Her aim is not to replicate history but to revise it. She freely admits, "I mix my metaphors and history" (LIV).

The knowledge gleaned from the Cabala brings her closer to the knowledge of "Paradise" (XXIX). Similarly, Elizabeth Dyer stole this knowledge from her uncle, and she, too, learned how to reach the trees in Paradise, "those same trees / with names of God, the same God" (XXIX); how to decipher "some seventy names or more, / inscribed in the

10. Mircea Eliade, *Myth and Reality,* trans. Willard R. Trask (New York: Harper and Row, 1963), p. 5.
11. Stanford Friedman, p. 109.   12. Stanford Friedman, p. 111.

circumference of this Flower"; and how to "find the special
Angel / and God's special name / that guides the soul from
birth."

In seeking the secret knowledge that brings the self closer
to divinity, Elizabeth dreams, remembers, and prays to Lilith,
Adam's first wife. H. D. follows the tradition that perceives
Lucifer as Adam, the "Light-bearer, / pre-Adamic of the sa-
cred *Luciferum*" (I). Lilith, unlike Eve, was "born of no man-
rib but a Tree" (I). Although "'Cursed shall she be'" (II), she
is the voice of the ancient goddess whose unjust desecration
throughout history H. D. rectifies, as Stanford Friedman
notes, by the "manipulation of shifting perspectives" and
by "revisionist mythmaking, woman's re-vision of masculine
tradition."[13]

In *Vale Ave*, she writes that she had written *Helen in Egypt*
"to break all barriers, to surpass" herself. *Vale Ave*, written in
Küsnacht when she was seventy and was recuperating from
a serious hip injury (LVI), shows H. D.'s ability to break fur-
ther barriers and to create "a new mythology" which pre-
pares the reader for the "sudden miracle" (LVI), that takes
place in *Hermetic Definition*, as noted in Lyric LXVI:

> I should be too old for exaltation,
> I am too old, but inexplicably,
>
> spring threatens with enchantment
> and I almost fear redemption through its beauty:
>
> doors open, one door shut inexorably,
> but I had sensed the depth and I was spared;
>
> I traveled, I was happy, even although
> the path had led from darkness
>
> on through darkness, back to illumination,
> and from illumination, to despair,

13. Stanford Friedman, p. 240.

and from despair to inspiration,
and as answer to a prayer,

the VALE AVE and the thought beyond the fear,
perhaps there'll be a miracle, after all.

Expressed in *Hermetic Definition* (1957–1960) is a firmly rooted resolve to reshape from intimate experience a poetry of epiphany — a poetry of "religion or majic" (*RRB* 2).[14] Private moments of insight are transformed into lyrics of visionary experience. In *Hermetic Definition,* H. D. defines the mysterious process by which the self, with the aid of cooperating angels, translates mundane existence into spiritual realism. It is at this level of heightened consciousness and "new intensity" (*RRB* 10) that the self, engaged in authentic prayer, participates in a "holy cosmos."[15] Reenactment of sacred space and time ushers in a sequence of epiphanies. *Hermetic Definition* is that "sudden miracle," the culmination of lifelong contemplation.

"Hermetic Definition," the title poem consisting of "Red Rose and a Beggar" (1961), "Grove of Academe" (1960), and "Star of Day" (1960), functions as a prelude to "Sagesse" (1957) and "Winter Love" (1959). Particularly in "Hermetic Definition," H. D. grapples with the human problem of tracing the self's heroic nature to its divine origins. "Sagesse," the second poem, places the self within sacred time. "Winter Love," the concluding poem, gathers all that her Helens have expressed since the very beginning of the quest. Helen is now an old goddess, a "Sage-Femme" (*WL* 27).

All these poems support the belief that human experience is epiphanous and sacred. The holiness of self is evident in its divine origins and in its communion with the angels. The

14. Abbreviations frequently cited in this chapter are listed under *Hermetic Definition* on Abbreviations page.
15. Mircea Eliade, *The Sacred and the Profane.* Tr. Willard R. Trask (New York: Harcourt, Brace, 1959), p. 65.

self, like God's throne, is surrounded by angels who facilitate communion with a divine sense of reality. Mircea Eliade defines this level of spiritual reality as a dynamic participation within what Otto describes as the *mysterium tremendum et fascinans* that envelops life.[16] It is the reality of this "wholly other" (*ganz andere*) level of existence that for H. D. translates mundane reality into a numinous existence of "spiritual realism."

Rudolf Otto originally explains this concept in *The Idea of the Holy*, subtitled "an inquiry into the non-rational factor in the idea of the divine and its relation to the rational." Otto's emphasis throughout the work is on the objective referential nature of the numinous. He clearly points out at the outset "that the rational and moral is an essential part of the content of what we may mean by holy or sacred: only not the whole of it."[17]

Although conceptually "*mysterium* denotes merely that which is hidden and esoteric, that which is beyond conception and understanding, extraordinary and unfamiliar," Otto posits that the numinous is also felt as "objective and outside the self."[18] Its feeling may come in various guises and shifting intensities, either pervading the mind "with a tranquil mood of deepest worship" or causing "sudden eruption up from the depths of the soul."[19]

The numinous experience, even in its highest expression,

16. Mircea Eliade, *The Sacred and the Profane*, pp. 8–13. Eliade discusses Otto's work in *The Sacred and the Profane*; Merton, although he does not directly allude to Otto's work, seems to reach similar conclusions throughout his work. It is also discussed by L. John Topel, *The Way to Peace* (p. 174). Topel states: "God is (1) mystery, that which is (wholly other) separate from people; therefore (2) 'tremendous,' 'awesome,' inspiring a fear which repels people; (3) and yet 'fascinating,' attracting people to the sweet depths of profoundest reality."

17. Rudolf Otto, *The Idea of the Holy*, tr. John W. Harvey, 2nd ed. (London: Oxford Univ Press, 1928), p. xvii.

18. Otto, p. 13 and p. 11.   19. Otto, p. 12.

is not totally free from a kind of "dæmonic dread" which impresses upon the worshipers a quality of *tremendum*, "uncanny" and "awful," which survives even in its sublime and exalted expression. Otto continues: "Its disappearance would be indeed an essential loss. The 'shudder' reappears in a form ennobled beyond measure, when the soul, held speechless, trembles inwardly to the farthest fibre of its being."[20] These expressions of the sacred, features of the *tremendum*, are often accompanied by a "consciousness of createdness," best described as the attribute of *majestas*, an "absolute overpoweringness" that affects a "plenitude of being" where transcendence is perceived as the sole and entire reality and epiphany is the modality of perception and vision.[21]

This sense of "wholly other" that pervades *Hermetic Definition* accounts for its most striking characteristic. The poem goes beyond the sphere of the usual, the intelligible, and the familiar, but at the same time is rooted in reality. The sense of the "wholly other" may derive from an everyday occurrence, such as a visit to a zoo or an article in a newspaper; at other times, it is brought forth by objects and entities which do not belong to the ordinary scheme of things, such as the continuing visitation of angels.

This "wholly other" reality brings moments of deep meditation, exaltation, self-fulfillment, and epiphany. H. D. conveys a complex sense of the sacred, richly charged moments of intense subjectivity. In her capacity for indepth contemplation, she creates a poetry of divination.

Hermetic Definition aims at changing the heart of the person praying. Transformation relies on interiorization of spiritual reality, grounded in the belief that divinity exists within the self. The covenant is between self and divinity: "I will put my law in their inward parts, and write it in their hearts (Jer. 31:33). With an ever-deepening consciousness and affective

20. Otto, p. 17.   21. Otto, pp. 18–21.

rituals (such as prayers and hermetic practices), H. D. pene-
trates the heart of the mystery. Written during the last four
years of her life, these poems express a passionate urge to
understand the mystery by reaching back to origins, thus
rendering this final stage of the quest a deliberate return to
imaginative primitiveness, which brings forth a further un-
folding of consciousness.

In "Red Rose and a Beggar" the act of entering the cathe-
dral of Notre Dame is a symbolic and spiritual reentry into
the *mysterium tremendum et fascinans*. Reentry is a return to
origins and an affirmation of the sacred past. As Eliade ex-
plains, it is as if she were repeating the paradigmatic recon-
struction of the cathedral, and, in so doing, repeating the
work of divinity. By entering the cathedral, the self enters
sacred space, since the cathedral "shares a different space
from the street in which it stands," and its doors, at this level
of existence, are the doors of the gods and hence places of
passages between heaven and earth.[22] Reentry into sacred
space is an epiphanous experience.

On another level, "Red Rose and a Beggar" deals with the
visitation of the love goddess. Although in old age the poet
views this visitation as incongruous and paradoxical, she also
recognizes it to be another key of reentry into a regenerative
existence. Love, symbolized by the red rose, disturbs the
tranquil old age of a beggar-poet. Venus (Aphrodite-Helen-
Isis) descends upon her with full vigor, so that instead of
being a parenthetical experience at this point in life, love
dominates her consciousness. Consequently, the power of
love seems "ridiculous / in this time, this place, / unseemly,
impossible, / even slightly scandalous" (*RRB* 1). No one can
subvert the power of love — "(nobody can stop that, / no im-
manent threat from the air, / not even the weather, / blighting
our summer fruit)" (1). The reddest rose unfolds and estab-

22. Eliade, p. 25.

lishes that love is the "unalterable law" (7) that reveals and keeps religion alive, "the fervour, / . . . the enchantment" (7). Recognition of the dominion of love enables her to abandon herself to the goddess: "Take me anywhere, anywhere; / I walk unto you / . . . you are my whole estate" (2). Religion and magic are the architectonics of the goddess' inner temple and these are "mated, exactly the same, / equal in power, together yet separate" (2).

In old age, then, the poet remains steadfast in her worship of the goddess and continues to reenact the proper rituals. The biting irony heard in the early "Demeter" poem where the goddess' catalog is an indictment of idolatry (attacking false worshipers who offer sacrifice to her while at the same time they ignore her suffering) is now absent. In contrast, the worshiper in "Red Rose and a Beggar" modifies her offering to suit the goddess-muse of poetry who is her "whole estate" (2) "stance" and "station" (5).

It is the goddess who commands her to write and who helps her to penetrate the mystery: "She draws the veil aside, / unbinds my eyes, / commands, / write, write, or die" (5). Her verse is dedicated to the goddess, or as she puts it, "This is my new prayer" (6) devoted to the "Isis-self" (6). In this poem the "Isis-self" manifests in the image of "Our Lady" (or "*Notre Dame*") whose place of worship "hold[s] secrets" (6).

During this last phase H. D. begins to sum up the achievement of the earlier poetry, yet another return to origins. The bronze doors, inscribed in 1257, bear relevance to the bronze roses sculpted in 1931, embodied and cast "for another bronze, 1960" (*RRB* 13). The work begun in *Red Roses for Bronze* now finds completion. In 1931, the "Red-Roses-for-Bronze / roses were for an abstraction" (*RRB* 12). In 1960, she draws upon the discoveries made in the earlier poetry: "So my *Red Roses for Bronze* (1930) / bring me to-day a prophecy, / . . . perhaps reach further into the future; / if it took

30 years for my *Red Roses for Bronze* / to find an exact im-
age" (14).

Her meditation returns to the angels, who guide her quest:
"I stand again on the threshold, / on my left are the angels
Astaroth, Lilith, / on my right, Raphael, Michael" (15). She
invokes the angels as "O most august / and sacred host"
(17), and pays tribute to them (lyrics 17 and 18). Addressing
them intimately, she states, "you know I offered you my best,

> hours, minutes, days, years spent
> to proffer a small grain
> of worship, incense,
>
> my last breath (I thought)
> to assemble in my song,
> lines competent to praise,
>
> of shame no taint, no *noms démoniaques*
> invoked, no fallen angel
> called by name[.]
>
> (*RRB*, 17, 6–15)

Asmodel, the "Mohammedan angel of Death" (*RRB* 18) ac-
centuates the urgency that accompanies a final reckoning
and summing up that take place in the following poem.

It is in "Grove of Academe" that H. D. arrives at the last
phase of the quest, "an end to the whole adventure, / it stops
here" (3). Ostensibly, the poem recounts the memorable ex-
perience of receiving the gold medal for poetry awarded to
her by the American Academy of Arts and Letters in 1960. It
is during this ceremony that she meets St.-John Perse, a poet
whom she reveres and whose poetry she greatly admires.
Perse, for H. D., belongs to the congregation of myth-
makers. Pearson recounts this meeting and its effect on her in
his Foreword to *Hermetic Definition*.[23]

_____

23. Norman Holmes Pearson, Foreword, *Hermetic Definition* (New
York: New Directions, 1973), pp. 2–3. Pearson writes: "She had broken
her hip in 1956, and never again could walk except with difficulty. Sitting

"Grove of Academe," however, is more than a synopsis of this meeting. She acknowledges that the creation of her own rosary of wild red roses (1), was influenced by Perse's *Exil:*

> how could I have known this?
> I could not have known it sooner,
> I had to experience
>
> the *roses, pourpre délice*
> and the *roseraies des roses rouges*
> before actually realizing
>
> the wild-rose
> precision, definition,
> image of divination.
>
> (*GA*, 1, 4–12)

Perse's poetry inspired her, especially his hermetic concept of "divination." She senses an affinity to his hermetic definition of reality. She writes, "I read of initiations, adepts, neophytes, / masters" (*GA* 2). His is also a poetry filled with angels. What she values most in Perse's poetry is its "miraculous" (*GA* 2) nature. Hers, too, is a poetry of divination, but her scope is less grand than his. She defines her poetry as an expression of "authentic prayer" (*GA* 10):

> I did not cheat
> nor fake inspiration,
> what I wrote was right then,
>
> auguries, hermetic definition.
>
> (*GA*, 3, 1–4)

She would have relinquished this fervent path ("I would have left initiates, many times," [3]) had she not felt com-

---

behind her chair, he reached out to help her. As H. D. wrote to me later, she remembered 'the gallant Léger Léger's gesture as I staggered — no swayed gracefully — from the reader's desk' where she had made her speech of acceptance. But mostly she remembered that they were, both, poets."

pelled to continue and had she not found sustenance in the
work of others who, like Perse, followed a similar path:

> but something sustained me,
> and when you greeted me,
> I was paid fully
>
> for the long search
> and the meagre lamp.
> (*GA*, 3, 7–12)

His acceptance is the recompense she has sought and the in-
spiration she has needed: "my hand worn with endeavor, /
our curious pre-occupation with stylus and pencil, / was re-
born at your touch" (3). His voyage, guided by his concepts
of "*transhumance*" and "*derivation*" (11), may be antithetical in
scope to hers, but both created "a miracle out of majic" (13).
Perse's *Exil* substantiates her own quest: it "transformed my
self-seeking / quest to content" (13).

Inspired, she imaginatively recreates the topoi of Perse's
poetry: "I breathe the aloes, the acacia, / of your senses,
tropic red spike, / trumpet flowers, indigo petal-drift / of
your remembrance" (6). Perse's "*promesse d'îles*" (*GA*, 6, 5) is
not her landscape. Hers suggests a starker reality, described
as "the weedy inlet / of my own *promesse*, / and a rock stark
as this, / and only small crabs / and a crab-net" (6). Perse's
antithetical landscape symbolizes a "giant-concept / of des-
erts, the earth entire / with water-fronts, sea-slopes, / storm,
wind and thunder-crash (7).

Moreover, she associates his cosmic law of derivation and
migration as a return to origins—to the goddess. After all,
she asks, "What is *Exil* but a gift's bestowal, / the goddess'
recompense?" (11). *Exil* and *Anabase* are "at one with Time
and the star-cycle" (12). For both poets, "Athené stands
guardian, / and there is ecstasy and healing / in her accep-
tance" (8). In "Grove of Academe" she is Athené Hygeia,
"small, intimate, not so august / as the Athenian Parthenos"

(5).[24] In essence, the "Grove of Academe" is the "Aegina temple," sacred to the goddess, as is the island where it stands. Significantly, it is the goddess-muse to whom she prays, "may Athené Hygeia be our near, / personal patroness" (5).

"Star of Day," part three of "Hermetic Definition," is on one level, an elegy of Lionel Durand, following along the lines of the apotheosis elegy.[25] Durand's death, nine months after their meeting, occasions this elegy. The apotheosized Durand becomes the angel Asmodel, now "integrated with the Star of Day" (*SD* 2), the goddess Venus.

Lyrics 1–4 reiterate the significance of their meeting. Durand's apotheosis as Asmodel occurs in lyrics 6–8. Asmodel rules one of the zodiac houses according to Cabala writings.[26] In the opening lyric, it is to Asmodel "to whom one may cry," (1) or voice her prayer, "*exhaussez mon incantation, ma prière*" (exhaust my incantation, / my prayer):

> raise up, lift up, receive my recognition,
> and this at last, with no reservation.
>
> (*SD*, 1, 5–6)

24. Thomas Bulfinch, *The Age of Fable* (Philadelphia: David McKay, 1898), p. 482. She is also "the goddess of health, and a daughter of Aesculapius, though some traditions make her the wife of the latter. In works of art she is presented as a virgin dressed in a long robe, and feeding a serpent from a cup." H. D.'s Hygeia also feeds "a serpent from a cup" (*GA*, 5, 9). The goddess conquers the serpent, which coils at her heel. The serpent associates the Greek goddess to her Egyptian role, where the serpent is also found in the "headdress of initiates" (*GA*, 10, 16). These sacred symbols, though "not always easy to decipher" (*GA*, 10, 20), remain "pertinent to us, here to-day" (*GA*, 10, 20).

25. In his Foreword to *Hermetic Definition* Norman Holmes Pearson writes that H. D. saw Lionel Durand only twice: "in April 1960 in Switzerland where he had come to interview her after the publication of *Bid Me To Live*, and in May in New York, where she had gone to receive the gold medal for poetry awarded by the American Academy of Arts and Letters. He died of a heart attack nine months after they first met." Lionel Durand was chief of the Paris Bureau of *Newsweek*.

26. Gustav Davidson, *Dictionary of Angels* (New York: The Free Press, 1967), p. 57.

Her sense of identity as a poet fulfills her and it is the angel-poet whom she asks for recognition. Through Asmodel, she also gets closer to the goddess, Venus, "Star of Day" (1). The goddess illumes her days, but the angels guide her toward this illumination.

Her days and nights are filled with rituals devoted to the angels. For H. D., ritual provides the continuity between past, present, and future. It is a solution to spiritual alienation. It is the vehicle toward transcendence. Eliade states that "by means of rites, religious man can pass without danger from ordinary temporal duration to sacred time."[27] Invocation of angels and reconstruction of an angelic calendar enable her to perceive sacrality in everyday reality. As regents of the hours, the angels facilitate a reenactment of sacred time, characterized by events that took place *in principio* but are also valid now. As Eliade points out, reenactment of rites makes "sacred time definitely recoverable, indefinitely repeatable."[28] Her reconstruction of a sacred calendar of the angels of the hours transforms temporal time into the "eternal moment," which she perceives and Eliade defines as "a sort of eternal mythical present that is periodically reintegrated by means of rites."[29]

By recreating a sacred calendar, she establishes continuity of sacred time as an existential dimension where rebirth can take place. The reality of a mythical past actualizes for her what Eliade refers to as *in illo tempore* of our spiritual heritage as it is actualized in the myths of the Golden Age and of Paradise, for example. By actively participating in daily rituals, she lives in another time by returning to the mythical *illud tempus*.[30] Her recreation of *heures sacrées*, sanctified by the angels of the hour and half-hour, actualize her return to *illud tempus*. The reconstruction of a sacred calendar devoted

27. Eliade, p. 68.   28. Eliade, p. 69.
29. Eliade, p. 70.   30. Eliade, p. 80.

to the angels is, then, the central important creation in *Hermetic Definition* and, perhaps, in all of her work. According to Eliade, "This ritual reactualizing of the *illud tempus*, in which the first epiphany of reality occurred, is the basis for all sacred calendars; the ritual is not merely the commemoration of a mythical (and hence religious event); it reactualizes the event."[31] By reenactment of the sacred calendar, she enters sacred time.

It is this ritualistic devotion to the angels that places "Star of Day" (and most of *Hermetic Definition*) within the context of the Practical Cabala. Particularly, H. D. chooses Ambelain's *La Kabbale pratique* as her source. Ambelain's esoteric work is made accessible by Gustav Davidson in *A Dictionary of Angels.* Davidson's indispensable angelology and the brilliant introduction to the Practical Cabala by Gershom Scholem in *Kabbalah* facilitate an understanding of the hermetic level of these poems. It is her assimilation of the Practical Cabala that defines her poems as hermetic experiences, "auguries, hermetic definition" (*GA* 3, 4).

Foremost, the Practical Cabala consists of white magic practiced by adherence to the angelic calendar and, as Scholem writes, "through the medium of the sacred, esoteric Names of God and the angels, the manipulation of which may affect the physical no less than the spiritual world."[32] As such, the cabalist (by extension the poet-as-cabalist) is a "master of the names." Since the Practical Cabala is defined by these activities, the cabalist is a magician, a Magus. Scholem points out that the practical side of the Cabala clearly signifies a primary concern with angelology and both the acceptance and practice of white magic (or "permissible magic").[33] H. D. adheres to the practices of the Practical Cabala by voicing and

31. Eliade, p. 81.
32. Gershom Scholem, *Kabbalah* (New York: New American Library, 1978), p. 182.
33. Scholem, p. 183.

offering prayers and other incantations addressed to the angels. Her hermetic poems, inspired by the angels, are to be seen in the tradition of what Davidson refers to as the so-called "eye-writing" or "angelic pens" attributed to the original angelic alphabet, whose "signs" are an intrinsic part of the Practical Cabala. In H. D.'s imagination, they are analogous to the hieroglyphs and other writing on the wall.[34]

In the Practical Cabala, and particularly in "Star of Day," the magical-neumatic powers of the angels are tapped through recitation and reenactment. In both the Practical Cabala and in H. D.'s poetry, the angels help to effect reentry into the world of spiritual realism.

The Practical Cabala is the perfect source for H. D. because it contains no fixed angelology. The names of the angels, as scholars demonstrate, have various forms. Often the names of the angels intermingle with the secret names of God, emphasizing only particular attributes of divinity. Sometimes a name designates both angel and God. The point is that the sacred names of the angels and of God occupy her thoughts. For H. D., the Cabala sustains a contemplative stance. The names always serve as an incentive to deeper meditation. "All the names," as Scholem points out, "of whatever kinds, have therefore a contemplative content."[35] Recitation and meditation of the names make possible the ascent to heaven. There is, then, throughout the Practical Cabala and throughout *Hermetic Definition* a tendency toward deep meditation, toward prayer, and toward contemplation of the mysteries of prayer.

In the Practical Cabala, the angels are part of "the great mystery." "Mystery" refers to "the earliest instructions on detailed meditations associated with basic prayers, according

34. For further discussion of angelic alphabets, "pens," of "eye-writing" see Davidson, *Dictionary of Angels (passim)* and Scholem, *Kabbalah,* p. 186, p. 188ff.

35. Scholem, p. 33.

to the concept of the Sefirot as stages in the hidden life of God, came from him."[36] Contemplation of the angels leads to communion with divinity. Through the angels, the aim is to attain "the beatitude of supreme communion."[37] The mystical intent of prayer (the "Kavvanah of prayer") serves as a vehicle for this communion.

Although there are other concerns and images in "Sagesse," the essence of the Practical Cabala — the angelology and the sacred calendar — are of central importance. Primarily, "Sagesse" deals with sacred time. The poem is occasioned by reading in *The Listener* an episode involving a caged owl, which affects her. Like the owl, she feels caged in the hospital room.[38] She can escape only by recourse to her sacred calendar, as she notes: "this is Whitsun, June the ninth, and I must find / the Angel or the Power that rules this hour" (*S* 1). For the hour, she finds "*Aneb* with the attribute, / *Dieu clément* . . . and for the day, / *Dieu propice* with the name of *Siré; / Viroaso* is the angel for the day, and for the hour, / we may invoke the angel, *Thopitus*" (*S* 1). The image of the angels merges with the image of the "white-faced Scops" owl caged in the zoo, an attribute of God — the "Kavvanah" of her contemplative prayer:

> May those who file before you feel
> something of what you are — that God is kept within

36. Scholem, p. 44 and p. 46.   37. Scholem, pp. 46 and 53.
38. Pearson, p. 3. Isolated in a convalescent home in Küsnacht, while recovering from a near-fatal hip injury, she too, feels caged. In the image of the owl, Pearson finds echoes of a caged Pound in Pisa and St. Elizabeth. There are echoes of herself looking at herself as the child in her father's study where the embalmed white owl is held in a bell-jar. In *Tribute to Freud*, the owl is a source of fascination and of intricacy, symbolizing her father's immense knowledge and wisdom of the stars. The owl, the traditional symbol of Athena or wisdom, is also a symbol of Sophia Pistis, the old church whose shards are scattered and found everywhere (see: *Trilogy*).

the narrow confines of a cage, a pen;
they will laugh and linger and some child may shudder,

touched by the majesty, the lifted wings,
the white mask and the eyes that seem to see,

like God, everything and like God, see nothing;
our small impertinence, our little worth

is invisible in the day; when darkness comes,
you will be no more a fool, a clown,   ʹ

a white-faced Scops, a captive and in prison,
but noble and priest and soldier, scribe and king

will hail you, sacrosanct, while frail women
bend and sway between the temple pillars,

till the torches flicker and fail,
and there is only faint light from the braziers

and the ghostly trail of incense, and cries of recognition
and of gladness in the fragrant air.

                                             (*S* 2)

A merciful and propitious God is invoked through Aneb, Siré,
Viroaso, and Thopitus, all angels invoked in incantation rites
of the Practical Cabala.[39] Her meditation inspires a vision of
God who remains insignificant and hidden to the multitude
but visible and holy to children and worshipers.

   "Sagesse" is a poem of synthesis and of integration. The
owl is within and without her. There is the "white-faced
Scops" in *The Listener;* there is God as the imprisoned owl;
there is the owl-as-the-caged-self; and there is the owl hoot-
ing outside her bedroom window: "An owl hooted out in the
darkness, / so the angel came" (*S* 4). This angel is Tara
whose attributes are *"Dieu fontaine de sagesse"* (*S*, 4, 3) —foun-
tain of wisdom. This wisdom integrates mundane with spiri-
tual reality: "how strange, how wonderful, that last night,"
she tells her nurse at the hospital, "was the first night that it

39. Davidson, p. 289.

came, / the distant summons, the muted cry, the call, / and my bones melted and my heart was flame, / and all I wished was freedom and to follow / the voice . . ." (*S* 4). She now intuits her own approaching death and the sense of freedom that will come with it. No longer will she be like the caged Scops.

The angels continue their visitation. Ptéchout, whose attributes are "*Dieu qui reçoit les pécheurs* / and *Dieu qui rejouit*" (*S* 6) (God who receives the sinners and God who rejoices). Another day is recreated by "this game of affirmations and of angels' names" (*S* 6). God receives, not rejects, sinners; "we have known the desperate day of Cain, / none of us blameless" (*S* 6). The angels reaffirm God's acceptance of us. There is, after all, the angel who says, "'I serve Him who receives the outcast,' and another says, / 'I bring happiness and serve God who rejoices'" (*S* 6).

Underlying this security of recurrence, there is the growing uncertainty that her recreation of a sacred calendar may be effective ritual but not effective poetry. Consequently, she expresses this doubt through the persona of her nurse:

> '. . . isn't it over-weighted?
> can you have so many angels' names,
> a list of dates, months, days,
> a prose in-set? or is it poetry? Egypt,
> hieratic rhythm, then the most ordinary association.'
>
> (*S*, 9, 1–5)

Isn't the desire to be "swept into a cycle / of majestic Spirits . . ." (*S* 9) an act of madness? Ironically, it is this dæmonic urge that compels her relentless invocation (*S* 11) and prayer (*S* 11) devoted to the angels who help her to effect a transformation of self (*S* 11). The angelic powers "'re-animate'" (*S* 13) and enable her to recreate a "'separate self'" (*S* 13), distinct from the "'dead pyre'" (*S* 13) of mortals who do not work out their spiritual salvation.

There are many angels who guide her way. She keeps vigil, awaiting their visitations, but most anxiously she awaits the appearance of the "star of day": "We should keep vigil, wait alert / till Venus 'strikes'" (*S* 15). What makes the day tolerable is knowing that the angels will come and bring "great joy" (*S* 15). It is Seket who comes at night, "while we sleep, 1.20 to be exact" (*S* 15), and she comes from Egypt.[40] Sotis, Sothis and other angels also come to her. Having their support, she asks, "what right have we to fear frustration and incompetence?" (*S* 15). Redemption and immortality are attainable; therefore, why should "we fret / and wear our nerves to shreds, / knowing the clock will 'strike,' / the rose and the camellia spread their flame, / when the early flowering of the peach is over" (*S* 15). Death is but a natural beginning of another level of existence made concrete and possible by the angels' assistance, the angels who make "our share of bliss . . . infinite" (*S* 15) and whose "names are symphonies" (*S* 15).

She acknowledges that these are the most intense of her poems, her epiphanies. Seket manifests as *"Dieu sauveur"* (*S* 16). Seket is another of God's attributes, but she is also an attribute of the Goddess. Seket is a manifestation of Mary, or "simply Mary's flower, / 'Marah' the *Grande Mer,* patron and protectress" (*S* 16). She is associated with flowers "sword-lilies on their stalks," (*S* 16) and, as *Créatrice de la Foi . . ."* (*S,* 16, 18), she is the source of faith. The association extends from Seket to Marah as the bitter sea and mother goddess, *"Sombre Mère Sterile* and *Brillante Mère Féconde"* (*S* 18) — the somber, sterile Mother and the brilliant, fecund Mother, who controls the planets, holding them steadfast in their course. She is found everywhere and is always near, always by her side in her books. In this "picture-

40. Davidson, p. 265. In the Cabala, Seket is a "female angel who dwells in Egypt; she is the angel of part of an hour and appears when properly invoked."

book" (*S* 18), she is "Tara, Miri, Mara, / with mountain-cherries like the mountain-snow, / or golden weed washed up on golden sand" (*S* 18).

Sustained meditation brings faith and "ecstasy" (*S* 23) which few can endure. Rapt in ecstasy, she waits for her midnight messengers (*S* 23). Seket comes "from Egypt, / with the red Egyptian lily in her hand" (*S* 23). Then comes *"Oues-tucati,"* "Lady of chaste hands and the quiet mind" (*S* 24) who crosses the sea from the sands of *"Leuké"* and "the Hesperides" (*S* 24). To this "immaculate" spirit she offers her prayer:

> O chaste, immaculate, accept our feeble effort,
> our faint prayer; in you, there is no conflict
>
> with the hours, the seasons and the minutes;
> we would bear a flickering taper to you,
>
> O most fair; unworthy, we would pray
> your intercession for us; grant us strength,
>
> a little strength to serve your Power,
> O *Leuké*-lily of this morning hour.
>
> (*S*, 24, 11–18)

The angel is a manifestation of Venus-Helen in Leuké, the goddess of love and transcendence. She, then, concludes her meditation, *"∂aignez m'éclairer, me gar∂er, me ∂irigez, / Ange ∂u Seigneur"* (*S* 25) by invoking "Siêmé," ("I beseech you to enlighten me, to keep me, to guide me, / Angel of God").

An experience of supreme communion is reached in lyric 26, the concluding lyric in "Sagesse," when the God-Sun manifests in full splendor. As the eternal groom, he awaits the bride-self. When Venus strikes at eight, he comes and takes her.

> *Dans le Soleil, il a placé sa tente,*
> *at c'est Lui-même qui s'avance,*
>
> *comme un Epoux hors ∂e la couche nuptiale.*
>
> (*S*, 26, 1–3)

("In the sun he has placed his tent, / and it is He, himself, who advances / as a Husband from the nuptial bed").

The search for the eternal lover and supremacy of love resurge in "Winter Love," subtitled ("Espérance"). In "Winter Love," an old Helen seeks and hopes to find — espérance — her "winter-love, a winter-lover" (*WL* 3). Although she returns to the panoply of the Trojan War and sums up the epiphanies experienced in Egypt and Leuké, her intent is to recreate Helen before the war and as an aging goddess who continues her search for a supreme lover. Lyrics 1–4 recapitulate Helen's experiences: "Fate, Fortune, Defamation, / Treachery, Adultery, War" (4). They linger over her entanglements with Menelaus, Paris, and Achilles. All these loves, like her first love for Odysseus, remain unfulfilled (*WL* 5). It is at this point that she focuses on Odysseus and recalls her prewar existence. Contemplation of his name calls up a whole sequence of reveries.

She recalls Odysseus' ship, because it is when walking toward his ship that Helen stops "under the oleanders" (*WL* 6) and experiences the epiphany of Helen of Troy. She foresees herself as the hated woman of history:

> so Helen stared, a Maiden, still a Maiden,
> though last night, escaped the grandam,
>
> Helen was conceived under the oleanders,
> that is, Helen, the future Helen
> that wrecked citadels, was born.
>
> (*WL*, 6, 20–24)

Her tryst with Odysseus ironically initiates Helen's tragedy as the femme fatale. Lyric 7, or "Chorus Strophe," accentuates the tragic doom of impending catastrophe and unavoidable destiny. "Heavy the hand of Fate" (*WL* 7) poignantly foreshadows the tragedy that falls upon Helen and the Greeks. The irony is that Helen, at this point, is helpless against "the weight of Destiny" (*WL* 7). The images of chains and bonds of fate give way to the insurmountable des-

olation Helen is yet to experience. Clearly, "there is no es-
cape / from pre-destined torture and agony" (*WL* 7).

In contrast to the "heavy hand of fate" stands a young girl
aroused by love. Lyric 8, the "Antistrophe," suggests the
frailty of Helen's character. "Frail is the thread and long, /
pale is the hand and fragile, / busy upon the loom," (8) against
the seeds of destruction ("the poisonous weeds; / the deadly
seeds of mandragora," (9, "Strophe"). Lyric 10, the "Anti-
strophe," functions as a cautionary homily, "Heed not the
dissonance, / heed not the hiss of Death, / Helen, immacu-
late one, / in a maiden-dress." The young, Spartan goddess,
symbol of unravaged beauty and innocence, is, however,
affected: she "is caught / in the tangle of grass" (10). The
stage for the fall is set by Odysseus' sudden departure: "O,
Helen most blest, / O *Virgo*, unravaged" (10), victim of "first
love and last" (10).

In "Winter Love" H. D. returns to the lasting effect of an
unfulfilled first love experience. She contrasts Helen's inno-
cence to her desire to experience love and to follow her lover,
to "wander" with him "in the Elysian-fields" (*WL* 11).

Years of desolate wandering and hatred do not paralyze
Helen's imagination nor prevent her return to innocence.
Imaginatively, she returns to a paradisiacal existence, which
renders contentment in old age: "I am content, / besieged
with memories, / like low-swarming bees" (*WL* 11). Even
though she is old and "every bone aches with the cold" (*WL*
12), she is now able to return to her original concept of self:
"but I dare not move; this is reality; / I choose the spell, or
enchantment" (*WL* 13).

Her return to a prelapsarian state sheds further light. She
realizes that the gods affected her destiny long before they
played their partisan roles in the war. She asks who had re-
plenished with fire the "wine-jars" (*WL* 14) on the island of
Samos? Who had hidden the candles and made preparations
for future visits? Which of the gods? (*WL* 15). Who had

brought Odysseus to Samos? It is during this tryst that
Helen makes a fatal choice: "Helen was lost, she sought real-
ity, / let go the dream" (*WL* 15). However, nothing replaces
the contentment she now experiences in lyric 16:

> O, do not bring snow-water
> but fresh snow;
> I would be bathed with stars,
>
> new fallen from heaven,
> one with the cloud,
> my forehead ringed
>
> with icy frost, a crown;
> let my mind flash with blades,
> let thought return,
>
> unravel the thick skein,
> woven of tangled memory and desire,
> lust of the body, hunger, cold and thirst;
>
> our hidden lair was sanctified *Virgo,*
> the lost, unsatisfied, the broken tryst,
> the half-attained;
>
> love built on dreams
> of the forgotten first unsatisfied embrace,
> is satisfied.

Regaining her dream, she ventures further on the quest "to
conquer undiscovered worlds / with words — 'peace, peace'
— or with a Holy War" (*WL* 18).

Lyric 20 reiterates Helen's acceptance of her tragic past as
the phantom Helen recounts the experiences of Troy and
Egypt, and places her in Leuké once again. In Leuké, Helen
wears "the veils of widowhood" (*WL* 20), suggesting the final
stage of the quest and functioning as a requiem of the past:

> O Ebony island, O tall cypress-trees,
> now I am blessed anew as my dark veils
> cling close and close and make an image of me,
>
> a cypress-Helen, *vierge* and widow, the *femme-noire.*
>> (*WL*, 21, 1–4)

The myth-cycle reaches completion in the image of the goddess as the *"femme-noire"* — not the adulteress, but the old goddess whose life-cycle is nearing its end. Instead of profane wraps as upon the ramparts, she is now covered with a sacred shroud:

> now I am wrapped about
> with myrrh and incense,
>
> Egypt's balm and savour
> of the burnt Phoenix-nest,
> *l'île blanche* is *l'île noire.*
> (*WL,* 21, 6–9)

Complete transformation takes place in this funerary elegy. Helen, like the phoenix, undergoes death and rebirth in Egypt and in Leuké.

The elegiac strain perfectly suits the apotheosis of a goddess who has lived passionately and compassionately:

> tighten my bounds,
> O unseen and unknown,
> wrap me round and round
>
> with Egypt's linen as the dead are wrapped,
> mystically cut, cauterise
> as with fire, the wound from which
>
> the heart and entrails were drawn out;
> a shell? a shattered heart?
> no heart is left to heal.
> (*WL,* 21, 10–18)

Helen sheds her humanity and her ascent follows. The goddess is now ready to taste "The golden apples of the Hesperides" (*WL* 25) without fear of precipitating a second debacle.

Will this goddess be remembered, or will she be overshadowed by the phantom Helen of Troy.

> The golden apples of the Hesperides,
> the brushed-bloom of the pollen
> on the wing of ravishing butterfly or plundering bee;

the gold of evanescence or the gold
or heavy-weighted treasure,
which will out-weigh the other?

(*WL*, 25, 1–6)

In H. D.'s transformation of myth, Helen will be remembered as "the gold / of heavy-weighted treasure." In recreating and thereby perfecting her past, Helen is born anew. The goddess, *"Sage-Femme"* (27) acts as "midwife" (*WL* 27). Helen in "fantasy" and "remembrance" (*WL* 27) accomplishes her apotheosis: "I am delirious now and mean to be, / the whole earth shudders with my ecstasy" (*WL* 28).

Throughout the development of her poetry, H. D. sought to create an image of the authentic self in search of a spiritual reality. Finally in this last poem, she destroys the "phantom self," along with "the guilt, the blame, the desolation" (28). By the time she writes *Hermetic Definition*, H. D. is transformed into a *"Sage-Femme,"* a wise regent of "God's throne" (28). Her lifelong search for personal salvation and universal redemption through spiritual realism has led her to the deepest center of existence. As H. D. followed the Magus in the desert and found the path toward deliverance, she invites us, like the Magi, to follow the star, to read her *"star-script"* (*HE*, p. 204) — a poetry of portent, mystery, and epiphany.

Works Consulted

Primary Works

(Some of these sources are found in the Hilda Doolittle Collection of American Literature at The Beinecke Rare Book and Manuscript Library Yale University)

"Avon River." Original Typescript. Za Doolittle 6.

Des Imagistes: An Anthology. New York: Albert and Charles Boni, 1914.

End to Torment. New York: New Directions, 1979.

Euripides. Iphigenia in Aulis. Translated by H. D. Za D721 915Cb.

The Flowering of the Rod. London and New York: Oxford University Press, 1946. (Original wrappers). Za D721 946F.

"Gather for Festival (Songs from Cyprus)." Words by H. D. for The Dancers. Choral suite. Za D721 G 953W.

H. D. Collected Poems 1912–1944. New York: New Directions, 1983.

Helen in Egypt. New York: New Directions, 1961.

"Helen in Egypt." Typescript with Notes to Norman Holmes Pearson. Part 1–4. Dated September 23, 1954. Za Doolittle, 17–1, 2.

Heliodora and Other Poems. London: Jonathan Cape, 1924. Author's autographed presentation to Dorothy Richardson, Iq R 393 2z 924A.

Hermetic Definition. New York: New Directions, 1972.

"Hermetic Definition." Typescript. Some Notes. Za Doolittle 37-1, 2.

Hermione. New York: New Directions, 1981.

Imagist Anthology, 1930. New York: Covici, Friede, 1930. "Foreword" by Ford Madox Ford and Glenn Hughes. Za 721 930J.

Letters to Viola Jordan, 1920–1951. Za Jordan.

Notes on Thought and Vision. San Francisco: City Lights Books, 1982.

"Red Notebook." Typescript. "Background Notes" to Helen in Egypt. 11 pp. Za Doolittle 14.

Red Roses for Bronze. London: Chatto and Windus, 1931.

Selected Poems of H. D. New York: Grove, 1957.

Some Imagist Poets. Boston: Houghton Mifflin, 1915; 1916; and 1917.

The Collected Poems of H. D. (1925). New York: Boni and Liveright, 1925.

Three Poems from *The Islands* series, 1969. ("Amaranth," "Eros," and "Envy.") Za Doolittle 13.

The Tribute to Circe, Two Poems. Cleveland: Clerk's Private Press, 1917. Za D721 917T.

Tribute to Freud. Boston: David Godine, 1974.

Tribute to Freud. "Introduction" by Peter Jones. Oxford: Carcanet Press, 1971. Za D721 956Tc.

Tribute to Freud. With Unpublished Letters by Freud to the Author. New York: Pantheon, 1956. "Foreword" by Merrill Moore. Za D721 956T.

Tribute to Freud, "Writing on the Wall." "Foreword" by Norman Holmes Pearson, "Introduction" by Kenneth Fields. Boston: David Godine, 1974. Za D721 956Tf.

Tribute to the Angels. London and New York: Oxford University Press, 1945. Za D721 945T.

Trilogy. Cheshire: Carcanet Press, 1973. Za D721 973T.

Trilogy. New York: New Directions, 1973. Za D721 973T.

Vale Ave. In *New Directions 44.* New York: New Directions, 1982.

"Winter Love (Espérance)." Autograph manuscript, marked "First rough copy, January 3–April 5–1959," ZF names, in a notebook. This group of poems was written for Ezra Pound. Za Doolittle 37–1, 2: Za 41–1, 2, 3, 4.

Secondary Works

Aldington, Richard. *Complete Poems of Richard Aldington.* London: Wingate, 1948.

Barthes, Roland. "Is There Any Poetic Writing?" *Writing Degree Zero,* tr. Annette Lavers and Colin Smith. New York: Hill and Wang, 1983, 41–52.

―――. "Theory of the Text," in *Untying the Text: A Post Structuralist Reader,* ed. Robert Young. Boston: Routledge and Kegan Paul, 1981, pp. 31–47.

Blau DuPlessis, Rachael, and Susan Stanford Friedman. "'Woman Is Perfect': H. D.'s Debate With Freud." *Feminist Studies* 7 (1981), 417–430.

―――. "Family, Sexes, Psyche: An Essay on H. D. and the Muse of the Woman Writer." *Montemora,* 6 (1979), 137–156.

―――. *H. D. The Struggle of that Career.* Bloomington: Indiana University Press, 1986.

―――. "Romantic Thralldom in H. D." *Contemporary Literature.* 20 (2) 1979: 178–203.

Bloom, Harold. *Poetry and Repression.* New Haven: Yale University Press, 1976.

Bulfinch, Thomas. *The Age of Fable.* Philadelphia: David McKay, 1898.

Burkert, Walter. *Structure and History in Greek Myth and Ritual.* Berkeley: University of California Press, 1980.

Cassirer, Ernst. *Language and Myth.* Tr. Suzanne Langer. New York: Dover, 1946.

Christ, Carol P. *Diving Deep and Surfacing. Women Writers on Spiritual Quest.* Boston: Beacon, 1980.

Christian, Paul. *The History and Practice of Magic.* Tr. James Kirkup and Julian Shaw. Ed. Ross Nicolson. New York: Citadel, 1969.

Cixous, Hélène. "The Laugh of the Medusa." Tr. Keith and Paula Cohen. *Signs,* I, 4 (Summer 1976), 875–893.

Clark, Rundle R. T. *Myth and Symbol in Ancient Egypt.* London: Thames and Hudson, 1978.

Coffman, Stanley K. "H. D.": *Imagism: A Chapter for the History of Modern Poetry.* Norman, Oklahoma: University of Oklahoma Press, 1951, pp. 145–148 and passim.

Davidson, Gustav. *A Dictionary of Angels.* New York: Collier-Macmillan, 1969.

Dembo, L. S. *Conceptions of Reality in Modern American Poetry.* Berkeley: University of California Press, 1966, pp. 24–41.

———. "Introduction," *Contemporary Literature,* X (Autumn 1969), 433–434.

———. ed. "Norman Holmes Pearson on H. D.: An Interview," *Contemporary Literature,* X (Autumn 1969), 435–446.

de Rougemont, Denis. *Love in the Western World.* Tr. Montgomery Belgion. New York: Pantheon, 1956.

Duncan, Robert. "Beginnings: Chapter I of the H. D. Book," *Coyote's Journal,* V–VI (1966), 8–31

———. "From the Day Book," *Origin,* X (July 1963), 1–47.

———. "The H. D. Book, Part I: Chapter 2," *Coyote's Journal,* III (1967), 27–35.

———. "The H. D. Book: Part II, Nights and Days, Chapter 4," *Caterpillar,* II (April 1969), 27–60.

———. "In the Sight of a Lyre, a Little Spear, a Chair," *Poetry,* XCI (January 1958), 256–260.

———. "Nights and Days, Chapter One," *Sumac* (Fall 1968), 101–146.

———. "Part I: Beginnings: Chapter 5. Occult Matters," *Stony Brook Review,* I–II (Fall 1968), 4–19.

———. "Part II, Chapter 5," *Stony Brook Review,* III–IV (1969), 36–47.

———. "Rites of Participation, I," *Caterpillar,* I (October 1967), 6–29.

———. "Rites of Participation, II, "Caterpillar, II (January 1960), 125–153.

———. *Roots and Branches.* New York: New Directions, 1969.

———. "Two Chapters from H. D.," *Triquarterly,* XII (Spring 1968), 67–98.

Eliade, Mircea. *Myth and Poetry*. Tr. Willard Trask. New York: Harper and Row, 1963.

————. *Myth, Dreams, and Mysteries*. Tr. Philip Mairet. New York: Harper and Row, 1960.

————. *The Sacred and the Profane*. Tr. Willard R. Trask. New York: Harcourt, Brace, Jovanovich, 1959.

Fairclough, Henry Rushton. "The Classics and Our Twentieth-Century Poets." *Stanford University Language and Literature Series*, Vol. II, No. 2 Stanford, California: Stanford University Press, 1927, 271–314.

Fields, Kenneth. "Introduction," *Tribute to Freud* by H. D. Boston: David R. Godine, 1974.

Flint, F. S. "The Poetry of H. D." *The Egoist*, II (May 1, 1915), 72–73.

Friebert, L. M. "Conflict and Creativity in the World of H. D." *Journal of Women's Studies in Literature*, 1 (Winter 1979), 258–271.

————. "From Semblance to Selfhood: The Evolution of Woman in H. D.'s Neo-Epic *Helen in Egypt*." *Arizona Quarterly*, 36 (1980), 165–175.

Freud, Sigmund. *Interpretation of Dreams*. Ed. and tr. James Strachey. New York: Avon Library, 1966.

Gelpi, Albert. "H. D.: Hilda in Egypt," *Coming to Light: American Poets in the Twentieth Century*. eds. Diane Wood Middlebrook and Marilyn Yalom. Ann Arbor: University of Michigan Press, 1985, 233–253.

————. "The Thistle and the Serpent." Introduction to *Notes on Thought and Vision*. San Francisco: City Lights Books, 1982, 7–14.

Gibbons, Kathryn Gibbs. "The Art of H. D.," *Mississippi Quarterly*, XV (1962), 152–160.

Gilbert, Sandra M., and Susan Gubar. *The Madwoman in the Attic*. New Haven: Yale, 1979.

Graves, Robert. *The Greek Myths*. London: George Braziller, 1957.

————. *The White Goddess*. London: Faber and Faber, 1948.

Greenwood, E. B. "H. D. and the Problem of Escapism." *Essays in Criticism*, 21 (October 1971), 365–376.

Gregory, Horace. "Introduction to *Helen in Egypt*." New York: New Directions, 1961, vii–xi.

Gubar, Susan. "The Echoing Spell of H. D.'s *Trilogy*." *Contemporary Literature*, 19 (Spring 1978), 196–218.

Guest, Barbara. *Herself Defined. The Poet H. D. and Her World*. New York: Doubleday, 1984.

Guy, Davenport. *End to Torment*. Book Review. *New York Times Review of Books* (15 July 1979), p. 12.

"H. D." (Editorial tribute on occasion of H. D.'s death). *New York Times*, October 5, 1961, p. 36.

"H. D. Returns Home," Bethlehem, Pennsylvania. *Globe-Times*, October 31, 1961, p. 6.

Higgins, John J., S. J. *Thomas Merton on Prayer*. New York: Doubleday, 1973.

Holland, Norman N. "Freud and H. D." *International Journal of Psychoanalysis,* L (1959), 309–315.

––––––. "H. D. and the 'Blameless Physician,'" *Contemporary Literature,* X (Autumn 1969), 474–506.

––––––. *Poems in Persons.* (An Introduction to the Psychoanalysis of H. D.) New York: Norton, 1973.

Hughes, Glenn. "H. D.: The Perfect Imagist." *Imagism and Imagists: A Study in Modern Poetry.* Stanford, California: Stanford University Press, 1931, 109–124 and passim.

Jonas, Hans. *The Gnostic Religion.* Boston: Beacon Press, 1963.

Jones, Peter, ed. "Introduction." *Imagist Poetry.* Harmondsworth: Penguin, 1972, 1–43.

King, Michael. "Foreword," *End to Torment.* New York: New Directions, 1979, i–vii.

––––––. ed. *H. D. Woman and Poet.* Orono: National Poetry Foundation, 1986.

Jung, Carl Gustav, ed. *Man and His Symbols.* 1964; rpt. New York: Dell, 1968.

––––––. *Modern Man in Search of a Soul.* Tr. W. S. Dell and Cary F. Barnes. New York: Harcourt, Brace and World, 1933.

––––––. *Psyche and Symbol.* Ed. Violet S. de Laszlo. New York: Bantam Books, 1958.

Klees, Frederick. *The Pennsylvania Dutch.* New York: Macmillan, 1964.

Kunitz, Stanley. "A Tale of a Jar," (Review of *The Flowering of the Rod*) *Poetry,* LXX (April 1947), 36–42.

Lask, Thomas. "Hilda's Book." *New York Times* (25 February 1979), p. 47.

Lawrence, D. H. *St. Mawr and the Man Who Died.* New York: Vintage, 1953.

Levertov, Denise. "H. D.: An Appreciation." *The Poet in the World.* New York: New Directions, 1974, 244–248.

Lowell, Amy. "The Imagists: H. D. and John Gould Fletcher." *Tendencies in American Poetry.* New York: Macmillan, 1917, 235–280.

Martz, Louis. L. "Introduction," *H. D. Collected Poems 1912–1944.* New York: New Directions, 1983, xi–xxxv; and "Notes," 613–624.

––––––. *The Poetry of Meditation.* New Haven and London: Yale University Press, 1962.

Merton, Thomas. *Contemplative Prayer.* New York: Herder and Herder, 1969.

––––––. *Faith and Violence.* Notre Dame, Indiana: University of Notre Dame Press, 1968.

––––––. *The New Man.* New York: Mentor-Omega, 1961.

––––––. *New Seeds of Contemplation.* Norfolk: New Directions, 1961.

––––––. *Seasons of Celebration.* New York: Farrar, Straus and Giroux, 1964.

––––––. *Seeds of Contemplation.* Norfolk: New Directions, 1949.

––––––. *Zen and the Birds of Appetite.* New York: New Directions, 1968.

Monroe, Harriet, "H. D." *Poets and Their Art*, rev. ed. New York: Macmillan, 1932, 92–99, 319–320. (Reprinted essay).

———. "Some Imagist Poets" (Review). *Poetry*, VI, 3 (June 1915), 50–53.

Moore, Merrill. Foreword, *Tribute to Freud*. New York: Pantheon Books, 1956, vii–ix.

Newlin, Margaret. "Unhelpful Hymen!: Marianne Moore and Hilda Doolittle." *Essays in Criticism*, 27 (July 1977), 216–230.

Ostriker, Alicia. "The Thieves of Language: Women Poets and Revisionist Mythmaking," in *Coming to Light: American Poets in the Twentieth Century*. Eds. Diane Wood Middlebrook and Marilyn Yalom. Ann Arbor: University of Michigan Press, 1983, 7–30.

———. "The Poet as Heroine. Learning to Read H. D.," *Writing Like a Woman*. Ann Arbor: University of Michigan Press, 1983, 7–39.

Otto, Rudolf. *The Idea of the Holy*. Tr. John W. Harvey, 2nd ed. London: Oxford University Press, 1928.

Paige, D. D. *The Letters of Ezra Pound: 1907–1941*. New York: Harcourt, Brace, 1950, 36, 56, 63, 76, 77–79, 109, 112, 118, 161, 169, 222, 284, 288, 292, 400.

Parente, Pascal. *The Angels*. Meinrad, Indiana: Grail Publications, 1957.

Pearson, Norman Holmes. Collection of H. D.'s Papers. Letters and Unpublished Material. Za H. D.

———. Foreword, *Hermetic Definition*. New York: New Directions, 1972, n.p.

———. Foreword, *Tribute to Freud*. Boston: David R. Godine, 1974, vii–xvi.

———. Foreword, *Trilogy*. New York: New Directions, 1973, v–xii.

———. "A Selection of Poetry and Prose: Introduction," *Contemporary Literature*, X (Autumn 1969), 587–589.

Perse, St.-John (Alexis Leger). *Collected Poems*. Tr. W. H. Auden et al. Princeton: Princeton University Press, 1971.

"Poet Hilda Doolittle, On Yale Visit, Assails Imagist Label Used to Describe Her Work." *New Haven Register*, September 16, 1956, p. 10 (Interview).

Pondrom, Cyrena N., ed. "Selected Letters from H. D. to F. S. Flint: A Commentary on the Imagist Period," *Contemporary Literature*, X (Autumn 1969), 557.

P[ound], E[zra]. "H. D.'s Choruses From Euripides," *Little Review*, V (Nov. 1918), 16–17.

Pratt, William, ed. *The Imagist Poem —Modern Poetry in Miniature*. New York: E. P. Dutton, 1963, 16–21.

"Presentation to Hilda Doolittle of the Award of the Merit Medal for Poetry by Mark van Doren of the Academy." *Proceedings of the American Academy of Arts and Letters and the National Institute of Arts and Letters* No. 11 (1961), 40–41.

Quinn, Vincent. *Hilda Doolittle (H. D.)*. New York: Twayne, 1968.

————. "H. D.'s *Hermetic Definition:* The Poet as Archetypal Mother." *Contemporary Literature,* 18 (Winter 1977), 51–61.

Riddel, Joseph N. "H. D. and the Poetics of 'Spiritual Realism,'" *Contemporary Literature,* X (1969), 447–473.

Robinson, Janice, S. *H. D. The Life and the Works of an American Poet.* Boston: Houghton Mifflin, 1982.

Scholem, Gershom. *Kabbalah.* New York: Meridian, 1978.

Sievert, Rosario. "H. D.: A Symbolist Perspective." *Contemporary Literature Studies,* 16 (March 1979), 48–57.

Stanford Friedman, Susan. "Creating a Woman's Mythology: H. D.'s *Helen in Egypt." Women's Studies,* 5 (1977), 163–197.

————. "I Go where I Love: An Intertextual Study of H. D. and Adrienne Rich." *Coming to Light: American Poets in the Twentieth Century,* eds. Diane Wood Middlebrook and Marilyn Yalom. Ann Arbor: University of Michigan Press, 1985, 233–253.

———— and Rachael Blau DuPlessis. "The Fascinating Genius called H. D.—Why Was the Peer of T. S. Eliot and Ezra Pound Neglected Until Now?" *Ms.* Vol. X, No. 8, 36 (February 1982), 64–66.

————. *Psyche Reborn: The Emergence of H. D.* Bloomington: Indiana University Press, 1981.

————. "Who Buried H. D.? A Poet, Her Critics, and Her Place in 'The Literary Tradition.'" *College English,* 36 (1975), 801–814.

Steere, Douglas V. "Foreword," *Contemplative Prayer* by Thomas Merton. New York: Image Books, 1971.

"Stesichorus." *Greek Lyric.* Oxford: Clarendon Press, 1961, 74–128.

Stesichorus. *Storia della letteratura italiana.* Milan: Montadori, 1940–42, Vol. 1–3, 189–190, 277–281, 586.

Swann, Thomas B. *The Classical World of H. D.* Lincoln: University of Nebraska Press, 1962.

The Anagogic and Paideumic Review, vol. 1, nos. 3, 5, and 6, 1959. (Poems and brief critical commentary about H. D.) 2a + 2a nil.

Topel, L. John, S. J. *The Way to Peace.* New York: Orbis Books, 1979.

Vellacott, Philip, tr. Introduction. *Euripides. The Bacchae and Other Plays.* Harmondsworth: Penguin, 1972, 1–38.

Wagner, Linda Welshimer. "Helen in Egypt: A Culmination," *Contemporary Literature,* X (Autumn 1969), 523–536.

Watts, Harold H. "H. D. and the Age of Myth," *Sewanee Review* LVI (April 1948), 287–303.

Weigall, Arthur. *The Paganism in Our Christianity.* London: Putnam, 1928.

Wolle, Francis. *A Moravian Heritage* (1971). Za D721 + W 972w.

Index